C-4537　　CAREER EXAMINATION SERIES

This is your
PASSBOOK for...

Children and Youth Treatment Team Leader

Test Preparation Study Guide
Questions & Answers

NATIONAL LEARNING CORPORATION®

COPYRIGHT NOTICE

This book is SOLELY intended for, is sold ONLY to, and its use is RESTRICTED to individual, bona fide applicants or candidates who qualify by virtue of having seriously filed applications for appropriate license, certificate, professional and/or promotional advancement, higher school matriculation, scholarship, or other legitimate requirements of education and/or governmental authorities.

This book is NOT intended for use, class instruction, tutoring, training, duplication, copying, reprinting, excerption, or adaptation, etc., by:

1) Other publishers
2) Proprietors and/or Instructors of "Coaching" and/or Preparatory Courses
3) Personnel and/or Training Divisions of commercial, industrial, and governmental organizations
4) Schools, colleges, or universities and/or their departments and staffs, including teachers and other personnel
5) Testing Agencies or Bureaus
6) Study groups which seek by the purchase of a single volume to copy and/or duplicate and/or adapt this material for use by the group as a whole without having purchased individual volumes for each of the members of the group
7) Et al.

Such persons would be in violation of appropriate Federal and State statutes.

PROVISION OF LICENSING AGREEMENTS – Recognized educational, commercial, industrial, and governmental institutions and organizations, and others legitimately engaged in educational pursuits, including training, testing, and measurement activities, may address request for a licensing agreement to the copyright owners, who will determine whether, and under what conditions, including fees and charges, the materials in this book may be used them. In other words, a licensing facility exists for the legitimate use of the material in this book on other than an individual basis. However, it is asseverated and affirmed here that the material in this book CANNOT be used without the receipt of the express permission of such a licensing agreement from the Publishers. Inquiries re licensing should be addressed to the company, attention rights and permissions department.

All rights reserved, including the right of reproduction in whole or in part, in any form or by any means, electronic or mechanical, including photocopying, recording, or by any information storage and retrieval system, without permission in writing from the Publisher.

Copyright © 2025 by
National Learning Corporation

212 Michael Drive, Syosset, NY 11791
(516) 921-8888 • www.passbooks.com
E-mail: info@passbooks.com

PASSBOOK® SERIES

THE *PASSBOOK® SERIES* has been created to prepare applicants and candidates for the ultimate academic battlefield – the examination room.

At some time in our lives, each and every one of us may be required to take an examination – for validation, matriculation, admission, qualification, registration, certification, or licensure.

Based on the assumption that every applicant or candidate has met the basic formal educational standards, has taken the required number of courses, and read the necessary texts, the *PASSBOOK® SERIES* furnishes the one special preparation which may assure passing with confidence, instead of failing with insecurity. Examination questions – together with answers – are furnished as the basic vehicle for study so that the mysteries of the examination and its compounding difficulties may be eliminated or diminished by a sure method.

This book is meant to help you pass your examination provided that you qualify and are serious in your objective.

The entire field is reviewed through the huge store of content information which is succinctly presented through a provocative and challenging approach – the question-and-answer method.

A climate of success is established by furnishing the correct answers at the end of each test.

You soon learn to recognize types of questions, forms of questions, and patterns of questioning. You may even begin to anticipate expected outcomes.

You perceive that many questions are repeated or adapted so that you can gain acute insights, which may enable you to score many sure points.

You learn how to confront new questions, or types of questions, and to attack them confidently and work out the correct answers.

You note objectives and emphases, and recognize pitfalls and dangers, so that you may make positive educational adjustments.

Moreover, you are kept fully informed in relation to new concepts, methods, practices, and directions in the field.

You discover that you are actually taking the examination all the time: you are preparing for the examination by "taking" an examination, not by reading extraneous and/or supererogatory textbooks.

In short, this PASSBOOK®, used directedly, should be an important factor in helping you to pass your test.

CHILDREN AND YOUTH TREATMENT TEAM LEADER

DUTIES

As a Children and Youth Treatment Team Leader, you would plan, organize and supervise the implementation of a residential, habilitation, clinical, day center, or community program for mentally ill children and youth and those with intellectual and/or physical disabilities. You would have program and administrative responsibility for the treatment activities of an interdisciplinary treatment team and direct and coordinate a total program tailored to the individual needs of clients. You would be responsible for marshaling and assigning team resources to accomplish team goals, and evaluating team programs.

SUBJECT OF EXAMINATION:

The written test designed to evaluate knowledge, skills and /or abilities in the following areas:
1. Administrative techniques and practices;
2. Ensuring effective inter/intra agency communications;
3. Preparing written material; and
4. Characteristics and treatment needs of children and youth diagnosed with severe emotional disturbance.

HOW TO TAKE A TEST

I. YOU MUST PASS AN EXAMINATION

A. *WHAT EVERY CANDIDATE SHOULD KNOW*

Examination applicants often ask us for help in preparing for the written test. What can I study in advance? What kinds of questions will be asked? How will the test be given? How will the papers be graded?

As an applicant for a civil service examination, you may be wondering about some of these things. Our purpose here is to suggest effective methods of advance study and to describe civil service examinations.

Your chances for success on this examination can be increased if you know how to prepare. Those "pre-examination jitters" can be reduced if you know what to expect. You can even experience an adventure in good citizenship if you know why civil service exams are given.

B. *WHY ARE CIVIL SERVICE EXAMINATIONS GIVEN?*

Civil service examinations are important to you in two ways. As a citizen, you want public jobs filled by employees who know how to do their work. As a job seeker, you want a fair chance to compete for that job on an equal footing with other candidates. The best-known means of accomplishing this two-fold goal is the competitive examination.

Exams are widely publicized throughout the nation. They may be administered for jobs in federal, state, city, municipal, town or village governments or agencies.

Any citizen may apply, with some limitations, such as the age or residence of applicants. Your experience and education may be reviewed to see whether you meet the requirements for the particular examination. When these requirements exist, they are reasonable and applied consistently to all applicants. Thus, a competitive examination may cause you some uneasiness now, but it is your privilege and safeguard.

C. *HOW ARE CIVIL SERVICE EXAMS DEVELOPED?*

Examinations are carefully written by trained technicians who are specialists in the field known as "psychological measurement," in consultation with recognized authorities in the field of work that the test will cover. These experts recommend the subject matter areas or skills to be tested; only those knowledges or skills important to your success on the job are included. The most reliable books and source materials available are used as references. Together, the experts and technicians judge the difficulty level of the questions.

Test technicians know how to phrase questions so that the problem is clearly stated. Their ethics do not permit "trick" or "catch" questions. Questions may have been tried out on sample groups, or subjected to statistical analysis, to determine their usefulness.

Written tests are often used in combination with performance tests, ratings of training and experience, and oral interviews. All of these measures combine to form the best-known means of finding the right person for the right job.

II. HOW TO PASS THE WRITTEN TEST

A. NATURE OF THE EXAMINATION

To prepare intelligently for civil service examinations, you should know how they differ from school examinations you have taken. In school you were assigned certain definite pages to read or subjects to cover. The examination questions were quite detailed and usually emphasized memory. Civil service exams, on the other hand, try to discover your present ability to perform the duties of a position, plus your potentiality to learn these duties. In other words, a civil service exam attempts to predict how successful you will be. Questions cover such a broad area that they cannot be as minute and detailed as school exam questions.

In the public service similar kinds of work, or positions, are grouped together in one "class." This process is known as *position-classification*. All the positions in a class are paid according to the salary range for that class. One class title covers all of these positions, and they are all tested by the same examination.

B. FOUR BASIC STEPS

1) Study the announcement

How, then, can you know what subjects to study? Our best answer is: "Learn as much as possible about the class of positions for which you've applied." The exam will test the knowledge, skills and abilities needed to do the work.

Your most valuable source of information about the position you want is the official exam announcement. This announcement lists the training and experience qualifications. Check these standards and apply only if you come reasonably close to meeting them.

The brief description of the position in the examination announcement offers some clues to the subjects which will be tested. Think about the job itself. Review the duties in your mind. Can you perform them, or are there some in which you are rusty? Fill in the blank spots in your preparation.

Many jurisdictions preview the written test in the exam announcement by including a section called "Knowledge and Abilities Required," "Scope of the Examination," or some similar heading. Here you will find out specifically what fields will be tested.

2) Review your own background

Once you learn in general what the position is all about, and what you need to know to do the work, ask yourself which subjects you already know fairly well and which need improvement. You may wonder whether to concentrate on improving your strong areas or on building some background in your fields of weakness. When the announcement has specified "some knowledge" or "considerable knowledge," or has used adjectives like "beginning principles of..." or "advanced ... methods," you can get a clue as to the number and difficulty of questions to be asked in any given field. More questions, and hence broader coverage, would be included for those subjects which are more important in the work. Now weigh your strengths and weaknesses against the job requirements and prepare accordingly.

3) Determine the level of the position

Another way to tell how intensively you should prepare is to understand the level of the job for which you are applying. Is it the entering level? In other words, is this the position in which beginners in a field of work are hired? Or is it an intermediate or advanced level? Sometimes this is indicated by such words as "Junior" or "Senior" in the class title. Other jurisdictions use Roman numerals to designate the level – Clerk I, Clerk II, for example. The word "Supervisor" sometimes appears in the title. If the level is not indicated by the title, check the description of duties. Will you be working under very close supervision, or will you have responsibility for independent decisions in this work?

4) Choose appropriate study materials

Now that you know the subjects to be examined and the relative amount of each subject to be covered, you can choose suitable study materials. For beginning level jobs, or even advanced ones, if you have a pronounced weakness in some aspect of your training, read a modern, standard textbook in that field. Be sure it is up to date and has general coverage. Such books are normally available at your library, and the librarian will be glad to help you locate one. For entry-level positions, questions of appropriate difficulty are chosen – neither highly advanced questions, nor those too simple. Such questions require careful thought but not advanced training.

If the position for which you are applying is technical or advanced, you will read more advanced, specialized material. If you are already familiar with the basic principles of your field, elementary textbooks would waste your time. Concentrate on advanced textbooks and technical periodicals. Think through the concepts and review difficult problems in your field.

These are all general sources. You can get more ideas on your own initiative, following these leads. For example, training manuals and publications of the government agency which employs workers in your field can be useful, particularly for technical and professional positions. A letter or visit to the government department involved may result in more specific study suggestions, and certainly will provide you with a more definite idea of the exact nature of the position you are seeking.

III. KINDS OF TESTS

Tests are used for purposes other than measuring knowledge and ability to perform specified duties. For some positions, it is equally important to test ability to make adjustments to new situations or to profit from training. In others, basic mental abilities not dependent on information are essential. Questions which test these things may not appear as pertinent to the duties of the position as those which test for knowledge and information. Yet they are often highly important parts of a fair examination. For very general questions, it is almost impossible to help you direct your study efforts. What we can do is to point out some of the more common of these general abilities needed in public service positions and describe some typical questions.

1) General information

Broad, general information has been found useful for predicting job success in some kinds of work. This is tested in a variety of ways, from vocabulary lists to questions about current events. Basic background in some field of work, such as sociology or economics, may be sampled in a group of questions. Often these are principles which have become familiar to most persons through exposure rather than through formal training. It is difficult to advise you how to study for these questions; being alert to the world around you is our best suggestion.

2) Verbal ability

An example of an ability needed in many positions is verbal or language ability. Verbal ability is, in brief, the ability to use and understand words. Vocabulary and grammar tests are typical measures of this ability. Reading comprehension or paragraph interpretation questions are common in many kinds of civil service tests. You are given a paragraph of written material and asked to find its central meaning.

3) Numerical ability

Number skills can be tested by the familiar arithmetic problem, by checking paired lists of numbers to see which are alike and which are different, or by interpreting charts and graphs. In the latter test, a graph may be printed in the test booklet which you are asked to use as the basis for answering questions.

4) Observation

A popular test for law-enforcement positions is the observation test. A picture is shown to you for several minutes, then taken away. Questions about the picture test your ability to observe both details and larger elements.

5) Following directions

In many positions in the public service, the employee must be able to carry out written instructions dependably and accurately. You may be given a chart with several columns, each column listing a variety of information. The questions require you to carry out directions involving the information given in the chart.

6) Skills and aptitudes

Performance tests effectively measure some manual skills and aptitudes. When the skill is one in which you are trained, such as typing or shorthand, you can practice. These tests are often very much like those given in business school or high school courses. For many of the other skills and aptitudes, however, no short-time preparation can be made. Skills and abilities natural to you or that you have developed throughout your lifetime are being tested.

Many of the general questions just described provide all the data needed to answer the questions and ask you to use your reasoning ability to find the answers. Your best preparation for these tests, as well as for tests of facts and ideas, is to be at your physical and mental best. You, no doubt, have your own methods of getting into an exam-taking mood and keeping "in shape." The next section lists some ideas on this subject.

IV. KINDS OF QUESTIONS

Only rarely is the "essay" question, which you answer in narrative form, used in civil service tests. Civil service tests are usually of the short-answer type. Full instructions for answering these questions will be given to you at the examination. But in case this is your first experience with short-answer questions and separate answer sheets, here is what you need to know:

1) Multiple-choice Questions

Most popular of the short-answer questions is the "multiple choice" or "best answer" question. It can be used, for example, to test for factual knowledge, ability to solve problems or judgment in meeting situations found at work.

A multiple-choice question is normally one of three types—
- It can begin with an incomplete statement followed by several possible endings. You are to find the one ending which *best* completes the statement, although some of the others may not be entirely wrong.
- It can also be a complete statement in the form of a question which is answered by choosing one of the statements listed.

- It can be in the form of a problem – again you select the best answer.

Here is an example of a multiple-choice question with a discussion which should give you some clues as to the method for choosing the right answer:

When an employee has a complaint about his assignment, the action which will *best* help him overcome his difficulty is to
    A. discuss his difficulty with his coworkers
    B. take the problem to the head of the organization
    C. take the problem to the person who gave him the assignment
    D. say nothing to anyone about his complaint

In answering this question, you should study each of the choices to find which is best. Consider choice "A" – Certainly an employee may discuss his complaint with fellow employees, but no change or improvement can result, and the complaint remains unresolved. Choice "B" is a poor choice since the head of the organization probably does not know what assignment you have been given, and taking your problem to him is known as "going over the head" of the supervisor. The supervisor, or person who made the assignment, is the person who can clarify it or correct any injustice. Choice "C" is, therefore, correct. To say nothing, as in choice "D," is unwise. Supervisors have and interest in knowing the problems employees are facing, and the employee is seeking a solution to his problem.

2) True/False Questions

The "true/false" or "right/wrong" form of question is sometimes used. Here a complete statement is given. Your job is to decide whether the statement is right or wrong.

SAMPLE: A roaming cell-phone call to a nearby city costs less than a non-roaming call to a distant city.

This statement is wrong, or false, since roaming calls are more expensive.

This is not a complete list of all possible question forms, although most of the others are variations of these common types. You will always get complete directions for answering questions. Be sure you understand *how* to mark your answers – ask questions until you do.

V. RECORDING YOUR ANSWERS

Computer terminals are used more and more today for many different kinds of exams.

For an examination with very few applicants, you may be told to record your answers in the test booklet itself. Separate answer sheets are much more common. If this separate answer sheet is to be scored by machine – and this is often the case – it is highly important that you mark your answers correctly in order to get credit.

An electronic scoring machine is often used in civil service offices because of the speed with which papers can be scored. Machine-scored answer sheets must be marked with a pencil, which will be given to you. This pencil has a high graphite content which responds to the electronic scoring machine. As a matter of fact, stray dots may register as answers, so do not let your pencil rest on the answer sheet while you are pondering the correct answer. Also, if your pencil lead breaks or is otherwise defective, ask for another.

Since the answer sheet will be dropped in a slot in the scoring machine, be careful not to bend the corners or get the paper crumpled.

The answer sheet normally has five vertical columns of numbers, with 30 numbers to a column. These numbers correspond to the question numbers in your test booklet. After each number, going across the page are four or five pairs of dotted lines. These short dotted lines have small letters or numbers above them. The first two pairs may also have a "T" or "F" above the letters. This indicates that the first two pairs only are to be used if the questions are of the true-false type. If the questions are multiple choice, disregard the "T" and "F" and pay attention only to the small letters or numbers.

Answer your questions in the manner of the sample that follows:

32. The largest city in the United States is
    A. Washington, D.C.
    B. New York City
    C. Chicago
    D. Detroit
    E. San Francisco

1) Choose the answer you think is best. (New York City is the largest, so "B" is correct.)
2) Find the row of dotted lines numbered the same as the question you are answering. (Find row number 32)
3) Find the pair of dotted lines corresponding to the answer. (Find the pair of lines under the mark "B.")
4) Make a solid black mark between the dotted lines.

VI. BEFORE THE TEST

Common sense will help you find procedures to follow to get ready for an examination. Too many of us, however, overlook these sensible measures. Indeed, nervousness and fatigue have been found to be the most serious reasons why applicants fail to do their best on civil service tests. Here is a list of reminders:

- Begin your preparation early – Don't wait until the last minute to go scurrying around for books and materials or to find out what the position is all about.
- Prepare continuously – An hour a night for a week is better than an all-night cram session. This has been definitely established. What is more, a night a week for a month will return better dividends than crowding your study into a shorter period of time.
- Locate the place of the exam – You have been sent a notice telling you when and where to report for the examination. If the location is in a different town or otherwise unfamiliar to you, it would be well to inquire the best route and learn something about the building.
- Relax the night before the test – Allow your mind to rest. Do not study at all that night. Plan some mild recreation or diversion; then go to bed early and get a good night's sleep.
- Get up early enough to make a leisurely trip to the place for the test – This way unforeseen events, traffic snarls, unfamiliar buildings, etc. will not upset you.
- Dress comfortably – A written test is not a fashion show. You will be known by number and not by name, so wear something comfortable.

- Leave excess paraphernalia at home – Shopping bags and odd bundles will get in your way. You need bring only the items mentioned in the official notice you received; usually everything you need is provided. Do not bring reference books to the exam. They will only confuse those last minutes and be taken away from you when in the test room.
- Arrive somewhat ahead of time – If because of transportation schedules you must get there very early, bring a newspaper or magazine to take your mind off yourself while waiting.
- Locate the examination room – When you have found the proper room, you will be directed to the seat or part of the room where you will sit. Sometimes you are given a sheet of instructions to read while you are waiting. Do not fill out any forms until you are told to do so; just read them and be prepared.
- Relax and prepare to listen to the instructions
- If you have any physical problem that may keep you from doing your best, be sure to tell the test administrator. If you are sick or in poor health, you really cannot do your best on the exam. You can come back and take the test some other time.

VII. AT THE TEST

The day of the test is here and you have the test booklet in your hand. The temptation to get going is very strong. Caution! There is more to success than knowing the right answers. You must know how to identify your papers and understand variations in the type of short-answer question used in this particular examination. Follow these suggestions for maximum results from your efforts:

1) Cooperate with the monitor

The test administrator has a duty to create a situation in which you can be as much at ease as possible. He will give instructions, tell you when to begin, check to see that you are marking your answer sheet correctly, and so on. He is not there to guard you, although he will see that your competitors do not take unfair advantage. He wants to help you do your best.

2) Listen to all instructions

Don't jump the gun! Wait until you understand all directions. In most civil service tests you get more time than you need to answer the questions. So don't be in a hurry. Read each word of instructions until you clearly understand the meaning. Study the examples, listen to all announcements and follow directions. Ask questions if you do not understand what to do.

3) Identify your papers

Civil service exams are usually identified by number only. You will be assigned a number; you must not put your name on your test papers. Be sure to copy your number correctly. Since more than one exam may be given, copy your exact examination title.

4) Plan your time

Unless you are told that a test is a "speed" or "rate of work" test, speed itself is usually not important. Time enough to answer all the questions will be provided, but this does not mean that you have all day. An overall time limit has been set. Divide the total time (in minutes) by the number of questions to determine the approximate time you have for each question.

5) Do not linger over difficult questions

If you come across a difficult question, mark it with a paper clip (useful to have along) and come back to it when you have been through the booklet. One caution if you do this – be sure to skip a number on your answer sheet as well. Check often to be sure that you have not lost your place and that you are marking in the row numbered the same as the question you are answering.

6) Read the questions

Be sure you know what the question asks! Many capable people are unsuccessful because they failed to *read* the questions correctly.

7) Answer all questions

Unless you have been instructed that a penalty will be deducted for incorrect answers, it is better to guess than to omit a question.

8) Speed tests

It is often better NOT to guess on speed tests. It has been found that on timed tests people are tempted to spend the last few seconds before time is called in marking answers at random – without even reading them – in the hope of picking up a few extra points. To discourage this practice, the instructions may warn you that your score will be "corrected" for guessing. That is, a penalty will be applied. The incorrect answers will be deducted from the correct ones, or some other penalty formula will be used.

9) Review your answers

If you finish before time is called, go back to the questions you guessed or omitted to give them further thought. Review other answers if you have time.

10) Return your test materials

If you are ready to leave before others have finished or time is called, take ALL your materials to the monitor and leave quietly. Never take any test material with you. The monitor can discover whose papers are not complete, and taking a test booklet may be grounds for disqualification.

VIII. EXAMINATION TECHNIQUES

1) Read the general instructions carefully. These are usually printed on the first page of the exam booklet. As a rule, these instructions refer to the timing of the examination; the fact that you should not start work until the signal and must stop work at a signal, etc. If there are any *special* instructions, such as a choice of questions to be answered, make sure that you note this instruction carefully.

2) When you are ready to start work on the examination, that is as soon as the signal has been given, read the instructions to each question booklet, underline any key words or phrases, such as *least, best, outline, describe* and the like. In this way you will tend to answer as requested rather than discover on reviewing your paper that you *listed without describing*, that you selected the *worst* choice rather than the *best* choice, etc.

3) If the examination is of the objective or multiple-choice type – that is, each question will also give a series of possible answers: A, B, C or D, and you are called upon to select the best answer and write the letter next to that answer on your answer paper – it is advisable to start answering each question in turn. There may be anywhere from 50 to 100 such questions in the three or four hours allotted and you can see how much time would be taken if you read through all the questions before beginning to answer any. Furthermore, if you come across a question or group of questions which you know would be difficult to answer, it would undoubtedly affect your handling of all the other questions.

4) If the examination is of the essay type and contains but a few questions, it is a moot point as to whether you should read all the questions before starting to answer any one. Of course, if you are given a choice – say five out of seven and the like – then it is essential to read all the questions so you can eliminate the two that are most difficult. If, however, you are asked to answer all the questions, there may be danger in trying to answer the easiest one first because you may find that you will spend too much time on it. The best technique is to answer the first question, then proceed to the second, etc.

5) Time your answers. Before the exam begins, write down the time it started, then add the time allowed for the examination and write down the time it must be completed, then divide the time available somewhat as follows:
    - If 3-1/2 hours are allowed, that would be 210 minutes. If you have 80 objective-type questions, that would be an average of 2-1/2 minutes per question. Allow yourself no more than 2 minutes per question, or a total of 160 minutes, which will permit about 50 minutes to review.
    - If for the time allotment of 210 minutes there are 7 essay questions to answer, that would average about 30 minutes a question. Give yourself only 25 minutes per question so that you have about 35 minutes to review.

6) The most important instruction is to *read each question* and make sure you know what is wanted. The second most important instruction is to *time yourself properly* so that you answer every question. The third most important instruction is to *answer every question*. Guess if you have to but include something for each question. Remember that you will receive no credit for a blank and will probably receive some credit if you write something in answer to an essay question. If you guess a letter – say "B" for a multiple-choice question – you may have guessed right. If you leave a blank as an answer to a multiple-choice question, the examiners may respect your feelings but it will not add a point to your score. Some exams may penalize you for wrong answers, so in such cases *only*, you may not want to guess unless you have some basis for your answer.

7) Suggestions
    a. Objective-type questions
        1. Examine the question booklet for proper sequence of pages and questions
        2. Read all instructions carefully
        3. Skip any question which seems too difficult; return to it after all other questions have been answered
        4. Apportion your time properly; do not spend too much time on any single question or group of questions

5. Note and underline key words – *all, most, fewest, least, best, worst, same, opposite*, etc.
6. Pay particular attention to negatives
7. Note unusual option, e.g., unduly long, short, complex, different or similar in content to the body of the question
8. Observe the use of "hedging" words – *probably, may, most likely*, etc.
9. Make sure that your answer is put next to the same number as the question
10. Do not second-guess unless you have good reason to believe the second answer is definitely more correct
11. Cross out original answer if you decide another answer is more accurate; do not erase until you are ready to hand your paper in
12. Answer all questions; guess unless instructed otherwise
13. Leave time for review

b. Essay questions
1. Read each question carefully
2. Determine exactly what is wanted. Underline key words or phrases.
3. Decide on outline or paragraph answer
4. Include many different points and elements unless asked to develop any one or two points or elements
5. Show impartiality by giving pros and cons unless directed to select one side only
6. Make and write down any assumptions you find necessary to answer the questions
7. Watch your English, grammar, punctuation and choice of words
8. Time your answers; don't crowd material

8) Answering the essay question

Most essay questions can be answered by framing the specific response around several key words or ideas. Here are a few such key words or ideas:

M's: manpower, materials, methods, money, management
P's: purpose, program, policy, plan, procedure, practice, problems, pitfalls, personnel, public relations

a. Six basic steps in handling problems:
1. Preliminary plan and background development
2. Collect information, data and facts
3. Analyze and interpret information, data and facts
4. Analyze and develop solutions as well as make recommendations
5. Prepare report and sell recommendations
6. Install recommendations and follow up effectiveness

b. Pitfalls to avoid
1. *Taking things for granted* – A statement of the situation does not necessarily imply that each of the elements is necessarily true; for example, a complaint may be invalid and biased so that all that can be taken for granted is that a complaint has been registered

2. *Considering only one side of a situation* – Wherever possible, indicate several alternatives and then point out the reasons you selected the best one
3. *Failing to indicate follow up* – Whenever your answer indicates action on your part, make certain that you will take proper follow-up action to see how successful your recommendations, procedures or actions turn out to be
4. *Taking too long in answering any single question* – Remember to time your answers properly

IX. AFTER THE TEST

Scoring procedures differ in detail among civil service jurisdictions although the general principles are the same. Whether the papers are hand-scored or graded by machine we have described, they are nearly always graded by number. That is, the person who marks the paper knows only the number – never the name – of the applicant. Not until all the papers have been graded will they be matched with names. If other tests, such as training and experience or oral interview ratings have been given, scores will be combined. Different parts of the examination usually have different weights. For example, the written test might count 60 percent of the final grade, and a rating of training and experience 40 percent. In many jurisdictions, veterans will have a certain number of points added to their grades.

After the final grade has been determined, the names are placed in grade order and an eligible list is established. There are various methods for resolving ties between those who get the same final grade – probably the most common is to place first the name of the person whose application was received first. Job offers are made from the eligible list in the order the names appear on it. You will be notified of your grade and your rank as soon as all these computations have been made. This will be done as rapidly as possible.

People who are found to meet the requirements in the announcement are called "eligibles." Their names are put on a list of eligible candidates. An eligible's chances of getting a job depend on how high he stands on this list and how fast agencies are filling jobs from the list.

When a job is to be filled from a list of eligibles, the agency asks for the names of people on the list of eligibles for that job. When the civil service commission receives this request, it sends to the agency the names of the three people highest on this list. Or, if the job to be filled has specialized requirements, the office sends the agency the names of the top three persons who meet these requirements from the general list.

The appointing officer makes a choice from among the three people whose names were sent to him. If the selected person accepts the appointment, the names of the others are put back on the list to be considered for future openings.

That is the rule in hiring from all kinds of eligible lists, whether they are for typist, carpenter, chemist, or something else. For every vacancy, the appointing officer has his choice of any one of the top three eligibles on the list. This explains why the person whose name is on top of the list sometimes does not get an appointment when some of the persons lower on the list do. If the appointing officer chooses the second or third eligible, the No. 1 eligible does not get a job at once, but stays on the list until he is appointed or the list is terminated.

X. HOW TO PASS THE INTERVIEW TEST

The examination for which you applied requires an oral interview test. You have already taken the written test and you are now being called for the interview test – the final part of the formal examination.

You may think that it is not possible to prepare for an interview test and that there are no procedures to follow during an interview. Our purpose is to point out some things you can do in advance that will help you and some good rules to follow and pitfalls to avoid while you are being interviewed.

What is an interview supposed to test?

The written examination is designed to test the technical knowledge and competence of the candidate; the oral is designed to evaluate intangible qualities, not readily measured otherwise, and to establish a list showing the relative fitness of each candidate – as measured against his competitors – for the position sought. Scoring is not on the basis of "right" and "wrong," but on a sliding scale of values ranging from "not passable" to "outstanding." As a matter of fact, it is possible to achieve a relatively low score without a single "incorrect" answer because of evident weakness in the qualities being measured.

Occasionally, an examination may consist entirely of an oral test – either an individual or a group oral. In such cases, information is sought concerning the technical knowledges and abilities of the candidate, since there has been no written examination for this purpose. More commonly, however, an oral test is used to supplement a written examination.

Who conducts interviews?

The composition of oral boards varies among different jurisdictions. In nearly all, a representative of the personnel department serves as chairman. One of the members of the board may be a representative of the department in which the candidate would work. In some cases, "outside experts" are used, and, frequently, a businessman or some other representative of the general public is asked to serve. Labor and management or other special groups may be represented. The aim is to secure the services of experts in the appropriate field.

However the board is composed, it is a good idea (and not at all improper or unethical) to ascertain in advance of the interview who the members are and what groups they represent. When you are introduced to them, you will have some idea of their backgrounds and interests, and at least you will not stutter and stammer over their names.

What should be done before the interview?

While knowledge about the board members is useful and takes some of the surprise element out of the interview, there is other preparation which is more substantive. It *is* possible to prepare for an oral interview – in several ways:

1) Keep a copy of your application and review it carefully before the interview

This may be the only document before the oral board, and the starting point of the interview. Know what education and experience you have listed there, and the sequence and dates of all of it. Sometimes the board will ask you to review the highlights of your experience for them; you should not have to hem and haw doing it.

2) Study the class specification and the examination announcement

Usually, the oral board has one or both of these to guide them. The qualities, characteristics or knowledges required by the position sought are stated in these documents. They offer valuable clues as to the nature of the oral interview. For example, if the job involves supervisory responsibilities, the announcement will usually indicate that knowledge of modern supervisory methods and the qualifications of the candidate as a supervisor will be tested. If so, you can expect such questions, frequently in the form of a hypothetical situation which you are expected to solve. NEVER go into an oral without knowledge of the duties and responsibilities of the job you seek.

3) Think through each qualification required

Try to visualize the kind of questions you would ask if you were a board member. How well could you answer them? Try especially to appraise your own knowledge and background in each area, *measured against the job sought*, and identify any areas in which you are weak. Be critical and realistic – do not flatter yourself.

4) Do some general reading in areas in which you feel you may be weak

For example, if the job involves supervision and your past experience has NOT, some general reading in supervisory methods and practices, particularly in the field of human relations, might be useful. Do NOT study agency procedures or detailed manuals. The oral board will be testing your understanding and capacity, not your memory.

5) Get a good night's sleep and watch your general health and mental attitude

You will want a clear head at the interview. Take care of a cold or any other minor ailment, and of course, no hangovers.

What should be done on the day of the interview?

Now comes the day of the interview itself. Give yourself plenty of time to get there. Plan to arrive somewhat ahead of the scheduled time, particularly if your appointment is in the fore part of the day. If a previous candidate fails to appear, the board might be ready for you a bit early. By early afternoon an oral board is almost invariably behind schedule if there are many candidates, and you may have to wait. Take along a book or magazine to read, or your application to review, but leave any extraneous material in the waiting room when you go in for your interview. In any event, relax and compose yourself.

The matter of dress is important. The board is forming impressions about you – from your experience, your manners, your attitude, and your appearance. Give your personal appearance careful attention. Dress your best, but not your flashiest. Choose conservative, appropriate clothing, and be sure it is immaculate. This is a business interview, and your appearance should indicate that you regard it as such. Besides, being well groomed and properly dressed will help boost your confidence.

Sooner or later, someone will call your name and escort you into the interview room. *This is it.* From here on you are on your own. It is too late for any more preparation. But remember, you asked for this opportunity to prove your fitness, and you are here because your request was granted.

What happens when you go in?

The usual sequence of events will be as follows: The clerk (who is often the board stenographer) will introduce you to the chairman of the oral board, who will introduce you to the other members of the board. Acknowledge the introductions before you sit down. Do not be surprised if you find a microphone facing you or a stenotypist sitting by. Oral interviews are usually recorded in the event of an appeal or other review.

Usually the chairman of the board will open the interview by reviewing the highlights of your education and work experience from your application – primarily for the benefit of the other members of the board, as well as to get the material into the record. Do not interrupt or comment unless there is an error or significant misinterpretation; if that is the case, do not hesitate. But do not quibble about insignificant matters. Also, he will usually ask you some question about your education, experience or your present job – partly to get you to start talking and to establish the interviewing "rapport." He may start the actual questioning, or turn it over to one of the other members. Frequently, each member undertakes the questioning on a particular area, one in which he is perhaps most competent, so you can expect each member to participate in the examination. Because time is limited, you may also expect some rather abrupt switches in the direction the questioning takes, so do not be upset by it. Normally, a board member will not pursue a single line of questioning unless he discovers a particular strength or weakness.

After each member has participated, the chairman will usually ask whether any member has any further questions, then will ask you if you have anything you wish to add. Unless you are expecting this question, it may floor you. Worse, it may start you off on an extended, extemporaneous speech. The board is not usually seeking more information. The question is principally to offer you a last opportunity to present further qualifications or to indicate that you have nothing to add. So, if you feel that a significant qualification or characteristic has been overlooked, it is proper to point it out in a sentence or so. Do not compliment the board on the thoroughness of their examination – they have been sketchy, and you know it. If you wish, merely say, "No thank you, I have nothing further to add." This is a point where you can "talk yourself out" of a good impression or fail to present an important bit of information. Remember, *you close the interview yourself.*

The chairman will then say, "That is all, Mr. _____, thank you." Do not be startled; the interview is over, and quicker than you think. Thank him, gather your belongings and take your leave. Save your sigh of relief for the other side of the door.

How to put your best foot forward
Throughout this entire process, you may feel that the board individually and collectively is trying to pierce your defenses, seek out your hidden weaknesses and embarrass and confuse you. Actually, this is not true. They are obliged to make an appraisal of your qualifications for the job you are seeking, and they want to see you in your best light. Remember, they must interview all candidates and a non-cooperative candidate may become a failure in spite of their best efforts to bring out his qualifications. Here are 15 suggestions that will help you:

1) **Be natural – Keep your attitude confident, not cocky**
If you are not confident that you can do the job, do not expect the board to be. Do not apologize for your weaknesses, try to bring out your strong points. The board is interested in a positive, not negative, presentation. Cockiness will antagonize any board member and make him wonder if you are covering up a weakness by a false show of strength.

2) **Get comfortable, but don't lounge or sprawl**
Sit erectly but not stiffly. A careless posture may lead the board to conclude that you are careless in other things, or at least that you are not impressed by the importance of the occasion. Either conclusion is natural, even if incorrect. Do not fuss with your clothing, a pencil or an ashtray. Your hands may occasionally be useful to emphasize a point; do not let them become a point of distraction.

3) **Do not wisecrack or make small talk**
This is a serious situation, and your attitude should show that you consider it as such. Further, the time of the board is limited – they do not want to waste it, and neither should you.

4) Do not exaggerate your experience or abilities

In the first place, from information in the application or other interviews and sources, the board may know more about you than you think. Secondly, you probably will not get away with it. An experienced board is rather adept at spotting such a situation, so do not take the chance.

5) If you know a board member, do not make a point of it, yet do not hide it

Certainly you are not fooling him, and probably not the other members of the board. Do not try to take advantage of your acquaintanceship – it will probably do you little good.

6) Do not dominate the interview

Let the board do that. They will give you the clues – do not assume that you have to do all the talking. Realize that the board has a number of questions to ask you, and do not try to take up all the interview time by showing off your extensive knowledge of the answer to the first one.

7) Be attentive

You only have 20 minutes or so, and you should keep your attention at its sharpest throughout. When a member is addressing a problem or question to you, give him your undivided attention. Address your reply principally to him, but do not exclude the other board members.

8) Do not interrupt

A board member may be stating a problem for you to analyze. He will ask you a question when the time comes. Let him state the problem, and wait for the question.

9) Make sure you understand the question

Do not try to answer until you are sure what the question is. If it is not clear, restate it in your own words or ask the board member to clarify it for you. However, do not haggle about minor elements.

10) Reply promptly but not hastily

A common entry on oral board rating sheets is "candidate responded readily," or "candidate hesitated in replies." Respond as promptly and quickly as you can, but do not jump to a hasty, ill-considered answer.

11) Do not be peremptory in your answers

A brief answer is proper – but do not fire your answer back. That is a losing game from your point of view. The board member can probably ask questions much faster than you can answer them.

12) Do not try to create the answer you think the board member wants

He is interested in what kind of mind you have and how it works – not in playing games. Furthermore, he can usually spot this practice and will actually grade you down on it.

13) Do not switch sides in your reply merely to agree with a board member

Frequently, a member will take a contrary position merely to draw you out and to see if you are willing and able to defend your point of view. Do not start a debate, yet do not surrender a good position. If a position is worth taking, it is worth defending.

14) Do not be afraid to admit an error in judgment if you are shown to be wrong

The board knows that you are forced to reply without any opportunity for careful consideration. Your answer may be demonstrably wrong. If so, admit it and get on with the interview.

15) Do not dwell at length on your present job

The opening question may relate to your present assignment. Answer the question but do not go into an extended discussion. You are being examined for a *new* job, not your present one. As a matter of fact, try to phrase ALL your answers in terms of the job for which you are being examined.

Basis of Rating

Probably you will forget most of these "do's" and "don'ts" when you walk into the oral interview room. Even remembering them all will not ensure you a passing grade. Perhaps you did not have the qualifications in the first place. But remembering them will help you to put your best foot forward, without treading on the toes of the board members.

Rumor and popular opinion to the contrary notwithstanding, an oral board wants you to make the best appearance possible. They know you are under pressure – but they also want to see how you respond to it as a guide to what your reaction would be under the pressures of the job you seek. They will be influenced by the degree of poise you display, the personal traits you show and the manner in which you respond.

ABOUT THIS BOOK

This book contains tests divided into Examination Sections. Go through each test, answering every question in the margin. We have also attached a sample answer sheet at the back of the book that can be removed and used. At the end of each test look at the answer key and check your answers. On the ones you got wrong, look at the right answer choice and learn. Do not fill in the answers first. Do not memorize the questions and answers, but understand the answer and principles involved. On your test, the questions will likely be different from the samples. Questions are changed and new ones added. If you understand these past questions you should have success with any changes that arise. Tests may consist of several types of questions. We have additional books on each subject should more study be advisable or necessary for you. Finally, the more you study, the better prepared you will be. This book is intended to be the last thing you study before you walk into the examination room. Prior study of relevant texts is also recommended. NLC publishes some of these in our Fundamental Series. Knowledge and good sense are important factors in passing your exam. Good luck also helps. So now study this Passbook, absorb the material contained within and take that knowledge into the examination. Then do your best to pass that exam.

EXAMINATION SECTION

EXAMINATION SECTION
TEST 1

DIRECTIONS: Each question or incomplete statement is followed by several suggested answers or completions. Select the one the BEST answers the question or completes the statement. *PRINT THE LETTER OF THE CORRECT ANSWER IN THE SPACE AT THE RIGHT.*

1. From a habitation planning perspective, there are significant trends among persons whose primary diagnosis is either mental retardation, epilepsy, cerebral palsy, or dual diagnosis. These trends include

    A. less need among epileptics for assistance in language
    B. more need among mentally retarded persons for assistance in mobility
    C. significant group differences in the mean level of assistance scores on self-direction
    D. generally insignificant need among all groups for assistance in independent living

1._____

2. Any procedure that encourages a client to engage in the early steps of a sequence of behaviors is referred to as

    A. response priming
    B. prompting
    C. impulsion
    D. shaping

2._____

3. From a habilitation standpoint, quality of life is

    A. the outcome of individuals meeting basic needs in private
    B. basically an intrapersonal phenomenon and a product of self-perception
    C. defined by the consumer rather than the professional
    D. different for persons with and without disabilities

3._____

4. Which of the following conditions is produced only by congenital factors?

    A. Muscular dystrophy
    B. Epilepsy
    C. Myelomeningocele
    D. Cerebral palsy

4._____

5. The environmental assessment known as space coding is used to evaluate a(n)

    A. person's functional reinforcements
    B. person's behavioral setting
    C. organizational structure
    D. psychosocial climate

5._____

6. In adults, the diagnostic correlative to autism is known as

    A. dual diagnosis
    B. gross dysfunction
    C. apathy
    D. antisocial disorder

6._____

7. Which of the following is a behavior reduction procedure?

   A. Fading
   B. Response priming
   C. Extinction
   D. Shaping

8. Which of the following is a diagnostic condition that is most likely to result in emotional/behavioral impairment?

   A. Autism
   B. Anencephalus
   C. Cerebral palsy
   D. Traumatic brain injury

9. In general, a wheelchair-bound client with neuromuscular impairment should be bathed

   A. daily
   B. every other day
   C. twice weekly
   D. weekly

10. In the maintenance phase of a habilitation program, which of the following actions is associated with the agency's systems interface?

    A. Environmental assessments of necessary skills
    B. Altering or preserving interagency and intersector working agreements
    C. Committing resources to placement
    D. Allocation of staff to long-term supports

11. Which of the following is not a component of the limbic system?

    A. Hypothalamus
    B. Amygdala
    C. Pons
    D. Hippocampus

12. Which of the following conditions is likely to produce a neurological handicap?

    A. Amputation
    B. Muscular dystrophy
    C. Arthritis
    D. Epilepsy

13. For a client with cerebral palsy, ataxia will generally continue to improve until the age of approximately _____, at which time balance and coordination systems will reach maximum improvement.

    A. 8-10
    B. 12-15
    C. 15-18
    D. 19-25

14. Children with Down syndrome typically suffer from each of the following physical problems, except   14.____

    A. short limbs
    B. low muscle strength
    C. hypertonia
    D. high joint flexibility

15. Of the following skills, which would typically be taught to an autistic client first?   15.____

    A. Labeling objects and events using simple sentences
    B. Appropriate pronoun usage
    C. Responding to questions
    D. The use of two-word utterances to label pictures or events

16. Which of the following statements concerning an individual habilitation plan is true?   16.____

    A. It should be developed individually by the habilitation specialist
    B. It should name the agency that will provide the service, and then leave personnel assignments up to that agency
    C. A specific evaluation procedure and schedule for determining the achievement of objectives should be included in the plan
    D. Parents or guardians of clients should only be shown the plan after it has been written

17. Most language programs used in habilitation involve a behavioral approach to the acquisition of symbols and words known as   17.____

    A. phonics
    B. discrimination training
    C. gradual articulation
    D. whole language

18. Research has shown that the best way to teach emergency telephone skills to mentally retarded clients is to   18.____

    A. downplay the importance of the skill as it relates to their well-being
    B. integrate lessons into a generalized unit of telephone skills
    C. divide each emergency call into a series of sub-tasks
    D. conduct simulations that are as much like real emergencies as possible

19. What type of cerebral palsy is characterized by abnormally high muscle tone, tight or stiff muscle joints, and limited movement in affected areas?   19.____

    A. Diplegic
    B. Athetoid
    C. Ataxic
    D. Spastic

20. Which of the following is a social indicator of a community's quality of life?   20.____

    A. Material well-being
    B. Residential arrangement

C. Leisure
D. Psychological well-being

21. In the pre-vocational and vocational training of mentally retarded clients, which of the following forms of instructor assistance is generally most desirable?

    A. Physical assistance
    B. Modeling
    C. Physical prompting
    D. Verbal cue

22. Which of the following is not a transitional-situational disorder?

    A. Conversion reaction
    B. Adjustment reaction
    C. Suicide gestures
    D. Symptomatic alcoholism

23. For reducing the self-stimulatory behaviors of autistic or dual-diagnosis clients, effective approaches include
    I. overcorrection
    II. time-outs
    III. extinction
    IV. punishment

    A. I and II
    B. I and IV
    C. II, III and IV
    D. III and IV

24. Which of the following skill domains is relatively weak among clients with spina bifida?

    A. Long-term memory
    B. Writing
    C. Spelling
    D. Social cognition

25. A therapist used physical prompts to teach sign language to several profoundly retarded, autistic children. Training consisted of the therapist holding up an item (e.g., an apple) while saying "apple." If the child failed to make the sign for apple, the therapist guided the child's hand into the correct sign while repeating "apple." Once the child made the correct sign, reinforcement was provided. Eventually, the therapist provided less help to the child until the sign was made without assistance.
    This case illustrates the use of the technique of

    A. fading
    B. extinction
    C. differential reinforcement of other behavior
    D. response priming

KEY (CORRECT ANSWERS)

1.	A	11.	C
2.	A	12.	D
3.	C	13.	A
4.	C	14.	C
5.	B	15.	D
6.	A	16.	C
7.	C	17.	B
8.	A	18.	C
9.	A	19.	D
10.	B	20.	C

21. D
22. A
23. B
24. B
25. A

TEST 2

DIRECTIONS: Each question or incomplete statement is followed by several suggested answers or completions. Select the one the BEST answers the question or completes the statement. *PRINT THE LETTER OF THE CORRECT ANSWER IN THE SPACE AT THE RIGHT.*

1. For teaching specific competencies such as cognition and physical movements, one of the most useful instructional techniques would probably be to

    A. use a wide range of relevant stimulus and response variation
    B. conduct mass trials
    C. focus initially on demand more than reward
    D. present multiple training examples within individual sessions

2. The new behavioral/training technology used in habilitation programs focuses on the person-environmental perspective, and has each of the following characteristics, except

    A. environments are best described in terms of global names or functions, rather than specific demand characteristics
    B. the behavioral and competency requirements of environments can be objectively and reliably assessed
    C. personal and environmental attributes can be compared and discrepancies identified
    D. persons can be accurately described in terms of a set of concrete and measurable attributes

3. A number of agency-level factors are critical to an effective and efficient habilitation program. Which of the following factors includes the approaches used to assess an adult with disabilities on relevant performance requirements?

    A. Systems interface
    B. Habilitation strategies
    C. Natural environment
    D. Agency characteristics

4. In the human brain, functions associated with planning, initiating, and organizing generally originate in the

    A. amygdala
    B. occipital lobe
    C. frontal lobe
    D. pons

5. Overcorrection is a behavior reduction technique that

    A. requires fewer staff than other procedures generally do
    B. avoids physical or manual guidance
    C. is designed only to reduce problem behavior
    D. generally requires one-to-one supervision

6. In a typical habilitation plan documentation format, which of the following elements appears first?

    A. Interdisciplinary recommendations
    B. Existing prosthetics and environmental modifications
    C. Review of previous life-aim goals
    D. Service plan

7. A young client with myelomeningocele and a resulting neurogenic bladder should generally be expected to self-catheterize by around the age of

    A. 3 or 4
    B. 6 or 7
    C. 9 or 10
    D. 12 or 13

8. Which of the following skills are generally common to all types of habilitation curricula?

    A. living/work/recreation skills
    B. language
    C. social skills
    D. problem-solving/decision making

9. As quality-of-life measures, social indicators can accurately represent
    I. the collective quality of community life
    II. an individual's perceived quality of life
    III. outcomes from rehabilitation programs

    A. I only
    B. I and II
    C. II and III
    D. I, II and III

10. The main obstacle to the teaching of self-feeding skills to developmentally disabled clients is the

    A. infrequency of learning opportunities
    B. lack of social reference points or consequences for specified behaviors
    C. ethical problems inherent in the use of food as a reinforcement
    D. need for physical agility

11. A habilitation worker is training a client in the presence of a second trainer who will later assist the client's later efforts to work on the same task. This is a simple example of

    A. stimulus control
    B. generalization
    C. discrimination
    D. forward chaining

12. What is the behavioral term for the procedure used to teach successive approximations to a complex target behavior, until the client is able to perform the complete behavior?

    A. Chunking
    B. Overcorrection

C. Shaping
D. Normalization

13. Which of the following muscle groups will generally be most important for a client with T12 spina bifida?

    A. Glutei
    B. Gastrocs
    C. Hip flexors
    D. Anterior tibials

14. For adults with disabilities, Title _____ the Social Security Act delineates the maintenance program that is most likely to be used.

    A. II
    B. VII
    C. IX
    D. XVI

15. The specific diagnostic criteria for infantile autism include
    I. Peculiar speech patterns
    II. Delusions
    III. Onset before 30 months of age

    A. I only
    B. I and III
    C. II and III
    D. I, II, and III

16. Which of the following is a subjective measure of a client's quality of life?

    A. Available services
    B. Education
    C. Mobility
    D. Competence/productivity

17. Because of the complex difficulties involved in teaching or reducing the behaviors of developmentally disabled clients, which of the following techniques is generally most limited in it application among habilitation programs?

    A. Fading
    B. Overcorrection
    C. Response contingent stimulation
    D. Extinction

18. Which of the following is not a category in the Autism Behavior Checklist, the first component of the Autism Screening Instrument for Educational Planning (ASIEP)?

    A. Sensory
    B. Body and object use
    C. Language
    D. Associative

19. Which of the following is categorized as an anxiety disorder?

    A. Conversion reaction
    B. Adjustment reaction
    C. Lesch-Nyan syndrome
    D. Antisocial personality

20. A client is introduced to an integrated employment environment. If she is placed in competitive employment,

    A. most of the workers in her workplace or department will be disabled
    B. her wages will be at or above the prevailing or minimum rate
    C. whatever supports are provided will be at the job site
    D. she will not require ongoing job-related supports

21. A workshop instructor wants to increase the attentiveness of a 10-year-old child with mild mental retardation. With the help of an aide, the instructor reinforces the first occurrence of attentive behavior that occurs after 1 minute of the behavior has elapsed. This is an example of _____ reinforcement.

    A. variable interval
    B. fixed interval
    C. variable ratio
    D. fixed ratio

22. The most common functional disabilities resulting from a traumatic brain injury include
    I. Motor disturbances
    II. Fatigue
    III. Difficulty in maintaining concentration
    IV. Altered control and expression of emotions

    A. I and III
    B. I, III and IV
    C. I, III and IV
    D. I, II, III and IV

23. When used as a behavior reduction strategy, a response contingent stimulus should be each of the following, except

    A. strong enough to suppress the behavior
    B. consistently applied to every occurrence of the behavior
    C. begin as mildly as possible, and then increase in intensity
    D. applied immediately following the undesired behavior

24. Which of the following approaches is used to assess a client's psychosocial climate?

    A. Systems maintenance analysis
    B. Social ecology
    C. Space coding
    D. Physical setting analysis

25. Which of the following is characterized as a generalized positive reinforcer?

    A. A smile
    B. Food
    C. Praise
    D. Money

25.___

KEY (CORRECT ANSWERS)

1. B
2. A
3. B
4. C
5. D

6. A
7. B
8. D
9. A
10. A

11. B
12. C
13. C
14. D
15. B

16. A
17. D
18. D
19. A
20. B

21. B
22. D
23. C
24. B
25. D

EXAMINATION SECTION
TEST 1

DIRECTIONS: Each question or incomplete statement is followed by several suggested answers or completions. Select the one that BEST answers the question or completes the statement. *PRINT THE LETTER OF THE CORRECT ANSWER IN THE SPACE AT THE RIGHT.*

1. In working with adolescent groups, an important point to remember is to give

    A. guidance without taking matters out of the group's hands
    B. guidance to the youth leaders only
    C. assistance only when the groups ask for it
    D. direct assistance at every opportunity

2. The BASIC purpose to be kept in mind when programming group activities for delinquent adolescents is that

    A. group activities are natural for delinquents
    B. the activities should focus on control and discipline
    C. the youths should share in the program expenses
    D. the activities should focus on total freedom of expression

3. Workers assigned to your unit are experiencing difficulties with programming group activities. The programs seen to be out of context with the problems of the youths, and the youths are reported to be bored, evasive, and non-participating.
An important factor in programming that you, as unit supervisor, must teach them is

    A. to involve the group members in the planning and implementation of all programs
    B. to include current procedures like enounter, reality therapy, and crisis intervention
    C. that they must have individual meetings with key members to enlist their aid and assistance
    D. that they are not providing enough direction and control to the group meetings

4. The one of the following groups of characteristics which MOST correctly describes anti-social adolescent groups is

    A. fraternity, mutual respect, and interest in each other
    B. group loyalty, need to retaliate, and the necessity to fight
    C. divisiveness, mistrust, and self-centeredness
    D. none of the above

5. You are supervising a new worker who tells you, during his supervisory conference, that he feels that he has not been able to help his group to re-direct their energies into productive channels.
It would be BEST for you to advise this worker that

    A. he should not be discouraged because adolescents have boundless energy that is difficult to control
    B. adolescent groups respond to planning and direction, and that he should set up some simple form of organization
    C. the conflict and competition concept of group behavior requires group psychotherapy
    D. his anxieties are getting in the way of effective work with his group

6. A new worker in the unit under your supervision shows in his recording that he has been able to overcome his feelings of insecurity in his new role of working with his group and to work through the initial testing period imposed on him by the group. However, during his supervisory conference, you discover that he is extremely anxious because the group does not seem to be verbalizing their problems with him.
You should advise this worker in conference that

   A. these are hard-core youths who do not talk about their problems
   B. his recording is weak, and should be done in process style for the next six months
   C. his anxiety is probably being communicated to the group, inhibiting them from verbalizing their problems
   D. a marathon encounter with the group may help them to verbalize their problems

7. In preparation for a staff conference covering principles of working with alienated youth groups, you assign different aspects of the subject to different workers. In his notes, the worker who is to discuss *process in working with groups* lists the following:
   1. sensitivity to the pace of group movement
   2. resistance and resentment arising from domination by the worker
   3. time and place of meetings

   An IMPORTANT part that was omitted by the worker is

   A. realistic programming
   B. awareness of *where the group is at*
   C. the importance of sensitivity training
   D. supervision

8. A youth worker reports to you in a supervisory conference that the youths in his group are unfriendly and bossy with each other, but that when he leaves them, roughhousing breaks out.
The MOST likely explanation for this is that

   A. he is not exercising enough control
   B. he is probably too strict and tight with them
   C. this particular group of kids usually acts this way
   D. this is unusual behavior of alienated youth

9. The SIGNIFICANT factors that would distinguish a constructive and orderly group of adolescents from an anti-social gang are the

   A. aims, quality of the relationships, and behavior of the individuals
   B. aims, personality of the members, and locale
   C. age, problems, and behavior of the members
   D. locale, personality of the members, and leadership

10. Youth workers involved with groups of adolescent girls may have to deal with problems of sexual acting-out. Programming for girls involved in sexual acting-out should have as its BASIC purpose

    A. security building and developing a feeling of being needed and wanted
    B. sex information and a discussion of birth control and abortion
    C. rap sessions on dating, making out, and male-female psychology
    D. parties, dances, outings, and bus rides

11. Adolescents have many fears that they are ashamed to show because they are afraid of disapproval. Restraining these fears may lead to anxieties that could be even more troublesome.
    To help youths resolve such problems, youth service units should emphasize in their programming

    A. activities that help youths gain self-confidence
    B. rap sessions on anxiety
    C. activities that are not likely to produce fear
    D. hiking, swimming, wrestling, and basketball

12. All of the following are purposes of group counseling EXCEPT

    A. avoidance of treating pathology as such
    B. helping clients attain a better level of functioning
    C. modifying social and familial problems
    D. resolving intra-psychic conflicts

13. A MAJOR advantage of having group programs for local teenagers in Youth Services Agency neighborhood offices is that

    A. these programs are less expensive to operate
    B. the participating groups are mutual groups in their own environment
    C. this activity is necessary for suppressing riots
    D. such programs serve as good public relations

14. A worker reports about his youth council that one of the sub-groups in the council revolves around a boy who has many constructive ideas. However, this boy's participation is limited due to the rivalry between him and the elected president.
    The supervisor should advise the worker to

    A. have the leader of the sub-group excluded from the council
    B. help the leader of the sub-group participate more actively
    C. tell the leader of the sub-group to *play ball* with the rest of the council
    D. let the council settle this problem without outside assistance

15. One of your youth workers is having difficulty forming a group in a particular neighborhood. Parents in that area are upset about the idea of teenage groups. This worker plans to meet with some of these parents, and he asks your help in reaching a goal with them.
    As supervisor, you should advise him to approach this problem by

    A. helping the parents to see that group activities are a sign of a youth's growth, not of a lack of gratitude or affection for his parents
    B. informing the parents that it is the professional opinion of the Youth Services Agency that groups are necessary in order to serve youth constructively
    C. postponing this meeting until you can convince individual parents of the value of groups
    D. helping the parents to see that many of their teenagers are having difficulties at home and in school because they do not participate in group activities

16. Experts have described festivals, fairs, holidays, etc. as *nothing less nor more than excesses provided by law and which owe their cheerful character to the release which they bring.*
    The significance of this in programming unit projects is to

    A. have the workers assist the community in sponsoring fairs, block dances, etc.
    B. leave the sponsoring of fairs, dances, etc. to associations affiliated with the police department
    C. avoid involving large groups of people in public affairs because of the danger of fights, riots, etc.
    D. use a good part of the unit's budget for fairs, dances, bazaars, etc.

17. Which one of the groups listed below has the following four characteristics:
    1. Basic depressive character
    2. Intolerance for frustration and pain
    3. Lack of meaningful objects
    4. Artificial technique to maintain self-regard?

    A. College students B. Drug abusers
    C. Adolescents   D. Alienated youth

18. The MOST important consideration in evaluating the ego strength of an angry, deprived, mistreated, frustrated, evasive client is the client's ability to

    A. verbalize his problems
    B. redirect his anger
    C. form a relationship with an accepting worker
    D. hold a job

19. When a worker, in his first interview with a parent, tries to take down a developmental history of a boy, he usually gets many meaningless answers, such as *It was normal* or *I don't remember.*
    The worker should realize that

    A. this information is inaccurate and should be disregarded
    B. the parent is under stress at first, and should be able to give more factual information later
    C. the parent purposely is withholding valuable information about the boy
    D. the parent must be told that if he cannot cooperate he cannot be helped

20. One of the workers under your supervision is puzzled as to why a mother she was working with broke off contacts prermaturely. When you read the record of this mother, you learn that she had become overdependent upon the worker before suddenly stopping her visits.
    In the supervisory conference, you should help the worker to understand that this type of client

    A. is flighty, evasive, and has low reality testing
    B. is in need of deep psychotherapy
    C. is defending herself against this overdependence
    D. needs the chance to test her limits with an accepting person

21. When a worker is troubled because youths in his group ask him personal questions and he does not know how to answer them, as unit supervisor it would be BEST for you to advise the worker to

   A. interrogate the youths in detail about the reasons behind the questions
   B. tell the youths all they want to know, so that the worker appears friendly and human
   C. give a frank, brief, truthful answer and then immediately redirect the youths back to their own problems
   D. point out to the youths that the worker's personal life is not their business

22. Psychiatrists are usually concerned with the total functioning and integration of the human personality. Caseworkers usually concentrate on

   A. the same thing, but for shorter periods of time
   B. the same thing, but without prescribing medication
   C. helping the client to deal with the presenting problem
   D. all of the above

23. Some people feel that by cutting down temptations and stimuli, delinquency can be substantially decreased. Specific measures are curfews, eliminating the cruder forms of violence from the mass media, reducing the number of sexually stimulating publications available to youth, keeping down teenagers' resources for obtaining liquor, increasing recreational facilities, etc. The STRONGEST flaw in this approach is that

   A. it is not fair to non-delinquents
   B. it would not seriously affect the hard-core delinquent
   C. the community is not yet prepared for it
   D. it needs more time to prove itself

24. A COMMON error made by youth workers who are beginning to find out about the influence of unconscious desires and emotions on human behavior is to

   A. probe the client unnecessarily
   B. become over-assured that they can solve the client's problem
   C. slow up the pace of the interview
   D. look for the proper treatment method based on the client's neurosis

25. A basic technique which is used to obtain knowledge of the problem to be solved and sufficient understanding of the troubled person and of the situation, so that the problem can be solved effectively, is known as

   A. psychosomatics
   C. recording
   B. interviewing
   D. supervisory conferences

26. Which of the following is a CORRECT definition of the term *acceptance* as used in social work?

   A. A decision made at intake to accept the client as a case for the agency to handle
   B. The concept that the worker does not pass judgment on the client's behavior
   C. The concept of a positive and active understanding by the worker of the feelings a client expresses through his behavior
   D. Communication to the client that the worker does not condone and accept his antisocial behavior

27. Beginning youth workers are usually informed in a training session that they should be non-judgmental, should not become dependent on the client's liking them, and should not become angry. However, in an attempt to suppress these feelings, workers often behave in a stilted and artificial manner with clients.
As a supervisor, you should help your workers

   A. seek counseling to help them understand their angry feelings
   B. realize that they were not yet ready for that type of training
   C. understand that this artificiality will soon pass by as easily as it came
   D. recognize the naturalness of these feelings and learn to control their expression

28. A worker in the unit under your supervision has a youth in his group who has developed a strong antagonism toward him. You can find nothing that the worker has done to arouse such antagonism in the youth.
This antagonism is probably due to

   A. restrictions imposed on the client by the agency
   B. factors deeply hidden in the client's personality
   C. the youth's feeling of guilt because he has withheld information from the worker
   D. the fact that the worker may have promised the youth too much

29. The development of an emotional rapport, positive or negative, between the client and the worker is not abnormal, but inevitable. Sometimes the feelings that develop as a result of this rapport become excessively intense.
In those instances, the worker should

   A. request that the client be given another worker
   B. control the nature and intensity of the feelings
   C. ignore the feelings, which will disappear soon
   D. confront the client with the inappropriateness of these feelings

30. In social work, when we talk of ambivalence, we mean that the

   A. social worker refrains from imposing his moral judgments on the client
   B. supervisor assists the worker in understanding the psychological causes for client's behavior
   C. client has conflicting interests, desires, and emotions
   D. client is seeking someone who will understand the subjective reasons for his behavior

31. Although we can judge statements about objectively verifiable matters to be true or false, we are not similarly justified in passing judgments on subjective attitudes. This statement BEST explains the rationale behind the social work principle of

   A. empathy
   B. self-awareness
   C. non-judgmentality
   D. confidentiality

32. A psychological factor that explains why generally lawabiding individuals can become a part of a violent crowd is

   A. the deep urge for destruction and violence inherent in man
   B. the anonymity of the group would allow individuals to yield to restrained instincts
   C. that there is force in numbers, decreasing the likelihood of personal injury
   D. that man is basically a *herd animal,* so the mob is our natural environment

33. When you have learned that one of your workers has organized a protest, you should advise him to

    A. be aware that the group may not be able to defend themselves against the police
    B. alert the community to distract the police to another area
    C. call off the protest because of the probability of danger
    D. take precautions with his group in order to be sure that the protest will be orderly

34. Some local merchants are disturbed because they feel that a group of boys who *hang on the corner* will develop into a delinquent gang. They invite you, the unit supervisor, to address them at a meeting in order to describe the characteristics of delinquent gangs to them.
    In your talk to these merchants, you should

    A. describe how delinquent gangs make a career of hanging around, have a blind loyalty among members, and see destruction as their way of hitting back at society
    B. advise them to call off the meeting because the delinquent gang as such has disappeared
    C. assure them that they should not be concerned because you have a worker in that area who has this group under surveillance
    D. contact your area administrator because this involves a relationship with the community that is not on your level of responsibility

35. According to the REPORT OF THE NATIONAL ADVISORY COMMITTEE ON CIVIL DISORDERS, riots are dramatic forms of protest expressing

    A. hostility to government or private institutions
    B. undefined but real frustrations
    C. anger at the failure of society to provide certain groups with adequate opportunities
    D. all of the above

36. Many neighborhoods seem to develop a subculture in which forms of criminal and delinquent behavior and values are accepted as norms.
    If the unit area happens to be in one of these neighborhoods, the unit supervisor would be BEST advised to keep in mind that

    A. we know less about changing subcultures than we know about influencing groups and individuals
    B. it is easier to change subcultures than to influence groups and individuals
    C. subcultures are simple to identify, and helping the members to resolve their problems is comparatively easy
    D. this is only a theory and, therefore, should not influence the functioning of the unit office

37. The neighborhood drug abuse prevention network of the Addiction Services Agency is a series of broad-based community groups called

    A. CARE AND AWARE   B. EVIL AND WEAK
    C. RARE AND AWARE   D. NACE AND CARE

38. An agency whose sole purpose is to fight addiction through a comprehensive prevention and rehabilitation program is

    A. Daytop Village
    B. Narcotics Addiction Control Commission
    C. Addiction Services Agency
    D. Phoenix House

39. Agencies which have been traditionally used by the Youth Services Agency for the purpose of sponsoring approved group programs to help youth improve their behavior are:

    A. Madison-Felicia, Vocational Advisory Service, Catholic Youth Organization, United Neighborhood Houses, Federation Employment and Guidance Service, Community Centers
    B. Office of Economic Opportunity, Catholic Youth Organization, Police Athletic League, Federation Employment and Guidance Service, Vocational Advisory Service, Jewish Family Service, Federation of Protestant Welfare Agencies
    C. Catholic Youth Organization, United Neighborhood Houses, Young Men's Christian Association, Protestant Council, Police Athletic League, Builders For the Family and Youth
    D. Catholic Youth Organization, Young Men's Christian Association, Protestant Council, Police Athletic League, Office of Economic Opportunity, Builders For Family and Youth, Vocational Advisory Service

40. Agencies that are used by Youth Services Agency to provide individual casework treatment services for Youth Services Agency clients who need individual therapy for deep-seated problems are:

    A. Jewish Family Services, State Division for Youth, Catholic Charities, Staten Island Family Service, Salvation Army, Community Education
    B. Big Brothers, Catholic Charities, Jewish Board of Guardians, Jewish Family Services, Salvation Army
    C. Catholic Youth Organization, Vocational Advisory Service, Melrose Center, Federation Employment and Guidance Service, United Neighborhood Houses
    D. Catholic Charities, Jewish Family Service, Vocational Foundation, Vermont Program, Big Brothers, Boys' Harbor, Salvation Army

41. The Departments that make up the Human Resources Administration are:

    A. Manpower and Career Development, Office of Economic Opportunity, Commission on Civil Disorders, Youth Services Agency, Addiction Services, Social Services, Community Development
    B. Manpower and Career Development Agency, Office of Economic Opportunity, Youth Services Agency, Addiction Services Agency, Department of Social Services, Commission on Human Rights, Community Volunteers
    C. Human Resources Administration Central Staff, Manpower and Career Development Agency, Community Development Agency, Department of Social Services, Youth Services Agency, Addiction Services Agency, Office of Education Affairs
    D. Human Resources Administration Central Staff, Manpower and Career Development Agency, Department of Social Services, Youth Services Agency, Addiction Services Agency, Office of Economic Opportunity, Commission on Human Rights

42. A Youth Services Agency project that was developed in 1968 in response to the findings of the National Advisory Commission on Civil Disorders (Kerner-Lindsay Report) and which was designed to develop and demonstrate model approaches to engender interracial understanding between teenagers is the

    A. Youth Opportunity Center
    B. Demonstration and Training Unit
    C. Interdepartmental Neighborhood Service Center
    D. Vermont Project

42.____

43. Which one of the following is mandated to provide services to the poverty-stricken, to improve the quality of these services and the methods of delivering them, to carry out the legal commitment to the poor, and to help the poor to help themselves?

    A. Office of Economic Opportunity
    B. Environmental Resources Administration
    C. Community Action Program
    D. Model Cities Program

43.____

44. An indication of mature behavior to be sought for in the client and encouraged by the youth worker is the

    A. ability to become involved in issues of racism, urban life, and human rights
    B. development of some controls over the impulse to act out
    C. formulation of definite and specific goals in careers
    D. steady, consistent pattern of behavior that is relatively free of ambivalent feelings

44.____

45. That point in human development which marks a person's passage into adolescence is known as

    A. maturity   B. the Oedipal stage
    C. the genital stage   D. puberty

45.____

46. An important factor to remember about the mental, physical, social, and emotional growth of an adolescent is that the

    A. pace is uneven and individual
    B. pace is relatively even
    C. rate of growth is predictable
    D. growth has no special pattern

46.____

47. Adolescents are more likely to understand the concrete and the specific, rather than general ideas like justice, honesty, love, etc.
    The implication of this concept for the unit supervisor in guiding his staff is

    A. that programming should include recreation, job counseling, school help, and visits at times of crisis
    B. the necessity to make sure that the programs use a large part of their budget for *treats* for the youth
    C. to be sure the staff is directing much of their energy into pointing up the importance of these general concepts
    D. to help the youths understand that life has taught them to be mistrustful

47.____

48. The theory of juvenile delinquency that traces much of delinquency back to failures in family relationships during the early years of childhood, and to continuing family difficulties, offers help to the youth worker in

   A. forming a general picture of the typical delinquent
   B. understanding that fighting is one of the best ways to rise to the top
   C. identifying normal growth needs of adolescents and the obstacles against healthy maturity
   D. realizing that delinquents are children at heart and are best treated as children

49. The theory of juvenile delinquency which holds that youths from minority groups turn to anti-social behavior when they feel that their access to social, educational, and economic opportunities in legal and approved ways is blocked has had a strong impact on the establishment of agencies like the

   A. Job Corps
   B. Community Development Agency
   C. Youth Board of the 1950's
   D. Addiction Services Agency

50. Which of the following is a descriptive term for a client who is resistive, breaks appointments, withholds information, beclouds issues, relates to others in a primitive, often distorted, fashion, and acts out his wishes and conflicts in his contact with the worker?

   A. Psychotic
   B. Narcotics addict
   C. Schizophrenic
   D. Character disorder

KEY (CORRECT ANSWERS)

1. A	11. A	21. C	31. C	41. C
2. B	12. D	22. C	32. B	42. D
3. A	13. B	23. B	33. D	43. A
4. B	14. B	24. A	34. A	44. B
5. B	15. A	25. B	35. D	45. D
6. C	16. A	26. C	36. A	46. A
7. A	17. B	27. D	37. C	47. A
8. B	18. C	28. B	38. C	48. C
9. A	19. B	29. B	39. C	49. A
10. A	20. C	30. C	40. B	50. D

TEST 2

DIRECTIONS: Each question or incomplete statement is followed by several suggested answers or completions. Select the one that BEST answers the question or completes the statement. *PRINT THE LETTER OF THE CORRECT ANSWER IN THE SPACE AT THE RIGHT.*

1. Adolescents who become involved in delinquent behavior are usually angry or frustrated a large part of their time. Conscious awareness of the intensity of their needs makes them feel weak.
   For this reason, they frequently

   A. are easier to work with
   B. prefer strong male youth workers
   C. need to be controlled and disciplined
   D. have to show the world they don't care what happens

   1.____

2. Sociologists and behavioral scientists provided the ideas of cohesion, conflict, competition, cooperation, authority, leadership, and stratification that are clearly manifested in

   A. supervision
   B. addiction
   C. group behavior
   D. casework therapy

   2.____

3. The one of the following causes of juvenile delinquency among sub-lower class youth which has been given increased attention in recent years is the

   A. prevalence of the one-parent family
   B. failure of family relationships in the early years
   C. blockage of educational, vocational, and social opportunities
   D. emotional problems and psychiatric disorders of youth

   3.____

4. A high-ranking official recently stated that some youths have made suicide attempts in detention centers so that they would be transferred from the detention centers to hospitals.
   If the workers in a unit should bring this topic up for discussion in a staff meeting, the supervisor should

   A. instruct workers to inform the youths of the area about this method of getting out of a detention center
   B. have a worker visit a youth in detention in order to observe and report back to the unit so that a demonstration can be organized
   C. assign different workers to study various aspects of the problem in order to plan an intelligent, informed discussion
   D. point out that the worker does not directly become involved with this problem, and direct the discussion to a more pertinent topic

   4.____

5. The MOST significant characteristics of the daily lives of alienated youths can be described as

   A. their days are aimless, disorganized, and unproductive
   B. they spend most of their time in antisocial activity
   C. they spend a good portion of their time seeking a means of earning money
   D. they concentrate most of their energies on actingout

   5.____

6. A young man drops into the office to request help in finding a job. While he is waiting to see the office coverage worker, you notice he is nervous, sweating, yawning, and constantly blowing his nose.
   As a unit supervisor, you should

   A. overlook this because the youth is probably worried about getting a job, and is dirty and tired
   B. feel assured that the worker will observe this also and handle it in the best possible way
   C. advise the worker of your observations, and discuss the possible causes of this behavior with the worker
   D. do none of the above

7. The *battered child syndrome* is reported to be one of the most difficult problems facing health officials.
   When a worker knows of a case of a boy being severely abused physically by his parents, the supervisor should advise the worker to

   A. discuss this with a psychiatrist to find out why the parent is abusing the child
   B. tell the child to stay away from the parents as much as possible
   C. try to talk to the parents to help them see what they are doing wrong
   D. report the situation to the Bureau of Child Welfare of the Department of Social Services

8. Ghetto youth today present symptoms of delinquent behavior that are in many ways more disruptive than those of the anti-social gang members of the 1950's. Some of these symptoms are

   A. alienation, school drop-outs, drug addiction, loosely formed cliques
   B. interracial conflicts, community violence, few family ties, teenage drifters, and panhandlers
   C. promiscuity, alcoholism, vandalism, homosexuality, venereal disease
   D. all of the above

9. A psychological factor that tends to make the spread of drug abuse today easier among siblings in a family is the

   A. necessity for drug users to seduce others to join them
   B. need of siblings to rebel against parents
   C. fact that siblings can more easily *cover* for each other
   D. fact that older siblings can force younger siblings to take drugs

10. A parent complains to a worker that her teenage son is hanging around with a *bad bunch,* that money is strangely missing from the house lately, that his eating habits have changed, and that he spends long periods of time alone.
    When the worker discusses this with the unit supervisor, the supervisor should

    A. interview the parent as soon as possible to get more precise information
    B. advise the worker to refer the parent to a doctor to have her son examined
    C. help the worker to be supportive to the parent and try to make contact with the son
    D. assure him the parent is just jumpy over the drug scare and there is probably another explanation for the boy's behavior

11. A worker reports that the youths in his area think that *blowing pot* is all right because marijuana is not addictive, is harmless in small doses, and is far less dangerous than alcohol. The worker asks your help to talk the kids out of *blowing pot.*
You, as unit supervisor, should

    A. advise the worker to refer the youths to the nearest, best drug rehabilitation resource
    B. give the worker enough literature so the youths could learn more about the situation
    C. assure the worker that these facts are true
    D. help the worker to involve the youths in constructive group activities

11.____

12. It is important for the youth worker to understand that the adolescent's FIRST loyalty belongs to his

    A. peer group
    B. siblings
    C. parents
    D. best friend

12.____

13. One of the workers in a unit office reports that he is having some difficulty with his group of youths. It is apparent that the youth leader of the group is seriously disturbed.
The BEST action for the worker to take FIRST is to

    A. try to redirect the leader's activities into more constructive channels
    B. help the group select a leader who is more psychologically sound
    C. take steps to have the leader removed from the community into a setting where he can get psychiatric help
    D. show this leader where his behavior is hurting the group so that he can change his behavior

13.____

14. The pleasurable effect produced by heroin is the

    A. feeling of excitement and energy
    B. expansion of sense perceptions
    C. feeling of relaxation, sociability, and good humor
    D. suppression of fears, tensions, and anxieties

14.____

15. The many rumors that spread throughout the Youth Services Agency are harmful to the morale of the staff because they result in worry, suspicion, mistrust, and uncertainty. The BEST way the unit supervisor can stop a rumor is to

    A. disregard it
    B. deny it
    C. start a different one
    D. give the staff the true facts

15.____

16. Parental rejection and neglect damage the personality of the developing child, and orient the child toward his agemates in the neighborhood.
This statement would BEST describe the mechanism that leads to

    A. delinquency in urban industrial areas
    B. the establishment of neighborhood clubs
    C. the generation gap
    D. drug addiction

16.____

17. Many young people are introduced to drugs by friends. Youths don't like to be called *chicken,* they like to be *hip* like the rest, and they have to be a part of something. When a worker asks for your guidance on handling one of his youths who is being pressured into getting *high* by his friends, as the unit supervisor, you should help the worker 17.___

    A. gradually move this youth into another group of youths who are *straight*
    B. make the worker realize this is his problem, in his area, and that he must work it out the best way
    C. involve this youth and his group of friends in the programs and activities of the unit
    D. tell the youth he must work this out himself

18. Youth workers must help angry alienated adolescents to learn how to 18.___

    A. control their anger by learning when it's worthwhile to get angry
    B. suppress their angry feelings
    C. realize that anger is an unconscious emotion
    D. take part in aggressive demonstrations and takeovers

19. Of the following, an IMPORTANT reason why certain youths are stereotyped by the police and are therefore treated unfairly by them is that 19.___

    A. delinquent youths deserve to be treated more severely because they cause trouble for others
    B. these are only allegations and rhetoric made up by revolutionary elements who are hostile to the police
    C. the prevalence of *turnstile justice* results in hasty judgments by the police
    D. police officers in the field have no immediate data concerning the youths' backgrounds and react to their behavior at the moment

20. Group approaches are COMMONLY used for 20.___

    A. encounter, discussion, training, and administration
    B. education, counseling, therapy, and recreation
    C. counseling, recreation, catharsis, and crisis intervention
    D. competition, leadership, administration, and training

21. A worker under your supervision is having difficulty reaching some of the youths he is working with on a one-to-one basis. The recording on these youths shows that they have had little opportunity for healthy interpersonal relations.
    You should advise this worker to 21.___

    A. involve these youths in group counseling in order to help them overcome their reluctance in sharing experiences with another person
    B. refer these youths for psychiatric services because they are not likely to be reached by a youth worker
    C. assign these youths to Big Brothers or Big Sisters because they need to share a normal family experience
    D. give these youths more time to get to know and trust the worker

22. Planning, organization, methods, direction, coordination, budget and fiscal management, public relations, personnel administration, training, and supervision are the ESSENTIAL elements of

   A. group psychotherapy
   B. ego-oriented casework
   C. consultation
   D. administration

23. If a supervisor is unaware of a new worker's limitations and makes demands which are beyond the worker's capabilities, this will

   A. undermine the worker's confidence in functioning up to the limit of his actual capacities
   B. provide an incentive for the worker to further his training and improve services
   C. demonstrate the need for the agency to provide better orientation and in-service training for staff
   D. encourage the worker to function at a level higher than his present capacities

24. A high government official has announced: *We're looking for possible consolidation of services, for overlapping, for frills, for some built-in bureaucratic procedures that have been kind of historic but that no one has ever taken a long look at to see if time and technology have made them obsolete.*
    For the unit supervisor, the implication of this statement is that it is his responsibility to

   A. ignore this announcement since it pertains to matters beyond his responsibility
   B. report all matters of bureaucratic inefficiency directly to this high government official
   C. inform his workers at a staff meeting that there will be no funds for programs for the next few months
   D. try to involve the staff in a realistic reappraisal of the unit's program and discuss suggestions for cutbacks with the area administrator

25. Assume that you are a new unit supervisor in the Youth Services Agency and your workers bring many grievances to your attention.
    The BEST way for you, the supervisor, to reduce grievances in your unit is to

   A. have the workers submit fully documented written grievances
   B. consider each grievance seriously and eliminate the cause if possible
   C. make workers realize that grievances reflect their immaturity and rejection of authority
   D. refer the workers' grievances to the area Administrator

26. Of the following, BASIC subject areas to be discussed in staff conferences are:

   A. Job responsibilities, agency structure, social work concepts, needs and resources of people
   B. Case-studying, interviewing, individual growth and development, sources of information other than the client
   C. Community resources, work organization, child welfare services, and standards of performance
   D. All of the above

27. The discussion method in teaching provides a way to help staff integrate knowledge and thus make it available for application to day-to-day work.
To help workers integrate knowledge and develop skill is an IMPORTANT aspect of

    A. professional training
    B. memos, directives, and position papers
    C. staff and individual conferences
    D. job descriptions

28. The subjects of discussion in staff meetings cannot be isolated from what the unit supervisor

    A. thinks is most important
    B. reads in books, journals, etc.
    C. hears at supervisors' meetings
    D. discusses in individual conferences

29. Interplay between persons appears to speed up the learning process; discussion of the material provides an opportunity for a sharing of knowledge and experience and allows for a testing out of new ideas and application of theory.
These are the objectives for

    A. Sensitivity Training
    B. T-Groups
    C. Staff Conferences
    D. Administrative Training

30. A leadership which aims to develop the individual staff member's skill and knowledge, and to direct activities of the staff in such a way as to bring about improvements in the agency's services given to the client. This is a description of GOOD

    A. staff development
    B. psychological direction
    C. public accountability
    D. supervision

31. In addition to familiarity with techniques in administrative planning and professional knowledge, the MOST important element in good supervision in a social agency is skill in

    A. office management
    B. human relations
    C. business methods
    D. psychological evaluation

32. If an agency does not have clear and specific unit and job functions, the MOST probable result will be

    A. a gross breakdown in services
    B. gaps and overlaps in responsibility and authority
    C. an inability to function according to the city charter
    D. a violation of the union contractual agreement

33. The one of the following which is the MOST important thing for a unit supervisor to keep in mind regarding the organizational structure of his unit is the

    A. preparation of time sheets and monthly reports
    B. two-way communication and maximum delegation
    C. geometric executive relationships
    D. critiques and controls

34. Budget and fiscal management is one essential practice of administration. 34.____
    A unit supervisor should see budgeting and fiscal management as a

    A. planning instrument
    B. fiscal control
    C. mandate from the civil service commission
    D. prerequisite of a union contractual agreement

35. Public relations with the community is one of the responsibilities of the unit supervisor. 35.____
    Good public relations means

    A. organizing the community to put pressure on officials in behalf of the agency
    B. getting reports from workers about the malcontents in the community and dealing with them in a diplomatic manner
    C. assuring the community that the unit will provide staff to problem areas
    D. getting understanding and cooperation from the community with which the agency is concerned

36. Problems and misunderstandings that arise from the lack of effective intraorganizational 36.____
    communication are apparent in many organizations.
    Of the following, the means to be employed by the unit supervisor to establish effective communication are

    A. supervisory and staff conferences
    B. manuals, bulletins, and periodic reports
    C. bulletin boards, memos, and unit newsletters
    D. all of the above

37. A personnel problem facing supervisors in public service more than in private industry is 37.____

    A. union management and negotiation
    B. budget and fiscal control
    C. systematic selection and tenure
    D. advisory boards and political connections

38. Which of the following three types of records are COMMON to most social agencies? 38.____

    A. Administrative, budgetary, and case
    B. Administrative, statistical, and case
    C. Administrative, budgetary, and statistical
    D. Budgetary, statistical, and case

39. Even after several supervisory conferences on a case, a worker in your unit seems not to 39.____
    be giving effective help. In a burst of anger, the worker tells a coworker that the supervisor expects him to learn in a short time what the supervisor has taken years to learn.
    Of the following, the BEST description of the supervisory relationship here is that the

    A. supervisor is so intent on seeing that the necessary service is given that he is unaware of the worker's inability to perform the service
    B. worker's behavior shows that he is too immature to be working in such a difficult field

C. worker is unaware of casework principles and techniques and their application to such a difficult case
D. supervisor is unable to give the worker effective guidance in the supervisory conference, which indicates that the worker needs academic professional training

40. The one of the following which is NOT an essential ingredient of a good staff development and training program
is that it should

A. include all members of the agency
B. meet the specific needs of the staff in relation to their job responsibilities
C. be a continuing process
D. give out the necessary rules and regulations of the agency

41. One of the areas in which consultation differs from supervision is that consultation

A. is not in the direct administrative line of authority
B. is offered by someone skilled in a specific area
C. relates to procedure rather than function
D. requires special training

42. The supervisor should make sure the unit office keeps records about the youths it serves and their families since these records help in diagnosing and understanding the problems.
Of the following, as the PRIMARY source of information for case records, the workers should use

A. reports from psychiatrists, doctors, etc.
B. all other agencies involved with the family
C. teachers, friends, local indigenous leaders
D. the parents and the youths themselves

43. Statistical records are needed for planning, research, and accountability although many workers feel that statistics are dull and boring. On the unit level, statistics can come alive when they are

A. recorded in non-technical language
B. compiled by the unit expert in mathematics
C. collected selectively and used against a background knowledge of the community
D. elaborate, detailed, and accurate

44. With the passage of time, case records

A. become more valuable
B. decline in usefulness
C. produce more information
D. become cumulative records

45. In general, the purpose of a case record is to

A. improve staff training and development
B. make statistics pertinent and real
C. provide data for research
D. further professional service to a client

46. A unit supervisor finds after an intensive in-service training course in case recording that his workers tend to postpone their recording and summaries.
The MOST likely explanation for this is that

   A. recording is not valuable enough to waste that amount of time on
   B. sufficient leadership was not given in the development of case records
   C. the workers are too busy in the field to have time to record
   D. the latest trend in social work is towards shorter records

47. A unit supervisor who has fewer youth workers in his unit than he can supervise effectively will be likely to

   A. make his staff overdependent on him
   B. lack the desire to train his workers effectively
   C. confuse his staff because of lack of direction
   D. supervise his staff too closely

48. The one of the following which is MOST likely to be seriously impaired as a result of poor supervision is the

   A. attitude of youth workers
   B. area of inter-departmental relations
   C. maintenance of case records and reports
   D. staff training and development program

49. It is generally good practice for the supervisor to ask for the opinions of his staff members before taking action affecting them.
The GREATEST disadvantage of following this principle when changing schedules or assignments is that staff may

   A. believe that the supervisor is unable to make his own decisions
   B. take advantage of the opportunity to present grievances during the discussion
   C. be resentful if their suggestions are not accepted
   D. suggest the same action as the supervisor had planned to take

50. The expansion of community relations or human relations units is a development resulting from the ghetto riots of the past few years.
The MOST important function such a unit can perform is to

   A. preach brotherhood and racial equality
   B. serve as a means for local city agency officials to develop city policy in accordance with local needs
   C. serve as a means of communication between people with grievances and policy makers who can take action
   D. give awards to prominent citizens who have promoted inter-racial understanding

KEY (CORRECT ANSWERS)

1. D	11. D	21. A	31. B	41. A
2. C	12. A	22. D	32. B	42. D
3. C	13. C	23. A	33. B	43. C
4. C	14. D	24. D	34. A	44. B
5. A	15. D	25. B	35. D	45. D
6. C	16. A	26. D	36. D	46. B
7. D	17. C	27. C	37. C	47. D
8. D	18. A	28. D	38. B	48. A
9. A	19. D	29. C	39. A	49. C
10. C	20. B	30. D	40. A	50. C

EXAMINATION SECTION
TEST 1

DIRECTIONS: Each question or incomplete statement is followed by several suggested answers or completions. Select the one that BEST answers the question or completes the statement. *PRINT THE LETTER OF THE CORRECT ANSWER IN THE SPACE AT THE RIGHT.*

1. With respect to the degree of supervision needed by subordinates, a senior children's counselor will USUALLY find that children's counselors with many years of experience

    A. do not need supervision
    B. do not need to be as closely supervised as newly appointed children's counselors
    C. need the same degree of supervision as newly appointed children's counselors
    D. need to be supervised very closely since their methods tend to be old-fashioned

2. When a senior children's counselor does not understand the instructions given in a staff memorandum, the one of the following staff members she should ask for an explanation is

    A. the assistant superintendent of the institution
    B. another senior children's counselor
    C. the one who wrote the memorandum
    D. her immediate supervisor

3. Of the following, the MOST probable result of having too many children's counselors under a senior children's counselor's supervision is that

    A. the performance of the senior children's counselor improves
    B. the senior children's counselor is unable to give each children's counselor enough attention
    C. each children's counselor learns her job more quickly
    D. the children get better care and closer attention from the children's counselors

4. When a senior children's counselor finds that all the children's counselors under his supervision make repeated errors in carrying out their duties, this is USUALLY an indication that the

    A. senior children's counselor is not an effective supervisor
    B. senior children's counselor is not supervising his subordinates severely enough
    C. children's counselors have not been given proper orientation
    D. children's counselors are not very alert

5. The MOST important tool for the in-service training of children's counselors is the

    A. all-day institutes conducted by various schools of social work
    B. institution's manual
    C. ongoing supervisory process
    D. orientation program

6. Assume that a children's counselor under your supervision disagrees with an order handed down by the superintendent of the institution. Of the following, the action you should take FIRST is to inform the counselor

A. of the reasons for the order
B. that he must follow the order even if he disagrees with it
C. he will be disciplined if he does not follow the order
D. that some exceptions to the order may be allowed

7. As a senior children's counselor, you notice that a children's counselor under your supervision becomes very upset when you discuss with her any mistakes she has made in handling her group. Of the following, it would be BEST for you to

   A. report this problem to your supervisor
   B. explain to her that she is too nervous to be an effective children's counselor
   C. talk to her about her reasons for being upset
   D. recommend to your supervisor that the children's counselor be transferred to another unit

8. Assume that a children's counselor under your supervision complains to you that another children's counselor gets more favorable treatment from you than she does. Of the following, the BEST way to handle this situation is to

   A. tell the counselor that she is imagining she is not being treated fairly
   B. inform the counselor that you will not listen to her complaint unless she can give you proof of any incident
   C. humor the counselor by agreeing that you have not treated her fairly
   D. ask the counselor to point out specific incidents in which she was not treated fairly

9. The senior children's counselor reviews adjustment reports on each child, which are prepared by the children's counselors. Which of the following statements should GENERALLY be omitted from a child's adjustment report? The child

   A. has recurrent nightmares
   B. seems to resent any children's counselor assigned to his group
   C. lost a glove on last week's trip
   D. enjoys school and her grades are good

10. Assume that a senior children's counselor in your institution follows the practice of telling each children's counselor under his supervision exactly how to treat each child in the counselor's group. Such a practice is

    A. *advisable;* in this way, the children's counselors will always know the correct methods to use with the children
    B. *advisable;* the senior children's counselor has more experience than his subordinates in handling children
    C. *inadvisable;* the senior children's counselor is not responsible for care of the children
    D. *inadvisable;* children's counselors must be able to act independently in the routine care of the group

11. Assume that a children's counselor under your supervision disagrees with the performance evaluation you have given him. Of the following, the BEST way to approach this situation is to

    A. point out to him that you can judge his performance more objectively than he can
    B. advise him to speak to the supervising children's counselor

C. discuss with him specific aspects of his performance which he needs to improve
D. tell him to submit his grievance to you in writing and that you will review the evaluation

12. Assume you are a senior children's counselor. You observe that a children's counselor under your supervision has a rejecting attitude toward one child in her group, although she relates very well to the other children in the group. Of the following, the BEST action for you to take FIRST is to

    A. discuss this matter with the counselor in order to determine why she reacts badly toward the child
    B. recommend that the child be transferred to another group immediately since this counselor cannot deal with her properly
    C. ask the child what she did to cause the counselor to behave this way
    D. tell the counselor to change her attitude toward this child or you will have to give her an unsatisfactory service rating

13. The senior children's counselor prepares special reports on unusual behavior describing significant incidents involving children in her dormitory. In preparing these reports, the senior counselor should

    A. include his own recommendation as to whether the children involved should be transferred out of the institution
    B. make the report as long as necessary and as detailed as possible
    C. use professional technical language to describe the problems of the children involved
    D. state who was involved, what happened, and when and where the incident took place

14. Assume that a new children's counselor under your supervision has shown both strengths and weaknesses in the performance of her duties. As a senior children's counselor, you are planning to hold the first evaluation conference with her. Of the following, the BEST method to use during the conference is to

    A. praise the strengths she has displayed and indicate that you will discuss her mistakes at a later conference
    B. discuss the mistakes she has made and indicate how she can improve her performance
    C. have her evaluate her own performance and then offer your criticisms
    D. praise her for the areas in which her performance is good and then discuss how she can overcome her weaknesses in performance

15. Assume that a newly appointed children's counselor assigned to your unit seems to be nervous and doubtful about her ability to succeed on the job. The BEST way for you, as the senior children's counselor, to make her feel more at ease is to

    A. introduce her to as many experienced children's counselors as possible on her first day
    B. have her read the manual several times
    C. give her extra attention and encouragement
    D. tell her that the job is difficult, but you are sure that she will succeed

16. A newly appointed children's counselor generally has many questions to ask about her new job. These questions are useful, from the senior children's counselor's point of view, CHIEFLY because they

    A. can be used as part of the training process
    B. give the senior children's counselor an opportunity to show her knowledge
    C. inform the senior children's counselor how well the new counselor is performing
    D. indicate the areas in which the institution's manual does not give enough information

17. A senior children's counselor who finds it necessary to discipline a children's counselor under his supervision should do so in a way that will

    A. show his own authority and power
    B. use the situation to improve the counselor's performance
    C. discipline the counselor in front of other counselors
    D. get the discipline over with as soon as possible

18. It is important for a senior children's counselor to meet with the children's counselors under his supervision on a regular basis to discuss any problems the dormitory may have. At one such conference, a children's counselor discusses the difficulty he is having in helping a child in his group adjust to the institution. It would be proper for the senior children's counselor, in conducting this conference, to

    A. tell the children's counselor how to handle this child
    B. encourage the other children's counselors to participate and to suggest solutions
    C. let the group reach its own conclusions, without any guidance from him
    D. put off discussing this problem, since it doesn't affect the whole group at this time

19. Assume that you discover a fire in a dormitory. No children are in the room, but several children are in another room far down the hall. Of the following, the FIRST action you should take is to

    A. run to the room down the hall and tell the children to go quickly down the stairs to the lobby
    B. get a fire extinguisher and try to put out the fire
    C. sound the fire alarm
    D. call the superintendent's office for instructions

20. A children's counselor under your supervision complains that a child in her group misbehaves often by quarreling with the other children, more often when the counselor is present. As a senior children's counselor, you should advise her that this child

    A. obviously needs psychiatric help
    B. is probably expressing her need for attention
    C. should be punished for this behavior
    D. should be transferred to another group

21. Most children do not want to go to bed. Of the following, the BEST technique for a children's counselor to use in getting the children in his group to go to bed is to

    A. provide very strenuous recreational activities before bedtime so that the children will become tired quickly
    B. let them know that bedtime is approaching, so they can finish what they are doing

C. warn them that they will be punished if they do not go to bed on time
D. tell them that the hour for bedtime was set for their own good

22. A children's counselor under your supervision notices that a two-year-old boy in his group occasionally plays with dolls. As the senior children's counselor, you should advise the counselor that

    A. such behavior is abnormal and should be reported to the psychologist
    B. children at this age do not make much of a distinction between masculine and feminine activities
    C. this child is showing slight homosexual tendencies
    D. boys should not be allowed to play with dolls

23. Assume that a three-year-old child in your dormitory sometimes tells you stories about his adventures which you know could not possibly be true. Of the following, the MOST appropriate way for you to view this situation is to realize that this child

    A. is already showing a tendency to become a liar
    B. has an exceptional creative ability
    C. must be having bad dreams at night
    D. is behaving normally for his age

24. Assume that a four-year-old child in your dormitory is afraid of the dark and starts crying as soon as the lights go out, keeping the other children in his room awake. Of the following, the BEST way to approach this problem is to

    A. give the child his own room, so he won't keep the other boys awake
    B. tell the child how silly his fear of the dark is
    C. recommend that this child be sent to the psychiatrist for help
    D. let the child take his favorite toy to bed with him for reassurance

25. A children's counselor under your supervision tells you that a boy of six in his group still wets his bed. Of the following, you should advise the counselor that this child is probably still wetting his bed

    A. in order to get revenge on the counselor
    B. in order to cause trouble
    C. because he doesn't have any shame
    D. because of unconscious feelings

26. While you are in your office writing a report, a seven-year-old child in your dormitory who has just returned from the swimming pool runs in excitedly and announces he has learned how to swim. He wants to tell you all about it, although you are quite busy. As a senior children's counselor, you should

    A. ask the child to come back later, since you are busy now
    B. stop what you are doing and listen to the child
    C. let the child talk while you continue to work on the report
    D. ask the child to sit down and wait quietly for you to finish the report, before he tells you about his new experience

27. A children's counselor under your supervision tells you that a seven-year-old child in her group lies to her constantly. As a senior children's counselor, you should advise the counselor that

   A. it is normal for children of that age to lie to adults often
   B. this child's lying may be a symptom of some problem that the child cannot bring herself to discuss with her
   C. children lie only when the counselor is not strict enough with them
   D. this child is probably dishonest and should be watched very carefully

27.___

28. Assume that you are a senior children's counselor. You notice that a nine-year-old boy in your dormitory is quite upset after his parents' visits. When you ask him why he is upset, he tells you that his parents yelled at him. You know from this boy's case record that his parents have mistreated him in the past. Of the following, the BEST way to approach this problem is to

   A. ask the boy's parents to visit him less often since their visits upset him
   B. speak to your supervisor about preventing the boy's parents from visiting him until his attitude toward them changes
   C. tell the boy that his parents are probably experiencing emotional difficulties
   D. bring this matter to the attention of the boy's caseworker

28.___

29. Assume that you see James, a nine-year-old boy in your dormitory, steal a dollar from another child in the group. Of the following, the BEST course of action to take is to

   A. tell James that you know what he did, and order him to return the stolen dollar
   B. tell the group that you know James took the dollar
   C. ask James in front of the group if he knows anything about the missing dollar
   D. ask James in private to give you the dollar and you will return it for him without mentioning his name

29.___

30. Of the following, the BEST way for a children's counselor to discipline a ten-year-old child in his group who has been fighting with other children during a group activity is to

   A. scold him in front of the other children
   B. remove him from the group until after the activity is finished
   C. assign to him chores that no one in the group likes to perform
   D. make him stand in a corner for two hours

30.___

31. When a girl in her group is extremely withdrawn, the children's counselor should

   A. ask another child in the group to become friendly with this girl
   B. ignore this girl so she won't feel conspicuous
   C. make a special effort to reach out to this girl
   D. realize that this girl probably cannot be helped

31.___

32. With respect to the rules in effect for a dormitory for adolescents, it is GENERALLY agreed that the adolescents will

   A. resent any rules established by the institution
   B. obey whatever rules their counselors tell them are important
   C. respect only strict rules
   D. appreciate reasonable rules

32.___

33. A thirteen-year-old child in your unit reports to you that his counselor struck him. This child has a reputation for being a liar. The counselor has a good relationship with the other children in his group. As the senior children's counselor, the MOST appropriate action for you to take is to

   A. discuss with the counselor the child's report that he was struck
   B. tell your supervisor that this child is causing you too much trouble
   C. recommend that the child be punished for his habit of lying
   D. ignore the child's complaint since he is a habitual liar

33.____

34. A fourteen-year-old girl in your dormitory has run away from the institution three times in a two-month period, but in each case she returned on her own after one night's absence. As the senior children's counselor, you should realize that this girl's running away is MOST likely a(n)

   A. indication that she hates the institution and does not want to remain there
   B. sign that she is a drug addict and had to run away to get a *fix*
   C. expression of her maladjustment and need for psychological help
   D. expression of her desire to return to community life

34.____

35. A children's counselor under your supervision tells you that two fourteen-year-old girls in her group are always fighting. She has spoken to them repeatedly about this, but they still cannot get along with each other. Of the following, the BEST solution to this problem is to

   A. transfer one of the girls to another group
   B. report their behavior to the superintendent
   C. tell the counselor to talk to the girls again
   D. warn the girls that they will be prevented from participating in group activities if they don't stop fighting

35.____

36. Assume you are a senior children's counselor. You observed that a children's counselor under your supervision viciously slapped a fifteen-year-old girl in her group when this girl used obscene language. Of the following, the action you should take FIRST is to

   A. tell the girl not to use obscene language again
   B. report the counselor's action to your supervisor
   C. ask the counselor to report to you any further use of obscene language by this girl
   D. advise the counselor to keep her temper under control

36.____

37. A fifteen-year-old boy in your dormitory has assaulted both children and counselors since being admitted to the institution. Although the staff has been patient in dealing with him, he has displayed an inability to adjust and is considered dangerous to the others. As a senior children's counselor, you should

   A. ask that this boy be transferred to another dormitory
   B. arrange for the other children in your dormitory to be kept away from this boy
   C. submit a report of this boy's behavior to the superintendent of the institution for possible court action
   D. speak to this boy about his behavior

37.____

38. Assume that a sixteen-year-old boy in your dormitory has a great deal of difficulty in completing his homework assignments. He is becoming very discouraged about his academic abilities and is thinking of quitting high school. As the senior children's counselor, you should

    A. try to arrange for tutoring for this boy
    B. ask this boy's counselor to do his homework for him so he won't quit school
    C. ask this boy's teachers to give him special treatment so he will pass all his subjects
    D. speak to this boy about finding a job after he quits school

39. A children's counselor under your supervision discovers that a boy in his group has a supply of amphetamines in his room and has been trying to sell them to the other boys. Of the following, the FIRST action that you should take as the senior children's counselor is to

    A. talk to this boy about the dangers involved in using these pills
    B. speak to the other boys to find out if any of them bought any pills
    C. report this situation to your supervisor
    D. search this boy's room for other evidence of drugs

40. One of the MOST common fears of early childhood is the fear of

    A. animals
    B. being separated from parents
    C. being rejected by peers
    D. having too much independence

41. The average child shows the FIRST signs of laughing responses

    A. before the age of six months
    B. between the ages of six months and one year
    C. at the age of about one year
    D. at the age of about fifteen months

42. A child is LEAST likely to choose a child of the opposite sex to play with at the age of

    A. two   B. four   C. seven   D. ten

43. When toilet-training a two-year-old child, the children's counselor should

    A. scold the child when she wets her pants
    B. take the child to the bathroom only when she asks to go
    C. have the child sit on the toilet for long periods of time
    D. keep the toilet-training routine free from tension

44. The average child of three years MOST often shows his anger by

    A. breaking things   B. crying
    C. threatening his mother   D. sulking

45. Children at the age of two or three occasionally have temper tantrums when they do not get what they want. Of the following, the BEST method for a children's counselor to use when faced with a temper tantrum by a two-year-old child in her group is to

    A. allow the child to have what he wants
    B. try to reason with the child by explaining why he cannot have what he wants
    C. wait until the worst of the temper tantrum is over and then make a friendly gesture toward the child
    D. order the child to stop this behavior

    45.____

46. All of the following are good principles to follow in administering punishment to a three-year-old child EXCEPT the

    A. punishment should be administered immediately after the incident of bad behavior
    B. child should be punished only if he understands why his behavior was bad
    C. specific punishment should be appropriate to the specific case of bad behavior
    D. punishment should be administered in an impartial manner

    46.____

47. The normal four-year-old child should be expected to

    A. cut her meat with a knife
    B. bathe herself without help
    C. care for herself at the toilet
    D. tell time to the nearest quarter hour

    47.____

48. It is usually not a good idea to take a child under the age of five to a movie that may frighten him MAINLY because young children cannot

    A. appreciate a cultural experience
    B. behave themselves in a movie theater
    C. distinguish clearly between real life and make-believe
    D. see movies without acting out what they see

    48.____

49. The average five-year-old child spends the MAJOR part of his play time

    A. playing by himself
    B. watching other children play
    C. playing cooperatively with other children
    D. playing competitive games involving teams

    49.____

50. A children's counselor faced with a question about sex from a six-year-old child in her group should

    A. tell the child she is too young to understand such things
    B. give the child as honest and simple an answer as possible
    C. realize that an older child must have told the six-year-old to ask that question
    D. answer the question in such a way as to discourage the child from asking any more questions about sex

    50.____

KEY (CORRECT ANSWERS)

1. B	11. C	21. B	31. C	41. A
2. D	12. A	22. B	32. D	42. D
3. B	13. D	23. D	33. A	43. D
4. A	14. D	24. D	34. C	44. B
5. C	15. C	25. D	35. A	45. C
6. A	16. A	26. B	36. B	46. B
7. C	17. B	27. B	37. C	47. C
8. D	18. B	28. D	38. A	48. C
9. C	19. C	29. D	39. C	49. C
10. D	20. B	30. B	40. B	50. B

TEST 2

DIRECTIONS: Each question or incomplete statement is followed by several suggested answers or completions. Select the one that BEST answers the question or completes the statement. *PRINT THE LETTER OF THE CORRECT ANSWER IN THE SPACE AT THE RIGHT.*

1. A six-year-old child should normally be expected to do all of the following EXCEPT   1.____

    A. play simple games
    B. put on a sweater without help
    C. draw with a crayon
    D. write in sentences

2. An educational television program developed especially for pre-school age children is   2.____

    A. Learning Your ABC's   B. Sesame Street
    C. The Number Game   D. The Partridge Family

3. Which of the following statements concerning masturbation in children is NOT true?   3.____

    A. Excessive masturbation can injure a child's genitals.
    B. Masturbation is practiced by most children at some point of their development.
    C. Masturbation may be a symptom of tenseness and nervousness in a child.
    D. There tends to be an increased urge to masturbate during adolescence.

4. A child's rate of physical growth is MOST rapid during the period   4.____

    A. from birth to six years   B. from six to nine years
    C. of pre-adolescence   D. of adolescence

5. In planning activities for a group of ten-year-old children, the children's counselor should   5.____

    A. encourage the children to participate in the planning
    B. schedule activities that are the easiest to plan
    C. realize that children at this age like to watch television
    D. insist that each child participate in each activity

6. A child of twelve would be MOST likely to find an outlet for his aggressive tendencies in   6.____

    A. watching television
    B. participating in athletics
    C. reading a history book
    D. playing checkers

7. Of the following, the statement which MOST accurately describes the physical development of boys and girls during adolescence is that   7.____

    A. girls generally mature earlier than boys
    B. boys generally mature earlier than girls
    C. boys and girls generally mature at about the same age
    D. physically active boys and girls generally mature earlier than physically inactive ones

8. The average child has not developed all the many abilities needed for beginning reading until the age of about

   A. two B. four C. six D. eight

9. The Stanford-Binet scale is a test given to children to measure

   A. mechanical ability
   C. musical ability
   B. intelligence
   D. anxiety

10. The Sabin oral vaccine is given to children to prevent

    A. German measles
    C. diphtheria
    B. tuberculosis
    D. polio

11. A common symptom of many childhood diseases is a rash. The one of the following diseases which is NOT usually accompanied by a rash is

    A. mumps
    C. scarlet fever
    B. impetigo
    D. chicken pox

12. Which of the following describes MOST accurately the intelligence of a child with an I.Q. of 50?

    A. Average
    B. Below average
    C. Borderline of average and above average
    D. Cannot be determined without knowing the child's age

13. In order to understand better the children in her group, a children's counselor should watch them during their play activities MAINLY because

    A. a child sometimes expresses in play feelings that she cannot express in words
    B. a child may commit a destructive act during play for which the counselor should punish her
    C. this is what the counselor is paid to do
    D. the counselor is expected to know what the children are doing at all times

14. The term *exceptional child* has been defined as one *who differs as a person to the extent that he is handicapped in his relationship with others.* According to this definition, which of the following can be classified as an *exceptional child?*
    A child

    A. with cerebral palsy
    B. of limited mental capacity
    C. with a severe speech problem
    D. all of the above

15. A child may be removed from his parents' custody and placed in a children's shelter by the

    A. Family Court, without the parents' consent
    B. Bureau of Child Welfare, without the parents' consent
    C. police department, upon the child's request if he is over 14 years of age
    D. child's probation officer, if he feels the home environment has a bad effect on the child

16. The ULTIMATE goal of institutional care should be to
    A. cure the child of any delinquent tendencies he may have
    B. help the child to accept his life situation
    C. return the child to family life in the community
    D. provide the child with care for a prolonged period of time

17. Of the following, the MOST important reason for keeping confidential the case record of a child in an institution is to
    A. protect the child case staff from the child's parents
    B. prevent the institution from getting bad publicity
    C. establish the fact that the institutional staff cares about the child
    D. respect the parents' and child's right of privacy

18. It is GENERALLY preferable to place a child in a foster home rather than in an institution because foster home placement
    A. is much cheaper than institutional care
    B. provides a child with more normal social and community relationships than an institution can provide
    C. offers an ideal setting for the diagnostic observation and study of the child
    D. gives the child a more structured environment than an institution does

19. The practice of having children's counselors of pre-school age children eat their meals together with the children is
    A. *advisable*; the counselor can teach good eating habits by example
    B. *advisable*; the counselor can keep the children completely quiet at meals
    C. *inadvisable*; the presence of the counselor will keep the children from eating what they want to eat
    D. *inadvisable*; the children resent the presence of an authority figure when they are eating

20. The practice of permitting children to bring some of their personal belongings to the institution at the time of placement is
    A. *advisable*; the institution will not have to supply the child with too many items, thereby saving money
    B. *advisable*; personal belongings help a child to retain his sense of identity
    C. *inadvisable*; a child's personal belongings may cause jealousy in other children
    D. *inadvisable*; the child will take more time to adjust to the institution if he is surrounded by memories of his previous experiences

21. In considering the relationships between a child in placement and the adults around him, an advantage of institutional placement over placement in a foster home is that the child
    A. care staff of an institution is trained to make more demands on the child than foster parents would make
    B. placed in an institution has to adjust to a minimum of adults
    C. placed in an institution receives more individual attention than foster parents can give
    D. care staff of an institution can more easily accept a child's aggressive behavior than foster parents could

22. The practice of having teenage children in a children's institution perform, on a voluntary basis, certain tasks in the institution for pay is 22.___

   A. *advisable;* the children in this program will learn to take on responsibility
   B. *advisable;* children who do not enjoy performing these tasks will not have to do them
   C. *inadvisable;* some children will be able to escape from performing their assigned tasks
   D. *inadvisable;* the institution will have to pay to have tasks performed which were previously done by the children without pay

23. Many children in the institution fear going to school and will resist leaving for school by suddenly developing ailnents, deliberately getting dirty, or dawdling. Of the following, the BEST way for a children's counselor to ease a child's fear of school is to 23.___

   A. point to other children in the group who like school
   B. assure him that he will appreciate his education when he grows up
   C. tell him that the counselor never feared school
   D. see him off to school with a few encouraging words

24. The one of the following which is an advantage of institutional placement as compared to foster family placement is that the child in an institution 24.___

   A. faces less of a threat of total loss through desertion by any one person
   B. learns to share adults with other children
   C. has more possibilities for individual choice because of the need for routines
   D. has many more opportunities to make decisions and learn to take responsibilities

25. Institutional placement offers the child the experience of being part of a peer group. The peer group can help the child build social and personal strengths by offering him the opportunity to 25.___

   A. find acceptance in a group in which he is not different from the other children
   B. learn positive group values and standards of behavior
   C. form relationships easily without having to seek them out
   D. do all of the above

26. It is important for the child in an institution to learn that the different articles he will use for his personal hygiene are his own personal belongings. The one of the following which would be the BEST way for the children's counselor to instill this idea is to 26.___

   A. provide a separate place for each child to store his personal things
   B. have each child buy a few inexpensive items, such as a comb and toothbrush, out of his allowance
   C. give the children in his group a lecture on hygiene
   D. inform the children that borrowing of personal items is not allowed

27. Having the child counseling staff select all the clothing for each child in the institution is 27.___

   A. *advisable;* the children are not mature enough to select the proper clothing by themselves
   B. *advisable;* the counselors know how to choose the garments that cost the least but wear well

C. *inadvisable;* the children may think that the Institution does not respect their feelings
D. *inadvisable;* the counselors may choose styles that are not *modern* enough

28. The child placed in an institution is LEAST able to cope with his problems at the times for

    A. rising and going to bed
    B. leaving for and returning from school
    C. eating meals
    D. receiving visitors

29. Children placed in an institution have a need for security : and safety. They want a predictable and orderly world.
    In order to avoid unnecessarily upsetting the children in his group, the child care worker should, whenever possible,

    A. inform them ahead of time if he expects to be absent from work
    B. change the group's routines so that the children become accustomed to change
    C. assure them that he will listen to their problems when he has time
    D. provide the group with an unstructured environment so that the children won't feel restricted

30. Which of the following situations indicates that the child is probably emotionally disturbed?
    A

    A. five-year-old girl suddenly starts behaving like a baby after the birth of her sister
    B. four-year-old boy keeps asking for his father, although he has been told repeatedly that his father has died
    C. ten-year-old boy has refused to play with other children since he first entered school five years ago
    D. all of the above

31. A child who has been shuffled from foster home to foster home before being placed in an institution would be MOST likely to react to the institutional placement by displaying a(n)

    A. fear of forming a close relationship with anyone
    B. immediate attachment to each of his counselors
    C. hatred for his parents
    D. desire to be removed from the institution and placed in another foster home

32. In the past few years, the agency-owned-and-operated group home has emerged as a new form of group care and treatment for certain children. The age group which can benefit MOST from this group home setting is

    A. pre-school   B. six to nine
    C. ten to twelve   D. adolescent

33. The approach and methods used in providing food to children in an institution are important in the care of each child MAINLY because

    A. mealtime should be a pleasurable experience in a relaxed atmosphere
    B. children must learn to eat different kinds of food

C. children find it boring to have the same menu every day
D. food has emotional significance for children who have been deprived of love

34. Which of the following drug treatment programs is administered by the Addiction Services Agency?

   A. Daytop Village
   B. Odyssey House
   C. Phoenix House
   D. Reality House

35. Methadone is a narcotic used in the treatment of addiction to

   A. marijuana   B. LSD   C. heroin   D. pep pills

36. The growing demand for day-care centers is a result of the

   A. increasing number of working mothers of pre-school age children
   B. higher rate of juvenile delinquency
   C. need for care of abandoned infants
   D. increase in the number of illegitimate births

37. *The child is constantly expressing his many needs and he constantly reaches out for fulfillment. When any child is so disturbed that he becomes engaged in delinquent behavior, he is telling us that something is wrong and that he is reaching out for satisfactions because of unmet needs.*
   The author of this paragraph feels that delinquent behavior should be looked upon as a(n)

   A. evil which should be severely punished
   B. expression of satisfied needs
   C. symptom of unfulfilled needs
   D. reaching out for a healthy way to fulfill needs

38. *The increasing rate of delinquency tells us more about our society and its problems than about the effectiveness of services for dealing with children in trouble.*
   The author of this statement is implying that the increasing rate of delinquency

   A. proves that services dealing with children in trouble are not effective
   B. is the cause of most of our society's problems
   C. suggests that society is not solving its problems
   D. can be stopped if more programs for delinquent children were available

Questions 39-43.

DIRECTIONS: Questions 39 through 43 are to be answered SOLELY on the basis of the following chart.

LENGTH OF STAY OF ADMISSIONS TO THE CHILDREN'S SHELTER OF PINE CITY
2004-2008

YEAR	ADMISSIONS	DISCHARGED WITHIN 90 DAYS	DISCHARGED AFTER 90 DAYS BUT WITHIN A YEAR	DISCHARGED AFTER 1 YEAR
2004	?	650	153	29
2005	975	720	205	50
2006	1120	887	?	45
2007	1055	775	247	33
2008	1190	816	312	62

39. The number of children admitted to the children's shelter in 2004 was

    A. 182	B. 650	C. 732	D. 832

40. The number of admissions to the children's shelter who remained for more than one year increased the MOST from

    A. 2004 to 2005	B. 2005 to 2008
    C. 2006 to 2008	D. 2007 to 2008

41. The number of children admitted to the children's shelter in 2006 who were discharged after 90 days but within one year was

    A. 188	B. 233	C. 333	D. 842

42. The average number of admissions to the children's shelter per year from 2005 to 2008 was

    A. 975	B. 1085	C. 2500	D. 4340

43. The percentage of admissions to the children's shelter in 2005 who were discharged within 90 days was MOST NEARLY

    A. 45%	B. 60%	C. 75%	D. 90%

Question 44.

DIRECTIONS: Question 44 is to be answered on the basis of the following passage.

Some adolescents find it very difficult to take the first step toward independence. Instead of experimenting as his friends do, a teenager may stay close to home, conforming to his parents' wishes. Sometimes parents and school authorities regard this untroublesome youngster with satisfaction and admiration, but they are wrong to do so. A too-conforming adolescent will not develop into an independent adult.

44. This passage implies that a teenager who always conforms to his parents' wishes 44.___

    A. should be admired by his teachers
    B. will develop into a troublesome person
    C. will become very independent
    D. should be encouraged to act more independently

Questions 45-46.

DIRECTIONS: Questions 45 and 46 are to be answered SOLELY on the basis of the following paragraph.

    The skilled children's counselor can encourage the handicapped child to make a maximum adjustment to the demands of learning and socialization. She will be aware that the child's needs are basically the same as those of other children and yet she will be sensitive to his special needs and the ways in which these are met. She will understand the frustration the child may experience when he cannot participate in the simple activities of childhood. She will also be aware of the need to help him to avoid repeated failures by encouraging him to engage in projects in which he can generally succeed and perhaps excel.

45. According to the above paragraph, it is important for the children's counselor to realize that the handicapped child 45.___

    A. should not participate in ordinary activities
    B. must not be treated in any special way
    C. is sensitive to the counselor's problems
    D. has needs similar to those of other children

46. According to the paragraph, the counselor can BEST help the handicapped child to avoid frustrating situations by encouraging him to 46.___

    A. participate in the same activities as *normal* children
    B. participate in activities which are not too difficult for him
    C. engage in projects which are interesting
    D. excel in difficult games

Questions 47-48.

DIRECTIONS: Questions 47 and 48 are to be answered SOLELY on the basis of the following paragraph.

    Behavior that seems strange to adults often is motivated by the child's desire to please his peers or to gain their attention. His feelings when ridiculed by his peers may range from grief to rage. It is difficult for the child to express such feelings and the reasons for them to adults, for to do so he must admit to himself the bitter fact that persons whose friendship he wants really do not like him. Instead of directly expressing his feelings, he may reveal them through symptoms such as fault-finding, fighting back, and complaining. As a result, adults may not realize that when he is telling them how much he dislikes certain children, he may really be expressing how much he would like to be liked by these same children, or how deeply he feels contempt of himself.

47. This paragraph implies that a child's constant complaints about certain other children may be his way of expressing   47._____

   A. his desire to be accepted by them
   B. his dislike of the adults around him
   C. ridicule for those he does not like
   D. how many faults those other children have

48. According to the paragraph, a child may find it difficult to express his grief at being rejected by his peer group because   48._____

   A. his rejection motivates him to behave strangely
   B. he knows that the adults around him would not understand his grief
   C. he may not be able to admit the fact of his rejection to himself
   D. his anger prevents him from expressing grief

Questions 49-50.

DIRECTIONS: Questions 49 and 50 are to be answered SOLELY on the basis of the following paragraph.

A very small child has no concept of right or wrong. However, as soon as he is sufficiently developed to be aware of forces outside himself, he will begin to see the advantage of behaving so as to win approval and avoid punishment. If the parents' standard of behavior is presented to the child in a consistent manner, the child will begin to incorporate that standard within himself, so that he feels the urge to do what his parents want him to do, whether they are there or not. Furthermore, he will feel uncomfortable doing what he thinks is wrong even if there is no probability of discover and punishment. If the parents' standard of behavior is not consistent, the child may grow up too confused to establish any ideal for himself. We then have a youngster who truly does not know right from wrong. He is in danger of having no firm standard of behavior, no conscience, and no feeling of guilt in defying the established community pattern.

49. The author of this passage implies that a child whose parents do NOT present him with a consistent standard of behavior   49._____

   A. will learn the difference between right and wrong when he is older
   B. may feel no guilt when committing delinquent acts
   C. will feel uncomfortable doing what he thinks is wrong
   D. is likely to establish his own ideal standards

50. The paragraph implies that when a child feels the urge to do what his parents want him to do, even if they are not present, it means that the child   50._____

   A. sees the advantages of behaving so as to avoid punishment
   B. has no concept of right and wrong
   C. has begun to develop a conscience based on his parents' standard of behavior
   D. is afraid that his parents will find out if he misbehaves

KEY (CORRECT ANSWERS)

1. D	11. A	21. D	31. A	41. A
2. B	12. B	22. A	32. D	42. B
3. A	13. A	23. D	33. D	43. C
4. A	14. D	24. A	34. C	44. D
5. A	15. A	25. D	35. C	45. D
6. B	16. C	26. A	36. A	46. B
7. A	17. D	27. C	37. C	47. A
8. C	18. B	28. A	38. C	48. C
9. B	19. A	29. A	39. D	49. B
10. D	20. B	30. C	40. D	50. C

EXAMINATION SECTION
TEST 1

DIRECTIONS: Each question or incomplete statement is followed by several suggested answers or completions. Select the one that BEST answers the question or completes the statement. *PRINT THE LETTER OF THE CORRECT ANSWER IN THE SPACE AT THE RIGHT.*

1. The BEST way for a supervisor to determine whether the counselors are doing their jobs effectively is to

    A. require that the counselors give daily written reports on all of their activities
    B. ask the children if they like their counselors
    C. schedule weekly group meetings at which the counselors may discuss problems under the supervisor's observation
    D. observe the counselors interacting with their groups, and hold regular individual conferences

1.____

2. Of the following, the MOST important factor that the supervisor should consider in evaluating a counselor's performance is

    A. the amount of work the counselor does on his shift
    B. his interest in the children and effectiveness in dealing with them
    C. how frequently he asks for help from the supervisor
    D. his willingness to be helpful and cooperative

2.____

3. A supervisor constantly stresses the inadequacies and failures of the counselors rather than complimenting them for their achievements. Of the following, the MOST likely outcome of continuing this practice is that the counselors will

    A. pamper the children
    B. become hostile and uncooperative
    C. try harder in working with the children
    D. develop better morale

3.____

4. A supervisor has received several complaints that counselors are sometimes absent from their assignments in the dormitories. The senior counselor in charge of staff assignments admits difficulty in exercising his authority over the counselors. The BEST action for the supervisor to take is to

    A. help the senior counselor with his problems in exercising authority over his subordinates
    B. help the senior counselor revise the assignment roster
    C. dismiss the counselors who have been absent from their assignments
    D. ask the senior counselor if he is afraid of the counselors and reassign him if he indicates that this is so

4.____

5. If an inexperienced counselor seems to be particularly tense about what might happen in his dormitory, the supervisor SHOULD

    A. stop by the dormitory once or twice during his shift to reassure the counselor
    B. tell the counselor that he will take over supervision of the dormitory at the first sign of trouble

5.____

51

C. order extra snacks for the children to distract them
D. tell the children that they will lose TV privileges if they do not obey the counselor

6. An inexperienced counselor is upset because Tom, one of the smaller boys in his group, disobeys him, and encourages several other boys to join him in disruptive behavior. The counselor sees Tom as a troublemaker and insists that he will lose control of the boys unless Tom is removed from his group.
Of the following, the MOST appropriate action for the counselor's supervisor to take FIRST is to

A. find another group for Tom
B. help the counselor see that Tom's misbehavior may arise from his own lack of experience in handling the boys
C. recommend that the counselor be given another group of boys
D. recommend that Tom be denied privileges until his disruptive behavior stops

7. After a particularly trying day, an inexperienced counselor, whose work has improved so that he is now performing satisfactorily, tells the supervisor that he feels unable to handle the children correctly.
The BEST course of action for the supervisor to take FIRST is to

A. reduce the number of children in the counselor's group until he feels more secure
B. transfer the counselor to a younger group
C. suggest to the counselor that he make an appointment with the staff psychologist to discuss his insecurity
D. encourage the counselor by citing instances in which he obviously handled the children well

8. While sitting around with the girls in her dormitory one night, a counselor was asked if she is a virgin. She was afraid to appear old-fashioned by not telling the truth. When she started to answer, however, the girls teased her and she began to cry.
As the supervisor, it would be BEST for you to tell the counselor that

A. she should have replied to the girls that they were disrespectful in asking this question and demanded that they apologize
B. you are certainly surprised that she was so naive as to walk right into this *trap*
C. it is not part of her job to carry on discussions about sex
D. she should have calmly refused to answer questions about her personal life or sex experiences

9. Assume that the following situation took place in one of the dorms on your floor: Richie, a 13-year-old, tried to avoid his chores by going to the infirmary whenever he could get away with it. His counselor thought and spoke of him as a *weakling;* this image was mirrored by the other boys and staff members, and he soon became the group scapegoat. The counselor and supervisory staff decided that Richie's attitude could not be changed, and finally had him transferred to another institution. Of the following, which is the BEST appraisal of this situation?

A. A supervisor can do little to help a counselor with a problem as complicated as this, for group life can be very rough.
B. The supervisor should have helped the counselor realize that the latter was making a bad situation worse by encouraging hostile reactions from the group.

C. If the counselor had forced Richie to do his chores and made it clear that he wouldn't take *this stuff,* Richie would have pulled himself together.
D. The counselor could have protected Richie and made him a kind of ward or mascot for the group.

10. When 8-year-old Doris was about to be discharged in the custody of her aunt, her counselor would not allow her to wear an attractive dress that her aunt had given to her. As a result, both Doris and her aunt were upset, and the latter made a *scene* with the social worker, who, in turn, made an issue of the situation with the supervisor.
Of the following, the BEST approach for the supervisor to have taken at this time was to

    A. order the counselor to apologize to the social worker
    B. tell the counselor quietly that she thinks everyone is making too much fuss about this situation
    C. inform the principal counselor of the social worker's interference
    D. help the counselor understand the feelings of Doris and her aunt

10.____

11. A supervisor has noticed that a new children's counselor is very restrained with the children and seems to be holding back from laughing and acting friendly towards them. The children in his group often go to other counselors with their questions and requests.
Of the following, the BEST advice that the supervisor could give the counselor in this case is that he

    A. had better change his ways as the children do not like him
    B. should insist that the children come to him with their questions and requests
    C. should ask the other counselors not to have anything to do with his group
    D. can let the children know that he likes them without losing their respect

11.____

12. Whenever a supervisor tactfully suggests improvements in a counselor's handling of the children, the counselor reacts by becoming angry and, on occasion, has walked out of the room, slamming the door.
The BEST of the following actions for the supervisor to take FIRST is to

    A. tell the counselor after he calms down that he acted foolishly
    B. suggest to the counselor that he get professional help about his uncontrollable temper
    C. speak with the counselor about his difficulty in handling criticism
    D. have the counselor transferred, after explaining the reason

12.____

13. When a supervisor finds that a counselor is punishing children for every little incident of disobedience, ignoring the extent and the child's motive, it would be MOST advisable for the supervisor to speak to the counselor and

    A. point out that disobedience is caused more by the adult than the child
    B. suggest that the counselor consult with a therapist about his unconscious motives
    C. suggest to the counselor that the children may not like him
    D. try to help him understand why he over-reacts to children's disobedience

13.____

14. A counselor asks his supervisor what to do about a group of boys who are *hanging around* during free periods because he believes they might be forming a delinquent group.
It would be BEST for the supervisor to recommend that the counselor should FIRST

14.____

A. let the boys know he is aware of what is going on
B. individually question the boys involved about their behavior
C. separate the boys involved
D. break up any group of more than three boys

15. Several of the girls' counselors place food on the children's plates without asking how much they want, and then insist that the girls eat everything before they can have dessert. The supervisor hesitates to do anything about this because the counselors have been on staff longer than she has.
Of the following, the BEST course of action for the supervisor to take would be to

   A. meet with the counselors who tend to be strict about children's eating habits and order them to reduce the portions they serve by one-third
   B. institute a system of allowing the children to serve themselves and requiring them to taste only small amounts of food they dislike
   C. order the counselors to stop forcing the children to finish their meals because this will have a bad effect on their physical health
   D. go to the dining room and overrule the counselors when they withhold dessert until the children clear their plates

15._____

16. Assume that the boys in one of the dormitories are constantly kicking or mauling each other in what their counselor thinks is a harmless and friendly way. Little by little, the counselor begins to take part in this, without being aware that this play has sexual overtones. Of the following, it would be MOST advisable for the counselor's supervisor to

   A. tell the counselor to immediately stop the boys from engaging in this kind of activity
   B. decide that it is all just good fun for the boys and the counselor
   C. talk to the counselor privately and give him guidance in checking a potentially serious situation
   D. order the counselor to tell the boys sharply that he will not wrestle with them any more

16._____

17. A counselor in a children's center for adolescents makes a practice of identifying the leaders among the boys in his group.
Of the following, the BEST evaluation of this practice is that it is

   A. *inadvisable*, chiefly because adolescents in a shelter do not have close interpersonal relationships with each other
   B. *advisable*, chiefly because a counselor will have a better understanding of the children's interaction if he knows who are the leaders in his group
   C. *inadvisable*, chiefly because it is best to control the situation by appointing kids he can trust to keep an eye on the others
   D. *advisable*, chiefly because it will be better if the tough kids control the group

17._____

18. A certain counselor has repeatedly neglected to get the children into the dining room or the showers at the appointed times, thus causing problems for the other counselors. The supervisor has made general suggestions about this on two occasions, but there has been no change in the counselor's behavior.
The BEST approach for the supervisor to take at this point is to

18._____

A. wait to see if the counselor has a plan of his own
B. assume that the counselor did not understand and make the suggestion again
C. recommend that the counselor be discharged
D. be more direct and specific in telling the counselor what is required

19. A supervisor observes a senior counselor making it known to several new counselors that he is *tough* and *hard to please.*
It would be ADVISABLE for the supervisor to tell the senior counselor that this behavior toward new counselors is

   A. *inappropriate,* because it will discourage a good working relationship with the counselors
   B. *appropriate,* because the senior counselor will be respected by the counselors if he lets them *know where they stand*
   C. *inappropriate,* because these new and inexperienced counselors are not likely to understand what the senior counselor means
   D. *appropriate,* because the counselors will realize that the senior counselor will not permit laziness on the job

20. Suppose that a counselor informs his supervisor that he is worried because some children who have been in the dormitory only for a few months often seem to be so bored that they are almost lifeless.
In this situation, the one of the following which is the BEST action for the supervisor to take FIRST is to

   A. tell the counselor that there is nothing to be concerned about
   B. determine what help the counselor needs in getting the children interested
   C. suggest that the children may not be getting enough sleep
   D. change the composition of the counselor's group

21. A supervisor finds that a counselor is feeling discouraged about a child of average intelligence who cannot seem to keep up with the daily schedule and, as a result, is occupying much of the counselor's time.
The BEST suggestion that the supervisor can make to the counselor is that the latter should

   A. plan an independent schedule for this child for the time being
   B. put this child in a group with other slow children
   C. demand more from this child in order to increase his motivation
   D. stop giving so much attention to this child, since it only encourages him to be slow

22. A counselor asks a supervisor how to handle a 12-year-old child he considers to be emotionally disturbed because he is always *asking about things of a sexual nature.*
The BEST approach for the supervisor to take is to

   A. advise the counselor to ask the child why he wants to know about *such things*
   B. suggest that the child be sent to the social worker as soon as possible
   C. suggest that the child's questions be ignored if possible
   D. ask the counselor why he thinks these questions indicate emotional disturbance rather than normal interest

23. A supervisor overhears a counselor discussing the theft of candy. A boy who is considered this counselor's *pet* has accused Johnny of stealing the candy from his locker, and the counselor seems to think that Johnny is guilty, even though Johnny denies it and has never been suspected of stealing before.
    In these circumstances, the supervisor's BEST course of action would be FIRST to

    A. apologize privately to Johnny for the attitude of the counselor
    B. speak to Johnny privately and question him thoroughly
    C. discuss the situation with the counselor privately and determine the basis for his belief
    D. tell the counselor in private that he will lose his effectiveness as a group leader if he continues to play favorites

24. Assume that the supervisor has just learned that Bob's counselor has ignored the fact that Bob, a ten-year-old boy who recently came to the shelter, has slipped out several times to the desk of the telephone operator in order to make a phone call.
    The CORRECT action for the supervisor to take FIRST is to

    A. discuss with the operator ways in which to handle Bob
    B. meet with Bob's counselor and Bob together
    C. recommend that the child be transferred to a counselor who has stronger control
    D. advise Bob's counselor to find out why Bob is making these calls

25. A counselor tells his supervisor about an eight-year-old boy who is new at the shelter. The boy dislikes the clothes provided for him and fights and resorts to *bad language* whenever the other children tease him about this dislike.
    It would be MOST appropriate for the supervisor to explain to the counselor that this behavior seems to be a(n)

    A. typical sign of homesickness
    B. attempt to become *little tough man* in the group
    C. normal result of strong feelings that many children have about clothing
    D. indication of serious emotional disturbance

KEY (CORRECT ANSWERS)

1.	D	11.	D
2.	B	12.	C
3.	B	13.	D
4.	A	14.	A
5.	A	15.	B
6.	B	16.	C
7.	D	17.	B
8.	D	18.	D
9.	B	19.	A
10.	D	20.	B

21. A
22. D
23. C
24. D
25. C

TEST 2

DIRECTIONS: Each question or incomplete statement is followed by several suggested answers or completions. Select the one that BEST answers the question or completes the statement. *PRINT THE LETTER OF THE CORRECT ANSWER IN THE SPACE AT THE RIGHT.*

1. On visiting day, a mother whose child has been placed in the shelter because of parental neglect complains to the counselor that the visitors' lounge is dirty and untidy. The lounge has been in normal use during the day and is not unusually untidy.
   It would be MOST appropriate for the counselor to

   A. make sure that the lounge is clean and tidy on the next visiting day
   B. realize that a mother who feels guilty may try to defend herself by showing that the institution is no better than she is
   C. ignore the complaint, since he is not responsible for the appearance of the lounge
   D. recommend that disciplinary action be taken against those who were responsible for cleaning the lounge

   1.____

2. A counselor's timesheet indicates that he began work at 7:00 A.M. At 8:30 A.M., the supervisor asks for him and is told by one of the counselor's subordinates that he has not seen the counselor that morning.
   Of the following actions, the BEST one for the supervisor to take FIRST is to

   A. say nothing to the counselor this time, but discipline him if he does it again
   B. discuss with the counselor the difference between the entry on the timesheet and the statement of his subordinate
   C. report the facts to the director, recommending that disciplinary action be taken against the counselor
   D. accuse the counselor of falsifying the timesheet and warn him of disciplinary action if he does it again

   2.____

3. Just before you go off duty, a counselor informs you that a busload of children has returned from an all-day outing with one child missing.
   As supervisor your FIRST action should be to

   A. consult with the administrator of the shelter
   B. leave a note for your relief supervisor to take care of the matter immediately
   C. notify the police and begin a search
   D. question the counselor who went on the outing in order to determine who is at fault in letting the child get lost

   3.____

4. Assume that a supervisor has called his subordinates to a meeting in order to try to determine the identity of some boys who threw bottles out the window at a passerby. The supervisor opens the meeting with his opinion of which boys are guilty.
   This action is

   A. *advisable,* chiefly because it might help the group reach their conclusions more quickly
   B. *inadvisable,* chiefly because it might cause the supervisor to be embarrassed later if he was wrong

   4.____

58

C. *advisable,* chiefly because it would be dishonest not to give his opinion
D. *inadvisable,* chiefly because it might influence the group's opinions before they have access to the facts

5. The MOST important reason for avoiding the assignment each day of two hours' overtime work to the staff of a children's institution is that

    A. staff cannot keep up peak performance if working hours are too long
    B. staff will take out their hostilities on the children
    C. hiring additional staff would be cheaper
    D. regular hours for staff make the children feel more secure

6. A supervisor calls a meeting to explain some new state health regulations to the senior counselors and counselors under his supervision. A counselor asks a question that the supervisor cannot answer.
It would be MOST appropriate for the supervisor to

    A. tell the counselor that if he wants an authoritative answer he should call the State Department of Health
    B. tell the counselor to ask the assistant superintendent of the shelter
    C. admit that he cannot answer the question and promise to get the information later
    D. ask the counselor to justify the practicality of the question

7. According to standards, during waking hours, a children's institution should assign one child-care worker to be responsible at any given time for the following number of children:

    A. 5 to 10   B. 10 to 12   C. 15 to 20   D. 20 to 25

8. If a group of counselors should complain about writing reports about the children and express doubts about their value, it would be advisable for the supervisor to tell the counselors that the GREATEST value of these reports is that they

    A. assist staff in understanding and helping the children
    B. are the supervisor's only source of information on how the counselors handle the children
    C. are necessary to help supervisory staff make up the yearly budget
    D. are required by law

9. Some supervisors read the counselors' logs mainly in order to check for incidents of trouble, and pay little attention to the good things that have been accomplished. The MOST likely result of such a practice is that many counselors will tend to

    A. be careful about what they write in the logs, in order to cover up troublesome events for which they may be held responsible
    B. record troublesome events in detail in order to call them to the attention of the supervisor for guidance and assistance
    C. work more diligently with the children in order to correct troublesome situations, so that they will not appear on the record
    D. exaggerate their accomplishments with the children in the logs in order to gain the supervisor's approval

10. A counselor has been unable to keep a child from running out of his dormitory into other dormitories without permission and disturbing the other groups. When the other counselors complain, the supervisor speaks to the counselor, who insists that almost all the children in his group are problem children.
    The FIRST thing that the supervisor should do is to

    A. determine whether the children like the counselor
    B. review the counselor's most recent performance rating
    C. decide whether the counselor is really interested in the children
    D. review the records of each child in this group

11. If the supervisor should find that most of the counselors under his supervision have trouble following the schedules, the BEST action to take FIRST would be to

    A. request consultation from the director
    B. meet with each counselor in order to discover why he fails to fulfill his assignments
    C. ask the senior counselors to work up new schedules for the counselors
    D. discuss the daily routine and possible improvements with all the counselors together

12. Assume that a supervisor finds that many children in the institution enjoy participating in group activities to a certain extent, but tend to withdraw at times and to limit their interaction with the group. He believes that these children may simply be fighting to assert their individuality.
    Of the following, the BEST method of handling this situation would be to

    A. allow voluntary participation in group activities
    B. reward these children when they stay with the group
    C. include periods without scheduled group activities in the daily program
    D. insist that these children interact with the group

13. A supervisor has been put in charge of a dormitory for the first time. Of the following, his PRIMARY concern in preparing for this assignment should be to

    A. find out whether the dormitory is clean and properly maintained
    B. determine whether enough supplies are available
    C. equalize the workload for each counselor
    D. learn as much as he can about the children in the dormitory

14. A counselor comes to the supervisor for advice on how to manage a 10-year-old child that presents a serious behavior problem.
    The BEST suggestion for the supervisor to make is that the counselor should

    A. punish the child appropriately for every instance of bad behavior
    B. try to discover the underlying reason for the child's behavior
    C. overlook misbehavior and reward the child for good behavior
    D. tell the child how much affection he will get if he is good

15. Assume that you are a supervisor and that some of your counselors tell you they feel that they have no leeway in carrying out routines and must rigidly follow regulations.
Of the following, the BEST way for you to encourage these counselors to exercise their initiative is to

    A. give them some of your responsibilities
    B. tell them to use their judgment and not to worry about the routines
    C. compliment the counselors whenever they make changes on their own
    D. ask them for suggestions about planning programs and assure them that their ideas will be considered

16. Assume that a children's institution has a problem because the children dislike certain foods served in the dining hall, and the counselors feel that the children are justified in their complaints.
Of the following, the BEST approach to use in order to make the menus more acceptable to the children would be to

    A. ask the children and staff to present menu ideas to the dietitian
    B. have the counselors try to convince the children that the foods they dislike are good for them
    C. instruct the counselors to see that the children taste small amounts of all foods
    D. have the dietitian temporarily remove foods disliked by the children from the menu

17. Assume that a counselor's written reports are always late and incomplete. When the supervisor discusses this problem with him, he complains of not having enough time during the day to do the reports properly. However, the supervisor knows that the counselor is not overloaded with work.
Of the following, the MOST appropriate action for the supervisor to take FIRST is to

    A. transfer the counselor to a less difficult group of children
    B. help the counselor reapportion his working time
    C. recommend that the counselor be disciplined for failure to perform his work
    D. ask the counselor to work overtime regularly

18. When a supervisor is put in charge of organizing the living arrangements in a dormitory for a group of new children, it is PARTICULARLY important for him to

    A. allow the children to arrange the furniture when they arrive
    B. avoid putting too much emphasis on getting the dormitory organized
    C. organize the dormitory and arrange the furniture before the children arrive
    D. organize the dormitory after he meets the children

19. The supervisor has become aware that the counselors are having difficulty getting the children into bed each night. There is excessive noise and activity in the television and reading corners when it is time for showers.
It would be advisable for the supervisor to meet with the counselors and tell them that the BEST way to get the children ready for bed is to

    A. take away television if they fail to cooperate
    B. advance bedtime by an hour if they fail to cooperate
    C. establish a quiet bedtime routine
    D. put out most of the lights

20. Assume that the director of a children's institution has assigned a supervisor to organize the entertainment for an *open house* day, and has asked the supervisor to do his best to get the participation of all counselors. This is an important assignment, since officials and community leaders are expected to attend.
Of the following, the MOST effective way to encourage the counselors' cooperation would be to

   A. give general assignments to the senior counselors and ask them to give specific responsibilities to each counselor
   B. issue a memorandum to all counselors giving detailed information about the program and including specific assignments
   C. call a meeting of all counselors and assign tasks based on decisions you have made previously
   D. hold an open discussion meeting with the counselors, ask them for suggestions, and permit them to volunteer for assignments of their choice, if possible

20.____

21. Community people often dislike having residences for children in their neighborhood because they fear that these children will be a bad influence on their own children.
Of the following, the BEST way for a children's institution to establish a constructive relationship with the community is to

   A. assure community leaders that the children will seldom be allowed out of the residence
   B. ignore the community's reaction and let the children come and go, accompanied by staff members
   C. invite community leaders to visit, in order to meet the children and staff and to learn about the function and purpose of the institution
   D. tell the children that they must be on their best behavior in order to dispel the hostility of community residents

21.____

22. Two volunteer workers who are excellent with the children frequently do not come in when expected. This is a source of disappointment for the children and causes serious problems for the counselors.
The appropriate action for the supervisor to take FIRST is to

   A. request that these volunteers be transferred from his floor
   B. tell the volunteers that, since they are not trustworthy, they should not return
   C. tell the children that volunteers can come and go as they please since they are not paid for their work
   D. explain to the volunteers how much their regular presence means to the children and the importance of not disappointing them

22.____

23. Assume that a neighborhood storekeeper has complained that a group of adolescents from the shelter *hang around* his store, damage his property, and steal candy and other merchandise. The adolescents have been identified as being in the group assigned to a counselor under your supervision.
Of the following, the MOST appropriate action to take FIRST is to

   A. call a meeting of all the counselors for the purpose of deciding what to do about this situation
   B. call in these children and confront them with their misbehavior

23.____

C. meet with the storekeeper and these children separately in order to determine the facts of the situation
D. forbid these children to leave the shelter unless accompanied by a counselor

24. Assume that the social worker calls a supervisor to the phone to speak to a parent who has not visited or written to his child for some time but is asking for a *report* on the child. This loss of contact with the parent has disturbed the child.
At this point, the supervisor's BEST approach would be to

    A. ask the parent why he is suddenly interested in the child
    B. say that the child is well and wants to visit, at which time the supervisor will *report* to the parent
    C. explain that confidential information cannot be discussed on the telephone
    D. give the *report* and demand that the parent visit the child

25. Of the following, the MOST important reason why children are placed in shelters maintained by the Department of Social Services is to

    A. provide a stable and comparatively inexpensive facility for their care
    B. provide temporary care for children who do not have competent parents or guardians
    C. provide the children with treatment facilities in a group residence
    D. give the responsible parent a chance to work and be removed from public assistance

KEY (CORRECT ANSWERS)

1.	B	11.	D
2.	B	12.	C
3.	D	13.	D
4.	D	14.	B
5.	A	15.	D
6.	C	16.	A
7.	B	17.	B
8.	A	18.	C
9.	A	19.	C
10.	D	20.	D

21. C
22. D
23. C
24. B
25. B

EXAMINATION SECTION
TEST 1

DIRECTIONS: Each question or incomplete statement is followed by several suggested answers or completions. Select the one that BEST answers the question or completes the statement. *PRINT THE LETTER OF THE CORRECT ANSWER IN THE SPACE AT THE RIGHT.*

1. During the first few days in a children's institution, some children will keep to themselves, refuse to take part in activities, and even refuse to eat.
   To help counselors deal effectively with such behavior, the supervisor should point out that these children are PROBABLY

   A. stubborn and they should be forced to take part in the activities
   B. behaving this way because they dislike their counselor
   C. feeling inferior, lonely, unwanted, and depressed
   D. showing signs of serious emotional disturbance

   1.____

2. Most children between the ages of six and eight are eager to show adults that they can do things for themselves such as getting their food, dressing, and taking care of their personal hygiene, and are apt to resent being *helped* or *watched* by adults.
   However, of the following, it is MOST important for child-care workers to realize that children

   A. will mature emotionally only if they are strictly supervised
   B. also want and need adults to be concerned about them
   C. should be told that they cannot be independent
   D. should be taught not to resent constant supervision by adults

   2.____

3. Assume a supervisor has learned that one of his subordinates punished a child he caught in the bathroom alone, masturbating.
   Of the following, the MOST appropriate action for the supervisor to take is to

   A. praise the subordinate for his action
   B. suggest that the child be given psychological consultation
   C. discuss with the subordinate his attitude about masturbation and the need to respect the child's privacy
   D. speak with the child privately and tell him he may be endangering his health

   3.____

4. A counselor asks the supervisor for advice about a seven-year-old boy who is often found with matches in his possession.
   The BEST suggestion the supervisor can make is that the counselor should FIRST

   A. find out whether the boy is smoking cigarettes
   B. watch the boy closely to find out what he is doing with the matches
   C. try to discover what psychological meaning the matches have for this boy
   D. tell the boy firmly about the danger of fire and take the matches away

   4.____

5. A thirteen-year-old boy who has committed thefts and was adjudged to be neglected is placed in a shelter.
   His *initial* attitude towards his counselor is MOST likely to be

   5.____

A. ambivalent
B. aggressively friendly
C. hostile and rejecting
D. sympathetic

6. If a counselor has a child in his group who stutters badly, finds it difficult to talk with the other children in his group, and is withdrawing into himself, he can *probably* BEST help the child by

   A. telling him that he will stop stuttering if he speaks slowly
   B. taking him aside as frequently as possible and giving him speech exercises
   C. stopping him every time he begins to stutter
   D. asking the other children to cooperate by not calling attention to the stuttering

7. A counselor complains frequently to the supervisor that the eight- to ten-year-old boys in his dormitory are not quiet at any time and are always creating disturbances. Of the following, the BEST suggestion the supervisor can make to the counselor is to

   A. examine carefully his relationships with the children
   B. give the children more things to do that interest them
   C. let the children know that many other youngsters find it hard to be quiet
   D. teach them the value of patience and the importance of learning to be quiet

8. Some eight- and nine-year-old children at the shelter refuse to take part in active outdoor sports, preferring to play quietly.
Assuming that these children have no physical or mental disability, the counselor should realize that

   A. children's choice of activities often depends on their experiences and skills
   B. when children are angry because they are placed in the institution, they show their anger by refusing to participate in group sports
   C. this behavior indicates emotional disturbance and requires psychiatric consultation
   D. organized games or group play are difficult for most children at this age

9. A ten-year-old boy seems to have difficulty reading any of the children's books that are available at the shelter. Of the following, the BEST recommendation that could be made in this situation is that

   A. books be found that will interest the child
   B. the child be told that reading is hard work
   C. the child be transferred to a younger age group
   D. the child be tested for reading ability

10. Counselors will often turn to the supervisor for on-the-spot solutions to problems that they have been unable to work out. Assume that a counselor has asked his supervisor what he should do when a 10-year-old child repeatedly asks for help in tying his shoelaces. The child does not seem to know how to begin.
It would be MOST appropriate for the supervisor to tell the counselor

    A. to patiently attempt to teach the child how to tie his shoelaces
    B. that the child is probably pretending that he does not know how to tie his laces in order to get special attention
    C. to recommend psychological consultation in the interest of the child
    D. that he should insist that the child learn to lace his own shoes

11. Susie, an eight-year-old, becomes terribly upset, abusive, and destructive when urged to eat certain foods that she has never eaten before.
    The BEST way for her counselor to help Susie is by

    A. insisting that she eat everything, for the benefit of her health
    B. rewarding her in little ways if she eats these foods
    C. ignoring her outbursts, since this will force her to eat
    D. accepting the fact that many children have a valid dislike for unfamiliar foods

12. Assume that a twelve-year-old boy, just admitted to the shelter, refuses to undress or even to take off his sweater.
    Of the following, the BEST thing for the counselor to do would be to

    A. talk with the boy about his reasons without pressuring him
    B. establish authority immediately by forcing the boy to undress
    C. punish the boy by taking away privileges until he conforms
    D. shame the boy by telling him he is acting like a baby

13. Assume that a supervisor has evidence that a children's counselor has brought marijuana and other drugs into the institution.
    The supervisor's FIRST action should be to

    A. report the situation to the director immediately
    B. warn the counselor that he will be discharged if he is found with drugs
    C. determine whether the counselor has introduced the children to drugs
    D. make a complete investigation and report his findings to the director

14. The CHIEF cause of death among people between 15 and 25 years of age is

    A. lead poisoning   B. drug abuse
    C. suicide   D. malnutrition

15. Recent studies show that there has been a trend toward an overall decline in the number of children cared for in institutions.
    The MOST important reason for this *decline* is that

    A. fewer children are adjudged to be neglected
    B. funds are lacking to provide institutional care in accordance with approved standards
    C. there is a shortage of qualified personnel to operate the institutions
    D. there is an increased life span of parents

16. Of the following, the MOST important role played by the mother in the healthy development of a young girl is to

    A. teach her to cook and clean
    B. protect her from immoral influences
    C. provide a female figure with whom she can identify
    D. encourage her to become popular with boys

17. The one of the following which is the MOST important factor in the present trend toward a lower birth rate in this country is the

    A. new morality   B. high cost of living
    C. women's liberation movement D. new abortion laws

18. Within the last few years, there has been a reorganization of public human service agencies in the city.
The Department of Social Services is now part of the

    A. Environmental Protection Administration
    B. Health Services Administration
    C. Board of Education
    D. Human Resources Administration

19. The agency that works mainly with the public school children who are having school adjustment problems is the

    A. Pupils' Placement Division
    B. Department of Mental Hygiene
    C. Department of Social Services
    D. Bureau of Child Guidance

20. The agency that has LEGAL authority to protect children frori mistreatment by adults is the

    A. S.P.C.C.   B. B.P.C.J.   C. S.P.C.A.   D. J.B.G.

21. An organization whose SOLE purpose is to help fatherless boys is the

    A. Angel Guardian Society
    B. Police Athletic League
    C. Sandlot Baseball Association
    D. Big Brothers

22. It is estimated that about one-fifth of the children in the United States live in families with poverty-level incomes.
The Federal Office of Economic Opportunity has established that a family of four is living in poverty if its income is *at or below*

    A. $10,800   B. $13,500   C. $18,000   D. $25,0.00

23. The one of the following that has recently gained widespread attention for its work to improve conditions for the poor in this country is the

    A. Social Security Administration
    B. Citizens' Committee for Children
    C. National Welfare Rights Organization
    D. Institute for Social Progress

24. The office of probation is doing away with the detention of adolescent offenders in security (locked-door) facilities MAINLY because this method

    A. is no longer needed since these offenders may now be let out on bail
    B. is no longer needed, due to the greater availability of foster homes for adolescents
    C. was often misused, and adolescents were mistreated instead of being educated or rehabilitated
    D. did not provide for any educational facilities

25. A counselor on the night shift reports that there has been an unusual amount of bedwetting in the intermediate boys' dormitory during the past two weeks. He has tried everything and now he thinks that they are doing it *just to be mean* to him. He names two or three boys who have probably put the others up to it.
Of the following, the MOST helpful action for the supervisor to take FIRST would be to

   A. find out whether anything upsetting happened to the boys in the previous two weeks
   B. meet with all the bedwetters in a group and tell them they will be punished if they wet their beds again
   C. question some of the boys to see whether the counselor correctly identified the leaders
   D. advise the night counselor to be more patient

25.____

KEY (CORRECT ANSWERS)

1.	C	11.	D
2.	B	12.	A
3.	C	13.	A
4.	D	14.	B
5.	C	15.	D
6.	D	16.	C
7.	B	17.	D
8.	A	18.	D
9.	D	19.	D
10.	C	20.	A

21.	D
22.	C
23.	C
24.	C
25.	A

TEST 2

DIRECTIONS: Each question or incomplete statement is followed by several suggested answers or completions. Select the one that BEST answers the question or completes the statement. *PRINT THE LETTER OF THE CORRECT ANSWER IN THE SPACE AT THE RIGHT.*

1. Many children in institutions feel such great resentment about their situation that they are angry at everybody and become disrespectful to counselors.
   The BEST way for supervisors to help counselors deal with this problem is to

   A. advise the counselors to mimic the children's angry responses in order to show them how difficult they are to live with
   B. take every opportunity to show the counselors what they have done wrong in handling these children
   C. discuss with the counselors the causes of the children's resentment and the importance of not reacting impulsively to their misbehavior
   D. provide the counselors with a reading list of books and articles on child development

   1.___

2. Assume that a usually quiet, rather obese boy started a fistfight when another boy teased him for being fat.
   Of the following, it would be BEST for the counselor to

   A. tell the boy who started the fight that he would not be teased if he lost weight
   B. help the boys settle the matter and warn them that they will be disciplined if they fight again
   C. punish both the fat boy and the boy who teased him
   D. punish the boy who started the fight

   2.___

3. A counselor comes to a supervisor asking for advice about a child that he frequently has to remind to be less noisy during the periods when the children are resting. The child temporarily quiets down when told to do so, but the counselor has become concerned about how to handle the situation.
   The supervisor should advise the counselor that his BEST approach would be to

   A. warn the child that he will be moved to another dormitory if he continues to be noisy
   B. find out if the other children are disturbed by this child before taking stronger disciplinary measures
   C. segregate him from the other children at rest periods and let him be as noisy as he pleases
   D. take away television privileges until the child improves

   3.___

4. The one of the following that would be a POOR way for a counselor to deal with tough and unfriendly teenagers is to

   A. suggest that they tell him when they think he fails to maintain the standards he demands of them
   B. resist their attempts to make him explain the reasons for new rules
   C. refrain from talking down to them
   D. encourage them to ask for an explanation whenever they do not understand something

   4.___

5. Assume that a child has just swallowed some turpentine that was accidentally left within his reach.
   Which of the following is NOT a recommended measure in giving first aid to the child before the doctor arrives?

   A. Keep the child warm
   B. Induce vomiting
   C. Give hot coffee or tea
   D. Give mineral oil

   5.____

6. Some professionals, such as psychiatrists, psychologists, teachers, and social workers, have a low opinion of the child-care worker's job and his value to the children.
   Of the following, the MOST serious consequence of such an attitude is that it may

   A. affect the children and their feeling of respect for their counselors
   B. discourage child-care workers from getting more education and professional training
   C. increase the children's hostility toward professionals on the institution's staff
   D. cause child-care workers to resent their supervisor as well as the professionals

   6.____

7. Assume that one of the boys becomes uncontrollable during the pottery-making periods on the weekly schedule, throwing materials around, upsetting equipment, annoying the other children, and refusing to work on any suggested projects. This does not occur at any other time. This boy's counselor tells his supervisor that he does not know how to handle this situation.
   The supervisor should suggest that the boy

   A. be excluded from recreational activities
   B. be put in another pottery group with a different counselor
   C. be given an activity that he prefers during this period
   D. has fears about getting his hands dirty

   7.____

8. A child tells a counselor that she does not wish to go on a picnic with her group, even though she has always gone willingly on such outings in the past. When urged to go, she becomes upset and says she is too tired.
   The MOST advisable action for the counselor to take FIRST is to

   A. tell the child that she will have to stay in the infirmary if she is too tired to go on the picnic
   B. tell the child that she has to go because all the arrangements have been made
   C. tell the child that she will lose other privileges if she does not go on the picnic
   D. try to determine the child's real reason for not wanting to go on this trip

   8.____

9. A 14-year-old boy is found with a knife, refuses to give it up, and threatens to *use it* on the counselor. Of the following, the BEST action for the counselor to take would be to

   A. order the boy to go to the director's office
   B. ignore the matter so that the other boys will not become involved
   C. tell the boy you will take this up with him later
   D. call the supervisor for assistance in handling the matter

   9.____

10. A counselor seeks advice from the supervisor about a child who has refused for the third time to help tidy up the dormitory.
    Of the following, the BEST suggestion for the supervisor to make would be that the counselor should

    10.____

A. have punished the child the first time he refused to help
B. pay no attention to this incident
C. ask the child whether he needs or wants help and also try to find out why he refused
D. try to *shame* the child in front of the other children for being lazy

11. A seven-year-old boy runs away from his group while on an outing, but is soon returned to the shelter by the police. This is the first time the boy has run away, and he has otherwise made a good adjustment at the shelter.
The MOST appropriate action for the counselor to take is to

    A. ask the other children to help keep an eye on him during future outings
    B. take away the boy's privileges until he *learns his lesson*
    C. ask the boy whether he wants to transfer to another group
    D. welcome the boy back and try to find out why he ran away and what happened

11.___

12. When a child in an institution is afraid or confused, the MOST appropriate action for his counselor to take FIRST is to

    A. recommend that he play with younger children
    B. consider psychiatric referral
    C. insist that he follow the daily routines without deviation
    D. give him sincere individual attention

12.___

13. Children in institutions often lie when they are questioned by adults.
The BEST way for counselors to approach this problem is to

    A. make these children aware that adults know they often lie
    B. promise the children that they will not be punished if they tell the truth
    C. listen objectively to the children's statements without assuming they are lying
    D. point out to the children that lying usually results in punishment

13.___

14. When a teenager is in trouble, the immediate reaction of many adults is to be unsympathetic and to *teach him a lesson.*
The BEST approach for a counselor to take FIRST with a teenage boy who feels that he has been treated unfairly by a recreation worker who has put him out of the gym for alleged misconduct is to

    A. ignore the boy's complaints and begin talking about something else
    B. listen to the boy's side of the story
    C. tell the boy he must learn not to question a person in authority
    D. quietly tell the boy to keep away from the recreation worker after this

14.___

15. Frequently a child who comes to a shelter says that he was sent away from his family because he was bad and his parents did not want him any more.
The BEST way for the counselor to begin to help such a child is to

    A. show his understanding of the child's feelings about leaving home and welcome him warmly
    B. tell him that he will be loved at the shelter if his behavior is good
    C. make him realize he was not bad by asking him to give you examples of his good behavior
    D. tell him that the social worker will explain to his family that he is not bad

15.___

16. The one of the following relating to young children which has received MOST attention from citizens and professional groups recently is   16.____

    A. the recurrence of poliomyelitis
    B. allowances for school lunches
    C. day care programs
    D. rubella immunization

17. The MAIN reason for transferring children from shelters to other institutions or foster homes is to provide   17.____

    A. another chance for the children to adjust
    B. a more permanent and stable living arrangement for the children
    C. a more economical method of caring for the children
    D. a structured environment for the children

18. Of the following, the experience that is LEAST likely to be a condition resulting in placement of a six-year-old child in a shelter maintained by the Department of Social Services is   18.____

    A. having little food in the house
    B. being threatened with a gun or a knife by a parent
    C. wandering away from home to an unfamiliar neighborhood
    D. being physically abused by a parent

19. When a child is remanded to the shelter by the court, the child's legal status is that his   19.____

    A. legal guardian is an appointee of the Commissioner of Social Service
    B. legal guardian is the court
    C. legal guardian is the superintendent of the shelter
    D. guardian is his parent

20. Assume that a child complains to a counselor of not feeling well. The counselor immediately tells the child to go to the nurse. When the child lingers, the counselor pushes him gently, but firmly, towards the nurse's station.
    Of the following, the BEST appraisal of this situation is that the counselor   20.____

    A. should have explored the child's complaint further, and accompanied him to the nurse
    B. was right in not exploring the child's complaint, since he has had no medical training
    C. need not have pushed the child, since his lingering showed he probably did not require medical attention
    D. was probably outsmarted by the child who was pretending he was ill

21. As the supervisor on your floor, you have noticed that several of the counselors speak to the children mainly in order to correct them for minor infractions.
    The BEST way to approach this situation is to   21.____

    A. tell the counselors that what they are doing is wrong, and order them to stop immediately
    B. explain to these counselors that the children need warmth and friendliness more than correction about minor matters

C. agree that most children do not pay attention if you speak kindly to them
D. suggest that the counselors appoint child monitors to correct the others

22. Assume that several counselors at a children's shelter have complained to one of the supervisors that the daily program schedules are too confining for the children and do not give the counselors enough freedom of action. The counselors want the schedules abolished.
It would be BEST for the supervisor to

   A. recommend that the counselors talk to the director about this matter
   B. help the counselors understand that the organization of time is important for these children as it helps to create order in their lives
   C. tell the counselors that schedules are the best method of keeping children out of trouble
   D. suggest that each counselor turn in his own schedule for approval

23. A supervisor overhears a group of children saying that they have to be pretty careful about what they do or say around their counselor because they *do not want to be slapped*.
The MOST appropriate action for the supervisor to take FIRST is to

   A. warn the counselor that he can be dismissed for slapping children
   B. report the situation to the director of the institution
   C. observe the counselor more closely and attempt to get the facts of the situation
   D. report the counselor to the Child Protective Unit on charges of child abuse

24. The one of the following which is an IMPORTANT reason why counselors should not strike children under any circumstances is that

   A. children may learn that violence is the only way to settle their differences with others
   B. older children are likely to strike the counselors in return
   C. they may injure the children so seriously that parents will prosecute them for child abuse
   D. strict laws against corporal punishment by teachers and counselors have recently been put into effect

25. A supervisor overhears a counselor telling a child that he will not be allowed to skip his evening shower, although the child took a shower earlier after swimming. The supervisor should tell the counselor later that his refusal to make an exception in this case was

   A. *incorrect,* because the second shower is wasting the child's time
   B. *correct,* because the other children would think the counselor is playing favorites and, therefore, lose their respect for him
   C. *incorrect,* because a counselor should consider individual needs whenever possible
   D. *correct,* because control will be lost when exceptions to rules are tolerated

KEY (CORRECT ANSWERS)

1.	C	11.	D
2.	B	12.	D
3.	B	13.	C
4.	B	14.	B
5.	B	15.	A
6.	A	16.	C
7.	C	17.	B
8.	D	18.	C
9.	D	19.	D
10.	C	20.	A

21. B
22. B
23. C
24. A
25. C

EXAMINATION SECTION
TEST 1

DIRECTIONS: Each question or incomplete statement is followed by several suggested answers or completions. Select the one that BEST answers the question or completes the statement. *PRINT THE LETTER OF THE CORRECT ANSWER IN THE SPACE AT THE RIGHT*

1. Which of the following statements is TRUE?

   A. The goal of normalization is to allow one to do whatever one likes.
   B. Normalization involves making a person become normal.
   C. Normalization advocates that whenever possible, people's perceptions of developmentally disabled individuals must be enhanced or improved.
   D. Normalization advocates encouraging the developmentally disabled to be just like everyone else.

2. It is important to view the developmentally disabled as

   A. helpless
   B. unable to make decisions
   C. deviant
   D. none of the above

3. All of the following would be considered good practice EXCEPT

   A. providing residential services in the community, rather than in an isolated area
   B. placing residential homes next to rural prisons
   C. providing access in residences to accommodate those who are non-ambulatory
   D. avoiding excessive rules that tend to separate staff from residents

4. All of the following are true in normalization EXCEPT

   A. family involvement in normalization is usually not helpful to achieving the goal
   B. clients should be involved, when possible, in selecting programming in order to develop independence
   C. program options should emphasize autonomy, independence, integration, and productivity
   D. it is a good idea when possible to have day programming located apart from the living setting

5. Benefits of normalization include all of the following EXCEPT

   A. development of self-confidence and self-esteem in the developmentally disabled
   B. social integration of the developmentally disabled
   C. positive changes in societal attitudes regarding the developmentally disabled
   D. societal acceptance of deviance

6. All of the following statements are true EXCEPT:

   A. Normalization means that normal conditions of life should be made available to developmentally disabled people
   B. Attitudes toward the mentally disabled have a great effect on the way they are treated, and, consequently, on their chances for living a productive, normal life

C. It is highly unlikely that efforts at normalization will succeed in most communities
D. What is normal or typical in one society may not be normal or typical in another

7. In normalization, the means used to teach a skill are as important as the skill itself. In teaching adults, which of the following would be MOST appropriate?

   A. Working individually with someone after dinner in order to teach him or her how to brush their teeth
   B. Teaching pouring skills with sand in a sandbox
   C. Teaching how to button clothes by using a doll for practice
   D. Teaching how to tie shoelaces by first working With a baby shoe

8. Which of the following statements is TRUE?

   A. Residents' chore duties in a community residence should only change three times a year.
   B. Entrance into a community residence should be solely determined by an individual's need for a place to live.
   C. Using a task analysis for a client would involve breaking down a complex task into smaller, more understandable parts.
   D. Clients should be allowed to eat when and what they choose.

9. Select the one statement below that is NOT true of supervised community residences. A supervised community residence

   A. can provide short-term residence for individuals who need only training and experience in activities of daily living after a period of institutionalization or as an alternative to institutionalization
   B. can provide an institutional setting for those people who need it
   C. can provide long-term residence for individuals who are unlikely to acquire the skills necessary for more independent living
   D. usually requires staff on site at all times

10. All of the following are goals of community residences EXCEPT

    A. providing a home environment for developmentally disabled persons
    B. providing a setting where clients can learn the skills necessary to live in the least restrictive environment
    C. providing a setting where the developmentally disabled can acquire the skills necessary to live as independently as possible
    D. the community residence allows for the maximum level of independence inconsistent with a person's disability and functional level

11. All of the following statements are true EXCEPT:

    A. A community residence does not need to adhere to the principle of normalization in its physical or social structure
    B. The term least restrictive environment refers to an environment which most resembles that of non-handicapped peers where the needs of developmentally disabled persons can be met

C. A person's length of stay in a community residence extends only until a person has attained the skills and motivation to function successfully in a less restrictive setting
D. The purposes of a community residence may vary so that people with different ranges of abilities and levels of functioning may be served

12. All of the following statements are true EXCEPT:

    A. Developmentally disabled persons residing in community residences must be afforded privacy, personal space, and freedom of access to the house as is consistent with their age and program needs
    B. Transportation should be available from the nearest institution so that people in community residences have access to the community
    C. The service needs of each person in a community residence should be individually planned by an interdisciplinary team
    D. An interdisciplinary team should include staff of the community residence, providers of program and support services, and, if appropriate, the developmentally disabled person's correspondent

13. All of the following statements are true EXCEPT:

    A. Supportive community residences are not required to provide staff on site 24 hours a day
    B. Residents in supervised community residences may need more assistance in activities of daily living than persons residing in supportive community residences
    C. An aim of a community residence is to maintain a family and home-like environment
    D. Those living in a community residence shall spend at least three hours per weekday and one evening per week in programs and activities at the residence

14. In working in treatment teams, it is MOST important for team members to

    A. communicate effectively with each other
    B. keep morale high
    C. attend meetings on time
    D. enjoy working with each other

15. All of the following statements are true EXCEPT:

    A. In teaching self-care skills, many tasks may need to be divided into sub parts
    B. Tasks which are easiest to learn should generally be taught first
    C. Changes in routine are very helpful when teaching the developmentally disabled a new skill
    D. The severely disabled do not learn as well from verbal instruction as they do from demonstration of a skill

16. All of the following statements are true EXCEPT:

    A. It is important to evaluate the client's readiness to attempt learning a particular task before starting to teach the task
    B. It is better to do a task for a client if the task may take much time and effort on his or her part
    C. People generally learn faster when their efforts lead to an enjoyable activity
    D. It is best when teaching a certain skill to begin with a small group when possible

17. All of the following statements are true EXCEPT:

    A. The expectations of a staff person of how well a client will be able to perform a certain task can influence daily living skills
    B. Environmental factors can influence daily living skills
    C. After seeing a skill demonstrated, a client should practice the skill
    D. A client will make a greater effort if he or she feels ill at ease with the instructor, and knows the instructor will become impatient if he or she continues to make mistakes

18. Of the following, the BEST way to teach a client an activity of daily living is to

    A. describe the steps to the client
    B. read the directions to the client
    C. break the activity into steps and have the client learn one step at a time
    D. have a client who can perform the task teach the client who cannot

19. All of the following are important steps in teaching a living skill EXCEPT

    A. defining the skill clearly
    B. determining the size of the skill
    C. breaking down each major step into substeps and sub-substeps as necessary
    D. rewarding the accomplishment of each step with candy

20. When teaching a daily living skill, it is important to keep in mind all of the following EXCEPT

    A. using concrete and specific language
    B. punishment can be a highly effective learning device
    C. matching the size of the skill to the client's ability level
    D. demonstrating what you want the resident to do

KEY (CORRECT ANSWERS)

1. C
2. D
3. B
4. A
5. D

6. C
7. A
8. C
9. B
10. D

11. A
12. B
13. D
14. A
15. C

16. B
17. D
18. C
19. D
20. B

TEST 2

DIRECTIONS: Each question or incomplete statement is followed by several suggested answers or completions. Select the one that BEST answers the question or completes the statement. *PRINT THE LETTER OF THE CORRECT ANSWER IN THE SPACE AT THE RIGHT.*

1. All of the following would be considered qualities of a developmental disability EXCEPT the disability

    A. may be attributable to autism
    B. has continued or can be expected to continue indefinitely
    C. can be easily overcome
    D. may be attributable to cerebral palsy or neurological impairment

2. The condition of autism

    A. applies to those people who have little or no control over their motor skills
    B. is hereditary
    C. is characterized by severe disorders of communication and behavior
    D. begins most frequently in adulthood

3. Secondary childhood autism differs from primary childhood autism in that

    A. primary childhood autism is more difficult to treat
    B. secondary childhood autism is secondary to disturbances such as brain damage
    C. secondary childhood autism is not as severe a disorder
    D. secondary childhood autism is less likely to interfere with behavior patterns

4. Which of the following would be LEAST adversely affected by autism?

    A. Interpersonal relations
    B. Learning
    C. Developmental rate and sequences
    D. Motor skills

5. Which of the following statements is NOT true?

    A. Cerebral palsy refers to a condition resulting from damage to the brain that may occur before, during or after birth and results in the loss of control over voluntary muscles in the body.
    B. Ataxic cerebral palsy is characterized by an inability to maintain normal balance.
    C. Someone with athetoid cerebral palsy would find it easier to maintain purposefulness of movements than someone with spastic cerebral palsy.
    D. Mixed cerebral palsy refers to the combination of two or more of the following categories of cerebral palsy such as the spastic, athetoid, ataxic, tremor, and rigid types.

6. All of the following are true about epilepsy EXCEPT

    A. epilepsy does not usually involve a loss of consciousness
    B. an *aura* often appears to the individual before a *grand mal* seizure occurs

C. people experiencing *petit mal* seizures are seldom aware that a seizure has occurred
D. status epilepticus, psychomotor, and Jacksonian are all forms of epilepsy

7. All of the following statements are true of developmental disability EXCEPT:

    A. The prevalence in the general total population is less than 3% of the population
    B. Approximately 89% of the disabled population is mildly disabled
    C. School-age children who are mildly disabled can usually acquire practical skills and useful reading and arithmetic skills
    D. Adults who are mildly disabled cannot usually achieve social and vocational skills adequate for minimum self-support

8. Which of the following statements is NOT true of intellectual disability?

    A. Approximately 6% of the disabled population has an I.Q. of 36-51, 3.5% of the population has an I.Q. of 20-35, and 1.5% of this population has an I.Q. of 19 and below.
    B. A severely disabled person could never achieve limited self-care.
    C. Moderately disabled adults may achieve self-maintenance in unskilled work or semi-skilled work under sheltered conditions.
    D. Severely disabled children can profit from systematic skills training.

9. All of the following refer to neurological impairment EXCEPT

    A. childhood aphasia is a condition characterized by the failure to develop, or difficulty in using, language and speech
    B. epilepsy
    C. minimal brain dysfunction is associated with deviations of the central nervous system
    D. neurological impairment refers to a group of disorders of the central nervous system characterized by dysfunction in one or more, but not all, skills affecting communicative, perceptual, cognitive, memory, attentional, motor control, and appropriate social behaviors

10. Which of the following statements is TRUE?

    A. Autistic children are below average in intelligence level.
    B. All cerebral palsied persons are developmentally disabled.
    C. Once an epileptic seizure has started, it cannot be stopped.
    D. Autism is due to faulty early interactional patterns between child and mother.

11. All of the following are false EXCEPT

    A. recent investigations have found that parents of autistic children have no specific common personality traits and no unusual environmental stresses
    B. cerebral palsied persons cannot understand directions
    C. it is not true that unless controlled seizures can cause further brain damage
    D. the majority of the developmentally disabled are in institutions

10. In serving the needs of autistic persons, the one of the following which is usually LEAST important is the need

    A. for training in social skills
    B. for language stimulation
    C. to deal with potentially self-injurious, repetitive, and aggressive behaviors
    D. to teach skills that would improve intelligence

11. In serving the needs of persons with cerebral palsy, the one of the following which is usually LEAST important is the need

    A. to experience normal movement and sensations as much as possible
    B. to develop fundamental movement patterns which the person can regulate
    C. for experience and guidance in social settings
    D. to restrict their environment

12. All of the following statements are true EXCEPT:

    A. It is important that epileptic persons have balanced diets
    B. Pica, a craving for unnatural food, occurs with all developmentally disabled persons
    C. It has been projected that 50% of those individuals who have cerebral palsy are also developmentally disabled
    D. When working with the developmentally disabled, it is important to encourage sensory-motor stimulation, physical stimulation, language stimulation, social skills training, and the performance of daily living skills

13. When working with neurologically impaired persons, all of the following are true EXCEPT:

    A. There is usually a need for perceptual training
    B. It is important to keep in mind that an individual may know something one day and not know it the next
    C. It may be necessary to remove distracting stimuli
    D. It is important to keep in mind that neurologically impaired persons usually have substantially lower I.Q.'s than the average person

14. The developmentally disabled do NOT have the right to

    A. register and vote in elections
    B. marry
    C. confidentiality of records
    D. hit someone who teases them

15. Which of the following statements is TRUE?

    A. It is important for staff members not to make all of the choices for their developmentally disabled clients.
    B. Distraction is not a good technique to use when trying to channel potentially violent or destructive behavior to a socially acceptable outlet.
    C. Severely and profoundly disabled children do not appear to have a strong need for personal contact.
    D. It is primarily the mildly or moderately disabled child that exhibits the behavior usually associated with developmental disability.

16. All of the following are causes of developmental disability EXCEPT

    A. organic defects
    B. brain lesions
    C. increased sexual activity
    D. chromosomal abnormalities

17. A developmentally disabled patient who is *acting out*

    A. may be trying to communicate that he or she is physically uncomfortable or needs something
    B. should be ignored
    C. should be severely punished
    D. feels comfortable in his or her surroundings

18. In working with the developmentally disabled, all of the following would be appropriate EXCEPT

    A. remembering that seemingly small things, both positive and negative, can be very important to the client
    B. allowing choices whenever possible
    C. maintaining a calm, level-headed attitude during an anxiety-producing situation will reassure clients and help them relax and feel safer
    D. after basic self-help skills have been mastered, it is not necessary to encourage further development

KEY (CORRECT ANSWERS)

1. C
2. C
3. B
4. D
5. C

6. A
7. D
8. B
9. B
10. C

11. A
12. D
13. D
14. B
15. D

16. D
17. A
18. C
19. A
20. D

EXAMINATION SECTION
TEST 1

DIRECTIONS: Each question or incomplete statement is followed by several suggested answers or completions. Select the one that BEST answers the question or completes the statement. *PRINT THE LETTER OF THE CORRECT ANSWER IN THE SPACE AT THE RIGHT.*

1. Marked improvement in a child's ability to draw a man over a brief period of time is MOST likely to be related to   1.____

    A. better social adjustment
    B. maturational effect
    C. the overcoming of a reading disability
    D. recovery from an illness

2. Phenylketonuria, which is associated with intellectual disability, is a disorder of   2.____

    A. the reticuloendothelia system
    B. metabolism
    C. cerebral damage
    D. gyral defect

3. A patient asserts, *I can't stand the agony I suffer when I go against my mother's wishes.* The therapist replies, *You really like to punish that momma inside of you for your dependency, don't you?*
   This response can be viewed as an example of   3.____

    A. reassurance   B. interpretation
    C. support   D. reflection of feeling

4. A shy young first grade boy becomes extremely attached to his teacher. He brings her presents, asks her to help him with his clothing a great deal, and wants to sit near her all the time.
   He is MOST likely manifesting the mental mechanism of   4.____

    A. introjection   B. sublimation
    C. reaction-formation D. transference

5. The peculiarities of language behavior in the schizophrenic arise from his extreme need of a feeling of   5.____

    A. personal security   B. self-denial
    C. isolation   D. disarticulation

6. The theory that psychical compensation for a feeling of physical or social inferiority is responsible for the development of a psychoneurosis is attributed to   6.____

    A. Adler   B. Horney   C. Freud   D. Sullivan

7. Which of the following terms refers to the maintenance of stability in the physiological functioning of the organism?

   A. Functional autonomy
   B. Canalization
   C. Homeostasis
   D. Maturation

8. Extensive studies of the personality and behavior of intellectually gifted children generally reveal that they

   A. are physically better developed on the whole than average children
   B. are more likely to be emotionally disturbed than average children
   C. are more prone to divorce in later life than average children
   D. more often come from homes in which emotional disturbance is present

9. Expert opinion of professional workers with the physically handicapped indicates that a list of behavior characteristics would be headed generally by feelings of

   A. aggression   B. hostility   C. inferiority   D. courage

10. Children with pykno-epilepsy suffer from _____ convulsions.

    A. diencephalic
    B. visceral
    C. psychic equivalent
    D. no

11. Children with albinism and aniridia may read MOST comfortably with levels of illumination that, in relation to average levels of illumination, are

    A. upper   B. middle   C. lower   D. uneven

12. Phenylpyruvic amentia has been traced to which of the following?

    A. Nutritional deficiency in the prenatal environment
    B. A single recessive gene
    C. Pathological nidation
    D. Effects of radiation

13. Age of mother has been found to be MOST closely associated with the incidence of which of the following?

    A. Cerebral palsy
    B. Cerebral angiomatosis
    C. Down syndrome
    D. Hydrocephaly

14. The so-called visual area of the cerebral cortex is located in the _____ lobe.

    A. frontal
    B. parietal
    C. occipital
    D. temporal

15. Hypothyroidism is due to _____ in childhood.

    A. thyroid insufficiency
    B. pituitary insufficiency
    C. thyroid excess
    D. pituitary excess

16. The inability to express oneself in words in spite of an adequate understanding and imaginal representation is called

    A. agraphia   B. aphemia   C. agnosia   D. aphexia

17. Clara Thompson saw psychoanalysis as a method of therapy primarily designed to   17._____
    A. give the individual new insights into his past experiences
    B. help the individual master his difficulties in living
    C. have the individual re-enact his relationships with his parents
    D. strengthen the individual's ego defenses

18. According to Freud, the source of the large majority of the dreams recorded during analysis is   18._____
    A. a recent and psychologically significant event which is directly represented in the dream
    B. several recent and significant events which are combined by the dream into a single whole
    C. one or more recent and significant events which are represented in the dream-content by allusion to a contemporary but indifferent event
    D. a subjectively significant experience which is constantly represented in the dream by allusion to a recent but indifferent impression

19. When an individual permits unpleasant impulses or thoughts access to consciousness but does not permit their normal elaboration in associative connections and in affect, the psychoanalytic adjustment mechanism involved is   19._____
    A. rationalization   B. conversion
    C. isolation   D. introjection

20. In psychoanalytic thinking, repression can BEST be thought of as a(n)   20._____
    A. attempt in projection
    B. special type of introjection
    C. reflection of acceptance of Id impulses
    D. temporal form of regression

KEY (CORRECT ANSWERS)

1.	A	11.	C
2.	B	12.	B
3.	B	13.	C
4.	D	14.	C
5.	A	15.	A
6.	A	16.	B
7.	C	17.	B
8.	A	18.	D
9.	C	19.	C
10.	D	20.	D

TEST 2

DIRECTIONS: Each question or incomplete statement is followed by several suggested answers or completions. Select the one that BEST answers the question or completes the statement. *PRINT THE LETTER OF THE CORRECT ANSWER IN THE SPACE AT THE RIGHT.*

1. The behavior pattern considered to be deviate by clinicians is   1.____

   A. infractions of the moral code
   B. generosity
   C. recessive personality
   D. resistance to authority

2. A symptom of dementia praecox is   2.____

   A. tick paralysis
   B. negativism
   C. extroversion
   D. eremophobia

3. According to classic psychoanalytic thinking, the disorder MOST responsive to psychoanalytic therapy is   3.____

   A. compulsive neurosis
   B. hysteria
   C. narcissistic neurosis
   D. obsessive neurosis

4. For the therapist, the MOST common meaning of resistance is that it is a(n)   4.____

   A. index of lack of suitability for treatment
   B. defensive attempt on the part of the patient
   C. reflection of superior therapeutic promise
   D. relatively rare phenomenon in psychotherapy

5. In a normal distribution, the percentage of children whose IQ's fall between 90 and 110 is APPROXIMATELY   5.____

   A. 40   B. 50   C. 60   D. 70

6. The pioneer in mental diseases who was the first to make a distinction between emotional disorder and intellectual disability was   6.____

   A. Kraepelin   B. Seguin   C. Esquirol   D. Galton

7. In psychoanalytic thinking, the term superego generally embraces the   7.____

   A. necessary social prohibitions as well as the higher cultural strivings and ideals
   B. unconscious strivings of the person as well as the ego-ideal
   C. unconscious reproaches of the person as well as the id strivings
   D. unconscious ego and its defense mechanism as well as the ego-ideal

8. A major contribution of Fromm to psychoanalysis can be considered to be his   8.____

   A. attempt to formulate the dynamics of orality and the concept of original sin
   B. belief that man has innate social feeling and a drive for perfection
   C. effort to relate the psychological forces operating in man to the society within which he lives
   D. effort to integrate the concept of psychosexual development with Rankian principles

9. José, a ten-year-old, has a hyperthyroid condition. It is MOST likely that his behavior will be characterized by

   A. shyness, withdrawal, and reticence
   B. negativism, aggressiveness, and uncooperativeness
   C. placidity, passivity, and psychomotor delays
   D. restlessness, irritability, and excessive activity

10. The etiology of intellectual disability which is attributed to mechanical damage to the fetus would be classified as

    A. exogenous   B. endogenous
    C. heterogenous   D. none of the above

11. The majority of children of intellectually disabled parents will have IQ's that in relation to the IQ's of their parents are

    A. somewhat lower
    B. somewhat higher
    C. lower for boys and higher for girls
    D. lower for girls and higher for boys

12. Stuttering and stammering are MOST likely to develop between the ages of _____ years.

    A. 2 and 5   B. 6 and 9
    C. 10 and 13   D. 14 and 18

13. Most cases of stuttering are PRIMARILY the result of

    A. changed handedness   B. hereditary factors
    C. physiological defects D. emotional problems

14. Anorexia is a condition which manifests itself in a loss of

    A. vision   B. appetite
    C. motor control   D. smell

15. Most differences in play activities and interests between boys and girls in the elementary school years can PROBABLY be attributed to

    A. inherent biological differences
    B. inherent emotional differences
    C. instinctual influences
    D. cultural influences

16. The rate and pattern of early motor development of children depend MAINLY upon

    A. experience   B. acculturation
    C. maturation   D. training

17. Of the following, the BEST index of the anatomical age of young children is

    A. brain weight   B. ossification
    C. basal metabolism   D. dentition

18. When children of very superior mental ability are compared in size and weight with children of the same age whose mental ability is average, the former children are found to be

    A. above average
    B. average
    C. below average
    D. either above or below average, depending on the age level

19. The average child speaks his first word at _____ months.

    A. 6   B. 9   C. 12   D. 15

20. In Pavlov's classical study of conditioning, the unconditioned stimulus was the

    A. food
    B. bell
    C. salivation
    D. electric shock

21. Contemporary reinforcement learning theory suggests that the MOST effective learning takes place when correct responses are _____ and incorrect responses _____.

    A. rewarded; ignored
    B. rewarded; punished
    C. ignored; punished
    D. none of the above

22. According to the literature, girls tend to develop physiologically and socially about

    A. the same as boys
    B. one to two years more slowly than boys
    C. one to two years more quickly than boys
    D. none of the above

23. The mother of a newborn infant is told by her physician that she will have to have corrective surgery performed within the next 2 years. It is expected that the operation in addition to her convalescence will keep her away from her baby approximately one month. The period during which the separation would be LEAST advisable from the standpoint of the child's emotional development is between the ages of _____ months.

    A. 1 and 6
    B. 8 and 16
    C. 16 and 20
    D. 20 and 24

24. Of the following, the term to which empathy is LEAST related is

    A. sublimation
    B. identification
    C. introjection
    D. projection

KEY (CORRECT ANSWERS)

1.	C	11.	B
2.	B	12.	A
3.	B	13.	D
4.	B	14.	B
5.	B	15.	D
6.	C	16.	C
7.	A	17.	B
8.	C	18.	A
9.	D	19.	C
10.	A	20.	A

21. A
22. C
23. B
24. A

EXAMINATION SECTION
TEST 1

DIRECTIONS: Each question or incomplete statement is followed by several suggested answers or completions. Select the one that BEST answers the question or completes the statement. *PRINT THE LETTER OF THE CORRECT ANSWER IN THE SPACE AT THE RIGHT.*

1. The psychologist whose name is MOST often associated with the theory that the experience of birth has a profound influence on personality development and that an individual who has a slow, prolonged birth is likely to have a personality which fights, struggles and plunges is

    A. Horney
    B. Freud
    C. Sullivan
    D. Rank

    1.____

2. Which of the following is the MOST correct statement concerning puberty and physical maturity?

    A. Boys and girls who experience early puberty will achieve physical maturity and cease growing later than will the late maturers.
    B. Boys and girls who experience early puberty will achieve physical maturity and cease growing sooner than will the late maturers.
    C. Boys and girls who experience early puberty will achieve physical maturity and cease growing at approximately the same time as the late maturers.
    D. None of the above

    2.____

3. The MOST prominent difficulties of the middle years of childhood revolve around

    A. relations with peer groups
    B. parent-child relationships
    C. schooling and the ability to learn
    D. physical development

    3.____

4. In the normal population, the range of achievement of children of the same age in grades 5 and 6 is approximately from

    A. 1 to 2 years
    B. 2 to 4 years
    C. 3 to 5 years
    D. 5 to 8 years

    4.____

5. The MOST accurate statement concerning anxiety, of the following, is that anxiety is

    A. needed for the socialization process
    B. not needed for the socialization process
    C. less produced by "mental" punishment than by physical punishment
    D. of negligible effect in producing neurosis

    5.____

6. Of the following, the area of greatest similarity among children is in their

    A. inherited traits
    B. rates of development
    C. sequences of development
    D. patterns of growth dimensions

    6.____

7. Of the following, which is the MOST significant factor in determining the choice of friends among children between the ages of six and ten?

   A. Mutual interests
   B. Similar personality traits
   C. Conveniently close location
   D. Social and economic standing of parents

8. Lewin, in defining his structural concepts of psychology, represented them

   A. topologically
   B. metrically
   C. geometrically
   D. orthographically

9. As part of the socialization process, the phenomenon of ambivalence is at its highest intensity during the

   A. toddler years
   B. preschool years
   C. early school years
   D. intermediate school years

10. The child's need to be a "goody-goody" and his willingness to conform are MOST frequently observed during the

    A. phallic period
    B. latency period
    C. prepubertal period
    D. adolescent period

11. Joe Flirp is a great health education teacher, to a large extent, because the boys model themselves after him. The foregoing illustrates the psychological mechanism of

    A. sublimation
    B. displacement
    C. regression
    D. identification

12. "You're much too authoritarian," said the principal to the teacher. "And I won't stand for that in my school." The principal is demonstrating the psychological mechanism of

    A. sublimation
    B. conversion
    C. projection
    D. identification

13. Margaret Snorble, unhappy because of her lack of friendship, devoted all her energy to studying. She became the number one student in her grade. Margaret is demonstrating the psychological mechanism of

    A. sublimation
    B. conversion
    C. introjection
    D. fantasy

14. Ben was ill now and then. However, each time after a short rest, he quickly became well. This tendency or process is known as

    A. redintegration
    B. regression
    C. homeostasis
    D. somatistation

15. Joanie asked for apple pie and was told that there was none left. "Oh, well," said she, "give me peach pie. I like it better anyway." Joanie is demonstrating the psychological mechanism of

    A. regression
    B. displacement
    C. rationalization
    D. sublimation

16. The principal had just left after telling Miss Jones she had to improve the quality of her lesson plans. Tears came to her eyes; she stamped her foot several times, pounded on the desk and then broke into uncontrolled sobbing. Miss Jones' behavior is an example of the psychological mechanism of

    A. introjection
    B. projection
    C. sublimation
    D. regression

17. Of the following statements concerning praise and punishment, which is LEAST in accord with modern psychological principles?

    A. When a child is bad, spank him.
    B. When a child is bad, say, "If you're not good, I won't love you any more."
    C. When a child is good, give him something to show your approval.
    D. When a child is good, say, "That's O.K. Let's try to do better next time."

18. Which one of the following is NOT characteristic of the development of a group?

    A. Emergence of collective goals
    B. Solidification of individual roles within the group structure
    C. Growth of group norms for behavior
    D. Development of a group atmosphere or social climate

19. The status of an individual in a group is determined, for the MOST part, by

    A. the possession of those qualities the group deems important
    B. his socio-economic level
    C. his status in other groups of which he is a member
    D. the amount of time and energy he is willing to devote to the purposes of the group

20. In comparison with other members of a group, the leader tends to

    A. hold himself in higher esteem
    B. be less spontaneous
    C. be more desirous of being of service to others
    D. be more willing to accept a low level of performance from members of the group

21. The individual who emerges as the leader of a group is usually

    A. the person who, in the judgment of the group, can best meet the demands of the particular problem
    B. superior to the other members of the group in a wide variety of abilities
    C. chosen on the basis of personal qualities rather than ability
    D. the same person, no matter in what activities the group participates

22. The degree of cohesiveness which has been established in a group is MOST likely to be lowered by

    A. unfavorable evaluation of the group by outsiders
    B. favorable evaluation of the group by outsiders
    C. decreasing the amount of interaction in the group
    D. increasing the degree of interaction in the group

23. Research has shown that neighborhood gangs tend to be more cohesive than groups of the same age functioning as clubs in more formal youth agencies. This would suggest that

    A. the club is potentially longer-lived than the gang
    B. young people join clubs only if they are not accepted by the gang
    C. clubs will not be able to function adequately in a given neighborhood until some way is found to destroy gangs already in existence
    D. the activities of the gang meet the needs of its members better than those of the club program do

24. Studies of the cohesiveness of small groups have indicated that the more cohesive a group, the

    A. more willing will the group be to defend itself against external criticism
    B. less likely is it that the group will permit internal disagreement with its objective or goals
    C. less perceptive is the group of its own solidarity
    D. more susceptible is the group to disruption caused by loss of a leader

25. According to Sullivan, anxiety serves as a defense against the danger of

    A. conditioned fears
    B. self-discovery
    C. destructive people on the outside
    D. interpersonal destructiveness

26. The system of classifying people into those who move towards, against, and away from people was devised by

    A. Alexander   B. Fromm
    C. Fenichel   D. Horney

27. Scientific investigators generally agree that the development of human behavior begins

    A. at the time of conception
    B. during the prenatal period
    C. at birth
    D. at the time of initial social interaction

28. Of the following, the MOST frequent reason why two 11-year old boys stop "being friends" is

    A. lack of agreement concerning activities to be undertaken
    B. lack of recent contact
    C. a clash of personalities
    D. parental disapproval

29. Of the following, the MOST important determinant of leadership in pre-adolescent children is the child's

    A. self-confidence   B. sex
    C. physical attractiveness   D. socio-economic status

30. Of the following, the one MOST likely to be associated with poor emotional development in a sixth-grade girl is

    A. lack of interest in boys
    B. striving for perfection in all her school work
    C. desire to please her parents in everything she does
    D. a strong interest in arithmetic, with only passive interest in other school subjects

31. The author of FOUNDATIONS OF READING INSTRUCTION is

    A. Paul Witty
    B. Emmett A. Betts
    C. David H. Russell
    D. Helen M. Robinson

32. The Dolch 220-word basic vocabulary consists of words that

    A. are most commonly used in fifteen basic readers on first and second grade levels
    B. are most commonly used in compositions by primary-grade children
    C. must be recognized as "sight words" because they do not follow regular phonetic principles
    D. make up fifty percent of reading matter used in the elementary schools

33. The MOST rapid rate of growth among children between the ages of 2 and 8 is found at age

    A. 2   B. 4   C. 6   D. 8

34. Studies of the relationship between sex and reading disability of elementary school pupils generally reveal that among pupils with reading disabilities the number of

    A. girls exceeds the number of boys
    B. boys and girls is about equal
    C. boys is slightly greater than the number of girls
    D. boys is about 3 times the number of girls

35. Research reports agree that the reading interests of groups of children

    A. begin to be different for boys and girls during the primary grades
    B. change consistently as children grow older
    C. center on animal stories during pre-adolescent years
    D. show no difference between boys and girls until junion high school years

36. The MOST accurate statement to make regarding the cause of reading disability is that research shows that most reading difficulties are primarily due to

    A. low intelligence
    B. familial discord
    C. insufficient motivation to read
    D. a complex of interrelated factors

37. Fernald's name is associated with a teaching procedure by which a child learns words by means of a

    A. look-and-say technique
    B. visual motor approach
    C. tracing-and-writing procedure
    D. letter sound blending approach

38. A diagnostic report of a child's reading states that he has no word analysis techniques. This diagnosis is equivalent to saying that he

    A. has a poor meaningful vocabulary
    B. cannot understand what he reads
    C. cannot sound out words
    D. cannot adjust his rate

39. Where mixed dominance is identified as a possible causal factor for a child who makes many reversal errors, it would be BEST for the teacher to

    A. stress left to right direction in reading
    B. change the child's hand preference
    C. change the child's eye preference
    D. stress an oral approach in reading

40. The mother of a first-grade child is concerned about her child's reading. It appears that the child can read only the words in her primer, but cannot sound out any words not in her book. Of the following, the BEST explanation to the mother would be that

    A. it is all right because the children are not taught phonics today
    B. it is all right because the child will learn to sound words
    C. it is serious and the child will get special help soon
    D. it is all right since children are taught to read whole words first, then the sounds

41. As a means of changing the current behavior pattern of an adolescent, which of the following forces will generally prove to be MOST potent? Disapproval of the behavior pattern by

    A. the adolescent's parents
    B. his classroom teacher
    C. a group of his peers
    D. an adult he admires

42. Of the following, the characteristic that is MOST important in determining an individual's status in a group of pre-adolescent girls is her

    A. school achievement
    B. socio-economic status
    C. ability to make friends
    D. intelligence

43. If the results of studies of boys' clubs are applicable to the school situation, one may expect the greatest amount of aggressive behavior to be noted in classes where the classroom climate may be described as

    A. permissive
    B. laissez-faire
    C. democratic
    D. autocratic

44. Which of the following authors would you be LEAST likely to recommend for information about child care?

    A. Sidonie Gruenberg
    B. Jean Piaget
    C. Ernest Harms
    D. Benjamin Spock

45. Of the following, which one is NOT an authority in reading? 45.____

    A. Gates   B. Russell
    C. Harris   D. Bullis

46. Studies have shown that the ratio of reading disability among boys as compared to girls is: 46.____

    A. 4 to 1   B. 3 to 1   C. 2 to 1   D. equal

47. Which of the following terms refers to the maintenance of stability in the physiological functioning of the organism? 47.____

    A. functional autonomy   B. canalization
    C. homeostasis   D. maturation

48. A recent comprehensive survey of child-rearing patterns in America found mothers of the working class when compared in their toilet-training practices with mothers of the middle class to be 48.____

    A. more permissive   B. more indifferent
    C. more severe   D. more accepting

49. Studies of the relationship of body build and character traits have in general been found to be 49.____

    A. positively correlated
    B. negatively correlated
    C. statistically significantly correlated
    D. inconclusive

50. The theory that psychical compensation for a feeling of physical or social inferiority is responsible for the development of a psychoneurosis is attributed to 50.____

    A. Adler   B. Horney
    C. Freud   D. Sullivan

KEY (CORRECT ANSWERS)

1. D	11. D	21. A	31. B	41. C
2. B	12. C	22. C	32. D	42. C
3. C	13. A	23. D	33. A	43. D
4. D	14. C	24. A	34. D	44. B
5. A	15. C	25. B	35. B	45. D
6. C	16. D	26. D	36. D	46. B
7. C	17. B	27. B	37. C	47. C
8. A	18. B	28. B	38. C	48. C
9. B	19. A	29. A	39. A	49. D
10. B	20. A	30. B	40. D	50. A

TEST 2

DIRECTIONS: Each question or incomplete statement is followed by several suggested answers or completions. Select the one that BEST answers the question or completes the statement. *PRINT THE LETTER OF THE CORRECT ANSWER IN THE SPACE AT THE RIGHT.*

1. Of the following, the MOST important consideration in distinguishing anxiety from fear is the

    A. intensity of the emotion
    B. extent of relation to subjective as distinguished from objective conditions
    C. actuality of danger
    D. strength of the personality organization of the one who is affected

    1.___

2. Wishes of children of elementary school age deal mainly with

    A. improvement of their own inner strength, character, or intelligence
    B. improvement of their personal appearance
    C. possessions, pleasant experiences, privileges, opportunities for enjoyment
    D. exploitation of family relationships

    2.___

3. The psychological climate of the home which influences adjustment of the child is MOST closely related to the

    A. number of children in the home
    B. educational level of the parents
    C. occupational level of the father
    D. attitudes of the parents

    3.___

4. With reference to emotional stability, intellectually gifted children as a group compared to average children are

    A. generally inferior   B. the same
    C. generally superior   D. unpredictably related

    4.___

5. Piaget distinguishes between two kinds of thought, logical and autistic. It is his thesis that the child's way of thinking is

    A. basically autistic
    B. either logical or autistic
    C. basically logical
    D. situated between the logical and the autistic

    5.___

6. According to research findings, the MOST effective way to help a child deal with a specific fear, such as a fear of dogs, is to

    A. have the parents and others who are close to the child set an example of fearlessness
    B. explain matters to him in terms he can understand readily
    C. help him by degrees to come actively and directly to grips with the situation
    D. try to effect "positive reconditioning" by presenting the feared stimulus with an attractive one

    6.___

7. A fundamental principle of the psychoanalytic school which has been accepted by most schools of psychology is the

   A. development of the collective unconscious
   B. theory of the existence of a dynamic unconscious
   C. development of an oedipus complex situation
   D. relationship between early psychosexual development and later adult behavior

8. In comparing the rate of biological growth for boys and girls between the ages of 5-7 and 7-10, the latter period shows

   A. a slightly more accelerated rate than the former
   B. a slightly less accelerated rate than the former
   C. a markedly more accelerated rate than the former
   D. a rate equal to the former period

9. The concept of "stages" in describing human development is LEAST applicable to

   A. Freud's psychoanalytic theory
   B. Piaget's cognitive theory
   C. Skinner's behavior theory
   D. Erikson's personality theory

10. The principal effect of nursery school attendance is upon the child's

    A. social development
    B. intellectual development
    C. perceptual development
    D. motor development

11. Which of the following terms is MOST clearly associated with stubborn reading disability?

    A. Apraxia   B. Dysplasia   C. Dyslexia   D. Aphasia

12. The boy who is encouraged or required to be more independent at an earlier age tends to develop a(n)

    A. low threshold for frustration
    B. inability to work well with others
    C. reluctance to accept adult authority
    D. strong need to achieve

13. Pioneering studies in eliminating children's fears were conducted by Mary Cover Jones. The methods used, which are consistent with present-day learning theory, included all but ONE of the following:

    A. Direct conditioning
    B. Social imitation
    C. Feeding responses
    D. Systematic desensitization

14. In contrast to upward mobile adolescents, downward mobile adolescents are

    A. less ambivalent in self-concept
    B. less interested in job security
    C. more confident in social relationships
    D. more dependent on their parents

15. In which of the following situations would a classroom atmosphere of competitiveness be LEAST detrimental to the cultivation of interpersonal relationships? Classmates are

    A. unfamiliar with one another, but equal in abilities
    B. familiar with one another and equal in abilities
    C. unfamiliar with one another and greatly disparate in abilities
    D. familiar with one another and greatly disparate in abilities

16. On group intelligence tests, Cyril Burt found the highest correlations between

    A. identical twins reared apart
    B. siblings reared together
    C. parents and own children living together
    D. identical twins reared together

17. An adolescent boy would like to have a girlfriend. As an example of sublimation, he might

    A. proclaim himself a "woman-hater"
    B. withdraw from all interpersonal relationships
    C. convince himself that girls are really crazy about him
    D. begin to write romantic poetry

18. Jim studies all night before an examination in an attempt to learn the entire course. This is an example of

    A. distributed practice   B. massed practice
    C. practice effect   D. spread of effect

19. The best-controlled studies of the influence of genetic factors on human behavior are found in investigations of

    A. newborn babies   B. identical twins
    C. fraternal twins   D. siblings

20. Terman's follow-up studies on a group of gifted children as compared to children of average intelligence revealed them to have

    A. better adjustment as shown on personality and character tests
    B. greater physical problems
    C. lower incomes
    D. more uneven academic achievement

21. Which one of the following is the MOST important determinant of leadership among pre-adolescent boys?

    A. Intellectual ability
    B. Physical size and strength
    C. Popularity with girls
    D. Sensitivity to the needs of others

22. Billy wants to be admired, but he is too clumsy to achieve this goal through sports. Therefore, although not a bright pupil, he studies long hours and earns very high grades. This may be cited as an example of

    A. compensation
    B. projection
    C. rationalization
    D. reaction formation

23. Of the following, the MOST important factor making for the development of friendship among young children is

    A. similarity in interests
    B. similarity in social class
    C. geographic proximity
    D. friendship among parents

24. Harlow's work on mothering in monkeys suggests that the affective bond between the infant and the mother is based on

    A. feeding
    B. grooming
    C. tactile contact
    D. primitive vocalization

25. The CORRECT order of Piaget's developmental stages is

    A. concrete operations, preoperational, sensorimotor, formal operational
    B. concrete operations, sensorimotor, preoperational, formal operational
    C. sensorimotor, concrete operations, preoperational, formal operational
    D. sensorimotor, preoperational, concrete operations, formal operational

26. Piaget's process which states that children invent increasingly more and better schemata for adapting to their environment is known as

    A. assimilation
    B. equilibrium
    C. accommodation
    D. conservation

27. Which of the following is NOT considered by Erikson to be a developmental task of adolescence?

    A. Development of a sense of shared identity with another
    B. Development of sexual identity
    C. Ability to see one's life in perspective
    D. Experimentation with different roles

28. A six-year-old child who is able to solve a conservation problem would be classified under which of the following stages described by Piaget?

    A. Sensorimotor
    B. Formal operations
    C. Preoperational
    D. Concrete operations

29. During adolescence, girls *generally* surpass boys in

    A. scientific ability
    B. mathematical ability
    C. ability to perform verbal tasks
    D. gross motor skills

30. The CORRECT order of Freud's stages of psychosexual development is:

    A. Oral, latency, anal, phallic, genital
    B. Oral, anal, phallic, latency, genital
    C. Phallic, oral, anal, latency, genital
    D. Latency, oral, genital, anal, phallic

31. According to Erikson, a MAJOR developmental conflict a child faces in the elementary school age period is the conflict between

    A. initiative and guilt
    B. identity and identity diffusion
    C. industry and inferiority
    D. trust and mistrust

32. According to Piaget, in the preoperational stage children

    A. begin to classify and order activities internally
    B. begin to integrate sensory and motor activities
    C. gain the ability to think logically about a problem
    D. are unable to transcend the here and now and are dependent on immediate perception

33. A pupil is able to reason simultaneously about whole and part and is able to classify according to two or three properties. According to Piaget, the pupil is in the _____ stage.

    A. sensory-motor   B. formal operations
    C. preoperational   D. concrete operations

34. According to Kohlberg, moral development proceeds through a sequence of stages that are

    A. dependent on the individual's personality and the way in which society reacts to that personality
    B. strongly influenced by individual differences in educational experience and religious training
    C. characterized by increasing symmetry, conventionality, and objectivity
    D. universal and invariant from one culture to another

35. The technique in which a particular form or sequence of behavior is established by reinforcing successively closer approximations to that behavior is called

    A. discriminative responding
    B. shaping
    C. classical conditioning
    D. fading

36. The HIGHEST need in Maslow's hierarchy of human needs is

    A. safety   B. love
    C. self-actualization   D. integration

37. According to Piaget, a child's thinking becomes completely general and capable of dealing with the hypothetical during the _____ stage.

    A. sensorimotor B. concrete operations
    C. preoperational D. formal operations

38. MOST child development specialists believe that a child's peer groups begin to replace the family as a socializing agent

    A. after the age of 5 or 6
    B. between the age of 2 or 3
    C. near the beginning of adolescence
    D. toward the end of adolescence

39. According to Erik Erikson, a key developmental task for the early elementary school years involves

    A. establishing a personal identity
    B. building confidence, resourcefulness, and enthusiasm
    C. surviving a psychosocial moratorium
    D. handling developmental discontinuity

40. Peter maintains that "everyone else in my class thinks I'm a crook." The mechanism of adjustment Peter is probably utilizing is usually referred to as

    A. projection B. rationalization
    C. compensation D. identification

41. Of the following, the BEST means of helping a child develop tolerance for tension is to

    A. protect the child from experiencing frustration
    B. make the child face reality through frequent experience of failure
    C. make sure that the child is uniformly successful
    D. help the child achieve some success and face some failure

42. Phil always develops a headache when he is called upon to complete a difficult task. Phil's headache is a(n)

    A. hysteroid reaction B. compensatory reaction
    C. reaction formation D. paranoid reaction

43. Which of the following is characteristic of the person who overcompensates?

    A. Projection B. Repression
    C. Self-repudiation D. Rationalization

44. A child who has been rejected by his parents tries to "show off" at every opportunity. Such a child is usually

    A. unaware of the nature of his frustration
    B. not capable of reacting more effectively
    C. reacting objectively to his stress situation
    D. deliberately trying to show his parents his need for affection

45. CHILD-CENTERED GROUP GUIDANCE OF PARENTS as described by Slavson deals 45.___
with

    A. the understanding of the behavior and specific acts
    B. of children and ways of dealing with them appropriately
    C. free-associative catharsis which uncovers anxiety-inducing memories, acts and situations
    D. diminution of guilt on the part of the parents
    E. intellectually recognizing and emotionally accepting latent, covert and repressed impulses and strivings in children

46. Which of the following statements BEST expresses the central theme in Bruno Bettelheim's book, LOVE IS NOT ENOUGH? The disturbed child needs to identify with a person who 46.___

    A. accepts his feelings
    B. clearly structures his environment
    C. permits regression
    D. is maternal and "giving"

47. The leisure time activities of the typical pre-adolescent boys' group are mainly given over to 47.___

    A. a succession of activities suited to a changing number of players
    B. games governed by a highly organized series of rules
    C. aimless circulation over a relatively large area looking for something to do
    D. just "hanging around with the boys"

48. The normal age range of reading ability between the best and the poorest reader in a typical sixth grade is about 48.___

    A. 2 years   B. 3 years
    C. 5 years   D. 7 years

49. Of the following books, the one NOT written by A.T. Jersild is 49.___

    A. IN SEARCH OF SELF
    B. CHILDREN'S FEARS
    C. LOVE IS NOT ENOUGH
    D. WHEN TEACHERS FACE THEMSELVES

50. Studies in child development at Yale University were done primarily under the direction of 50.___

    A. Lawrence K. Frank   B. Samuel R. Slavson
    C. Arnold Gesell   D. Albert Deutsch

KEY (CORRECT ANSWERS)

1. B	11. C	21. B	31. C	41. D
2. C	12. D	22. A	32. A	42. A
3. D	13. D	23. C	33. B	43. C
4. C	14. D	24. C	34. B	44. A
5. D	15. B	25. D	35. B	45. A
6. C	16. D	26. B	36. C	46. A
7. B	17. D	27. C	37. D	47. A
8. B	18. B	28. D	38. D	48. D
9. C	19. B	29. C	39. A	49. C
10. A	20. A	30. B	40. A	50. C

EXAMINATION SECTION
TEST 1

DIRECTIONS: Each question or incomplete statement is followed by several suggested answers or completions. Select the one that BEST answers the question or completes the statement. *PRINT THE LETTER OF THE CORRECT ANSWER IN THE SPACE AT THE RIGHT.*

1. The peer group serves the individual in the socialization process by

    A. showing him how to relate to other groups
    B. showing him how to be mature
    C. helping him to achieve an identity for himself
    D. helping him accept the discipline of his family

2. The age at which intelligence tests yield the MOST reliable prediction of future academic performance is

    A. 2-4   B. 4-6   C. 6-8   D. 12-14

3. Many studies have explored the effects of maternal deprivation on children. The findings indicate that such deprived children are MOST likely to be

    A. independent and active
    B. inert, withdrawn, mentally retarded and physically inferior
    C. less prone to infectious diseases because there is less danger of infection from others
    D. socially responsive to other adults

4. Of the following, which is MOST characteristic of the late maturing adolescent boy?

    A. Better adjustment to his age mates
    B. Greater independence of others
    C. Better acceptance of discipline
    D. Consistently negative evaluation of himself

5. Of the following, the major cause of juvenile delinquency is

    A. parental rejection   B. poverty
    C. culture conflict   D. inferior biological structure

6. In the recent research and study concerning the learning of disadvantaged youth, the MOST important single finding has been that

    A. the pre-school is the level of education which must be expanded
    B. the mother is the key factor in the enrichment of the socially disadvantaged
    C. the model the child identifies with must be well chosen
    D. little can be done for delinquent girls after seventeen years of age

7. An author who concerns himself with the "epigenetic principle of gradual unfoldings," the principle that the successive differentiations made during a lifetime provide a person with a developmental concept of self, is

    A. Esther Lloyd-Jones   B. Erik Erikson
    C. John Dewey   D. Edmund G. Williamson

8. The belief that power and status motives are MORE significant for behavior than broadly sexual motives was advocated by

   A. Freud
   B. Adler
   C. Jung
   D. Rank

9. Of all children, what percentage is generally considered to be mentally retarded?

   A. .5   B. 3.0   C. 10.0   D. 15.0

10. Studies of social acceptance show that gifted children are

    A. less socially acceptable than the average
    B. more socially acceptable than the retarded but less socially acceptable than the average
    C. more socially acceptable than the average and far more than the retarded
    D. no more socially accepted than the average

11. Of the following, the major characteristic of autistic type schizophrenic children is

    A. psychosomatic symptoms
    B. extreme withdrawal tendencies
    C. psychopathic symptoms
    D. extreme suspiciousness of adults

12. Of the following, the protective test MOST useful in studying the body-image of crippled children is the

    A. CHILDREN'S APPERCEPTION TEST
    B. BLACKY TEST
    C. MACHOVER DRAW-A-PERSON
    D. HOUSE-TREE-PERSON

13. The MOST serious problem for the cerebral palsied which contributes to learning difficulty in school, next to speech, is

    A. defective vision
    B. left-handedness
    C. hearing
    D. hand and eye coordination

14. Of the following symptoms, which is MOST characteristic of brain damaged children?

    A. Perseveration
    B. Echolalia
    C. Hallucinations
    D. Anorexia

15. Of the following, the organization that would be MOST helpful in working with a child suffering from athetosis would be the

    A. Association for the Help of Retarded Children
    B. United Cerebral Palsy Association
    C. Parents' Association for CRMD
    D. League for Epilepsy

16. The behavior patterns that develop during adolescence are

    A. genetically determined
    B. culturally determined
    C. physiologically determined
    D. found in all societies

17. According to Erikson, if a child has his needs thoroughly satisfied during his childhood, he is *most likely* to be an adolescent who is

    A. over-demanding
    B. unable to meet frustration
    C. over-achieving
    D. successful in personal-social development

18. Research evidence on girls' fears indicates that their fears during the oepidal period involve the type of anxiety known as

    A. separation
    B. fixation
    C. castration
    D. deprivation

19. In the University of Chicago study on identical twins reared apart, the GREATEST similarity found was in

    A. intelligence
    B. vocational choice
    C. personality
    D. physical appearance

20. In which of the following groups of adolescents are personal problems in adjustment MOST likely to arise?

    A. Early maturing boys and girls
    B. Late maturing boys and girls
    C. Early maturing girls and late maturing boys
    D. Late maturing girls and early maturing boys

21. The adolescent gang structure fulfills the unsatisfied needs of lower class youth through his acquisition of

    A. social skills
    B. intellectual and vocational interests
    C. athletic skills
    D. sanctions for his own aggression

22. The major limitation of the sociogram and sociometric test is that it does NOT disclose the

    A. status of the individual
    B. variety of choice
    C. organization pattern
    D. factors underlying choice

23. In establishing identity and sex role, the adolescent is MOST likely to be influenced by which of the following?

    A. Parents
    B. Siblings
    C. Peers
    D. Teachers

4 (#1)

24. Studies on the characteristics of intellectually dull adolescents indicate

   A. inferior physical development on the part of the dull as compared with normal children
   B. more frequent eye, ear and speech defects among the dull children
   C. no clear social or emotional difference between dull and normal children
   D. all of the above characteristics to be true

25. "I made the varsity basketball and football teams but the coach cut me off the track squad." This statement embodies which of the following ego-defense mechanisms?

   A. Projection   B. Sublimation
   C. Repression   D. Regression

26. Considering the various informal groups which exist in a school system, such as faculty friendship groups, student clubs, cliques, and gangs, it is noticeable that the members of each group tend to possess common information and common ideas in many respects. These group beliefs exist because

   A. of the initial self-selection of the group by its members
   B. information is filtered through group leaders
   C. members are subjected to the same range of information
   D. all of the above are true

27. Of the following, the information that a sociogram does NOT reveal is the

   A. general pattern of group organization
   B. network of group communication
   C. reasons for choices and rejections
   D. relative strength of choice status of individual members

28. The weaknesses in cross-sectional studies of adolescents lie in the fact that

   A. only those who survive through the high school are sampled
   B. only the lower levels of the socio-economic groups are sampled
   C. only some interrelationships of the aspects of growth are studied
   D. the lower levels of ability are also sampled

29. The stimulus-response theory of learning explains behavior in terms of

   A. subliminal motivational cues
   B. heredity and environment
   C. physiological processes
   D. learning by insight

30. Of the following, the major weakness of a sociometric test of social acceptability that asks only for positive choices is that it

   A. has a bad mental hygiene effect on the class
   B. crystallizes the groups' opinions of each other
   C. will give a good picture of the children in the middle range of acceptability
   D. fails to distinguish between the "overlooked" children and those who are rejected

31. In "Jonesville," middle class adolescents asked to name their best friends usually chose someone

    A. of their own social class
    B. of higher status than their own
    C. below them in social status
    D. they liked for personal reasons; their choices were distributed among all social classes

31.____

32. A common change in the personality defenses of the adolescent child is the development of

    A. greater intellectualism and isolation of affect
    B. a tendency toward avoidance and denial
    C. suspicion and withdrawal
    D. repression and literal-mindedness

32.____

33. Studies on the development of sex characteristics during pubescent growth indicate that

    A. the sequence in the development of sex characteristics is marked by great consistency
    B. the age at which specific sex characteristics appear is quite reliable
    C. the only differences in the age occurrence of specific characteristics is due to sex differences
    D. there is little range in size or variability of sex characteristics

33.____

34. Adler, Horney, and Rank are deviationists from which one of the following theories?

    A. Psychoanalytical   B. Rogerian
    C. Communications   D. Neobehavioral

34.____

35. All of the following are identified with behavioral counseling EXCEPT

    A. Williamson   B. Skinner
    C. Eysenck   D. Krumboltz

35.____

36. All of the following associations are correct EXCEPT

    A. endomorphy - softness and spherical appearance
    B. mesomorphy - hard and rectangular physique with a predominance of bone and muscle
    C. ectomorphy - a linear and fragile physique
    D. gynandromorphy - a physique that represents an exaggeration of sexual characteristics associated with the given sex

36.____

37. Psychiatrists generally agree that the three characteristics *usually* combined in a severely troubled child are

    A. laziness, hostility, withdrawal
    B. slight height, overweight, pallor
    C. lack of relatedness, a speech problem, an eating problem
    D. undernourishment, fatigue, lack of coordination

37.____

38. Directing an emotion toward a safe or acceptable object as a substitute for a dangerous or unacceptable object is a fairly good definition for which one of the following defense mechanisms?

    A. Displacement
    B. Repression
    C. Identification
    D. Rationalization

39. The "latency period" as a concept of psychoanalysis has reference to the

    A. years between early childhood and adolescence
    B. period during which successful toilet training (accommodation to time, place and manner) is normally achieved
    C. period during which the oedipal strivings reach their peak
    D. period of pubertal development

40. An unpopular girl frequently calls attention to the social deficiencies in others. Her behavior illustrates

    A. regression
    B. projection
    C. repression
    D. rationalization

41. Which one of the following was NOT supported by Kurt Lewin's research?

    A. People are more apt to change if they participate in a decision to change.
    B. It is easier to change individuals in a group situation rather than singly.
    C. Change brought about through groups was more lasting than that brought about singly.
    D. While pressures of group members upon individuals were very strong, they were not as influential as those of group leaders.

42. A six-year-old child should normally be expected to do all of the following EXCEPT

    A. play simple games
    B. put on a sweater without help
    C. draw with a crayon
    D. write in sentences

43. An educational television program developed especially for pre-school age children is

    A. Learning Your A B C's
    B. Sesame Street
    C. The Number Game
    D. The Partridge Family

44. Which of the following statements concerning masturbation in children is NOT true?

    A. Excessive masturbation can injure a child's genitals.
    B. Masturbation is practiced by most children at some point of their development.
    C. Masturbation may be a symptom of tenseness and nervousness in a child.
    D. There tends to be an increased urge to masturbate during adolescence.

45. A child's rate of physical growth is MOST rapid during the period

    A. from birth to two years
    B. from six to nine years
    C. of pre-adolescence
    D. of adolescence

46. In planning activities for a group of ten-year-old children, the children's counselor should   46.____

    A. encourage the children to participate in the planning
    B. schedule activities that are the easiest to plan
    C. realize that children at this age like to watch television
    D. insist that each child participate in each activity

47. A child of twelve would be MOST likely to find an outlet for his aggressive tendencies in   47.____

    A. watching television
    B. participating in athletics
    C. reading a history book
    D. playing checkers

48. Of the following, the statement which MOST accurately describes the physical development of boys and girls during adolescence is that   48.____

    A. girls generally mature earlier than boys
    B. boys generally mature earlier than girls
    C. boys and girls generally mature at about the same age
    D. physically active boys and girls generally mature earlier than physically inactive ones

49. The average child has not developed all the many abilities needed for beginning reading until the age of about   49.____

    A. two   B. four   C. six   D. eight

50. Which of the following situations indicates that the child is probably emotionally disturbed?   50.____

    A. A five-year-old girl suddenly starts behaving like a baby after the birth of her sister.
    B. A four-year-old boy keeps asking for his father, although he has been told repeatedly that his father has died.
    C. A ten-year-old boy has refused to play with other children since he first entered school five years ago.
    D. All of the above

KEY (CORRECT ANSWERS)

1. C	11. B	21. D	31. B	41. D
2. C	12. C	22. D	32. A	42. D
3. B	13. D	23. C	33. A	43. B
4. D	14. A	24. D	34. A	44. A
5. A	15. B	25. A	35. A	45. A
6. A	16. B	26. D	36. D	46. A
7. B	17. D	27. C	37. C	47. B
8. B	18. C	28. A	38. A	48. A
9. B	19. D	29. C	39. A	49. C
10. C	20. C	30. D	40. B	50. C

TEST 2

DIRECTIONS: Each question or incomplete statement is followed by several suggested answers or completions. Select the one that BEST answers the question or completes the statement. *PRINT THE LETTER OF THE CORRECT ANSWER IN THE SPACE AT THE RIGHT.*

1. The process by which children take to themselves the values, the thinking, and social behavior of their parents is called

    A. projection
    B. identification
    C. fixation
    D. sublimation

    1.___

2. Of the following, the characteristic that MOST clearly differentiates primary drives from secondary drives is that primary drives

    A. are related to biological needs that must be satisfied
    B. are learned early in the developmental cycle
    C. are derived from complex patterns of behavior
    D. may be observed after biological needs have been met

    2.___

3. Spitz and Goldfarb, in two different studies, have suggested that children who will have predictably lower I.Q's are those reared in

    A. institutions
    B. broken homes
    C. foster homes
    D. middle class homes

    3.___

4. One of the MOST common fears of early childhood is the fear of

    A. animals
    B. being separated from parents
    C. being rejected by peers
    D. having too much independence

    4.___

5. The average child shows the FIRST signs of laughing responses

    A. before the age of six months
    B. between the ages of six months and one year
    C. at the age of about one year
    D. at the age of about fifteen months

    5.___

6. A child is LEAST likely to choose a child of the opposite sex to play with at the age of

    A. two
    B. four
    C. seven
    D. ten

    6.___

7. When toilet training a two-year-old child, the children's counselor should

    A. scold the child when she wets her pants
    B. take the child to the bathroom only when she asks to go
    C. have the child sit on the toilet for long periods of time
    D. keep the toilet training routine free from tension

    7.___

8. The average child of three years MOST often shows his anger by

   A. breaking things
   B. crying
   C. threatening his mother
   D. sulking

9. Children at the age of two or three occasionally have temper tantrums when they do not get what they want. Of the following, the BEST method for a children's counselor to use when faced with a temper tantrum by a two-year-old child in her group is to

   A. allow the child to have what he wants
   B. try to reason with the child by explaining why he cannot have what he wants
   C. wait until the worst of the temper tantrum is over and then make a friendly gesture toward the child
   D. order the child to stop this behavior

10. All of the following are good principles to follow in administering punishment to a three-year-old child EXCEPT the

    A. punishment should be administered immediately after the incident of bad behavior
    B. child should be punished only if he understands why his behavior was bad
    C. specific punishment should be appropriate to the specific case of bad behavior
    D. punishment should be administered in an impartial manner

11. Helen, a 14-year-old girl, has two younger sisters who are more successful than she in school. Her mother complains that at home Helen constantly makes remarks intended to hurt their feelings. Helen's behavior is BEST characterized as a form of

    A. compulsion   B. sublimation
    C. rationalization   D. projection

12. Overlearning is primarily an outgrowth of

    A. removal of inhibitions   B. additional practice
    C. strong motivation   D. fear of failure

13. "The mind responds to relationships, not to fixed stimuli" is associated with the movement in psychology known as

    A. associationism   B. behaviorism
    C. Gestalt psychology   D. functionalism

14. Which one of the following is an example of "projection"?

    A. Calling other people hostile although the hostility is within oneself
    B. Playing sick in order to avoid responsibility
    C. Kicking the desk when one really wants to kick the teacher
    D. Giving other than the true reason for one's behavior

15. The basketball player who was dropped from the squad says, "Now I'll have time to study." If he really wanted to make the team, he is

    A. regressing   B. repressing
    C. projecting   D. rationalizing

16. Which one of the following reactions is generally instigated by frustration?

    A. Tolerance
    B. Aggression
    C. Identification
    D. Avoidance

17. A patient asserts, "I can't stand the agony I suffer when I go against my mother's wishes." The therapist replies, "You really like to punish that momma inside of you for your dependency, don't you?" This response can be viewed as an example of

    A. reassurance
    B. interpretation
    C. support
    D. reflection of feeling

18. A shy young first-grade boy becomes extremely attached to his teacher. He brings her presents, asks her to help him with his clothing a great deal, and wants to sit near her all the time. He is MOST likely manifesting the mental mechanism of

    A. introjection
    B. sublimation
    C. reaction-formation
    D. transference

19. When Billy was told he could not have a cookie, he lay down on the floor and pounded it with his fists. This could be an example of

    A. repression
    B. inhibition
    C. overcompensation
    D. regression

20. Habit formations in children such biting nails, picking at sores, masturbating, etc. are generally the result of

    A. poor parental supervision and training
    B. local irritations
    C. impaired general health
    D. emotional tensions

21. The attention span of a young child

    A. is not related to his mental ability
    B. can be increased if he has a high I.Q.
    C. cannot be changed before the child learns to read
    D. can be increased if the child is interested in what he is doing

22. Most young children need

    A. few media of expression
    B. to engage in independent planning
    C. many concrete experiences
    D. generalized explanations

23. The person with whom it is MOST important for a five-year-old child to have a good adjustment is

    A. father
    B. mother
    C. teacher
    D. sibling

24. At five, the normal, average child is able to play BEST

    A. alone
    B. in a large group
    C. with one other child somewhat older than himself
    D. in a small group of five or six children

25. Good education for five-year-old children stresses the importance of

   A. learning to sit still and wait for a turn
   B. opportunities to develop skill in crafts
   C. opportunities to explore and experiment
   D. learning to walk with a partner in line

26. Motor activities figure MOST importantly in a young child's intellectual enterprises because, through them, he

   A. learns how to meet new situations successfully
   B. acquires concepts of size, shape, balance, proportion
   C. learns how to live happily with other children
   D. gains confidence in himself as a person

27. Children can BEST be helped to make good choices through

   A. play with peers
   B. many experiences in making choices
   C. absorbing the teacher's sense of values
   D. imitating other children older than they

28. The timid, shy child who hesitates to join in activities and use of materials

   A. should be left alone
   B. should be praised for the work he does by himself
   C. should be drawn into the group and encouraged to participate as often as possible
   D. should have his mother come to his class to visit so that he will have a feeling of security

29. To understand the emotional life of the adolescent, it is MOST important to

   A. appraise the adolescent's emotions in the light of our own experience
   B. take into account the many forces, apparent as well as hidden, that operate in his life
   C. overlook impulsive behavior without apparent motive
   D. draw up a scholastic profile

30. The youngster who says, "I got an A in mathematics, but the teacher gave me a D in reading," is manifesting behavior which may be termed

   A. identification   B. projection
   C. regression   D. repression

31. Of the following comments which might be made by a teacher to a boy who has just misbehaved, the one likely to be MOST effective in correcting the behavior is:

   A. You are a bad boy who likes to misbehave.
   B. You are a silly boy and don't know how to behave.
   C. You are a poor, foolish boy who will get in trouble.
   D. You are a good boy but you made a mistake.

32. The personality development of young children is hampered MOST by

   A. the lack of good schools manned by adequately educated teachers
   B. dissension in the family
   C. the lack of love and affection
   D. failure in school I

33. It has been found that the gap between ability and achievement is generally SMALLEST in the

   A. gifted pupil
   B. dull pupil
   C. average pupil
   D. pupil of high socio-economic background

34. Extreme deviations in motor, adaptive, or language expression or personal-social behavior are

   A. a definite indication that a child is subnormal
   B. cause for alarm on the part of parent and teacher
   C. an indication of a temporary maladjustment
   D. reasons for seeking the advice of a specialist

35. Children's groups about the age of two typically show

   A. much cooperation
   B. sex segregation
   C. parallel activity
   D. all of these

36. Play and reading interests of boys and girls will be found to be MOST different at the age of

   A. three years
   B. six years
   C. ten years
   D. twelve years

37. As children in groups with very limited environments, such as canal-boat dwellers, "hollow-folk," etc., grow older, their I.Q. is found to

   A. increase
   B. increase greatly
   C. stay the same
   D. decrease

38. Transfer from one subject to another or to life situations will be increased if

   A. techniques and applications are emphasized
   B. the first subject is very difficult
   C. a good deal of drill is given in the first subject
   D. the situations seem quite different

39. A contemporary book by Sheldon and Eleanor Glueck reports their findings of a careful research study of juvenile delinquents. They state that

   A. most of their delinquents showed anti-social behavior beginning with their sixth year
   B. most of their delinquents did not show anti-social behavior until after their eleventh year
   C. the delinquents showed more physical defects than non-delinquents
   D. prediction tables can help to detect potential delinquents

40. Finger sucking in early childhood has long been a subject of discussion among psychiatrists. The one of the following statements which is GENERALLY accepted as true is that
    A. finger sucking denotes pending neuroses and the parents need psychiatric consultation
    B. finger sucking is a normal activity of early childhood and should not be interfered with
    C. finger sucking alters the child's facial contours and should be heavily discouraged
    D. finger sucking by a child over nine months old is due to emotional upset and needs treatment

KEY (CORRECT ANSWERS)

1. B	11. D	21. D	31. D
2. A	12. B	22. C	32. C
3. A	13. C	23. B	33. B
4. B	14. A	24. D	34. D
5. A	15. D	25. C	35. C
6. D	16. B	26. B	36. D
7. D	17. B	27. B	37. D
8. B	18. D	28. C	38. A
9. C	19. D	29. B	39. D
10. B	20. D	30. B	40. B

REPORT WRITING
EXAMINATION SECTION
TEST 1

DIRECTIONS: Each question or incomplete statement is followed by several suggested answers or completions. Select the one that BEST answers the question or completes the statement. *PRINT THE LETTER OF THE CORRECT ANSWER IN THE SPACE AT THE RIGHT.*

Questions 1-3.

DIRECTIONS: Questions 1 to 3 are based on the following example of a report. The report consists of ten numbered sentences, some of which are *not* consistent with the principles of good report writing.

(1) On the evening of February 24, Roscoe and Leroy, two members of the "Red Devils," were entering with a bottle of wine in their hands. (2) It was unusually good wine for these boys to buy. (3) I told them to give me the bottle and they refused, and added that they wouldn't let anyone "put them out." (4) I told them they were entitled to have a good time, but they could not do it the way they wanted; there were certain rules they had to observe. (5) At this point, Roscoe said he had seen me box at camp and suggested that Leroy not accept my offer. (6) Then I said firmly that the admission fee did not give them the authority to tell me what to do. (7) I also told them that, if they thought I would fight them over such a matter, they were sadly mistaken. (8) I added, however, that we could go to the gym right now and settle it another way if they wished. (9) Leroy immediately said that he was sorry, he had not understood the rules, and he did not want his quarter back. (10) On the other hand, they would not give up their bottle either, so they left the premises.

1. Only material that is relevant to the main thought of a report should be included. Which of the following sentences from the report contains material which is LEAST relevant to this report? Sentence
    "A. 2   B. 3   C. 8   D. 9

2. A good report should be arranged in logical order. Which of the following sentences from the report does NOT appear in its proper sequence in the report? Sentence
    A. 3   B. 5   C. 7   D. 9

3. Reports should include all essential information. Of the following, the MOST important fact that is *missing* from this report is:
    A. Who was involved in the incident   B. How the incident was resolved
    C. When the incident took place   D. Where the incident took place

4. The MOST serious of the following faults *commonly* found in explanatory reports is
    A. the use of slang terms   B. excessive details
    C. personal bias   D. redundancy

5. In reviewing a report he has prepared to submit to his superiors, a supervisor finds that his paragraphs are a typewritten page long and decides to make some revisions.
Of the following, the MOST important question he should ask about each paragraph is
   A. Are the words too lengthy?
   B. Is the idea under discussion too abstract?
   C. Is more than one central thought being expressed?
   D. Are the sentences too long?

6. The summary or findings of a long management report intended for the typical manager should, *generally*, appear _____ the report.
   A. at the very beginning of
   B. at the end of
   C. throughout
   D. in the middle of

7. In preparing a report that includes several tables, if not otherwise instructed, the typist should MOST properly include a list of tables
   A. in the introductory part of the report
   B. at the end of each chapter in the body of the report
   C. in the supplementary part of the report as an appendix
   D. in the supplementary part of the report as a part of the index

8. When typing a preliminary draft of a report, the one of the following which you should *generally* NOT do is to
   A. erase typing errors and deletions rather than "X"ing them out
   B. leave plenty of room at the top, bottom, and sides of each page
   C. make only the number of copies that you are asked to make
   D. type double or triple space

9. When you determine the methods of emphasis you will use in typing the titles, headings and subheadings of a report, the one of the following which it is MOST important to keep in mind is that
   A. all headings of the same rank should be typed in the same way
   B. all headings should be typed in the single style which is most pleasing to the eye
   C. headings should not take up more than one-third of the page width
   D. only one method should be used for all headings, whatever their rank

10. The one of the following ways in which inter-office memoranda *differ* from long formal reports is that they, *generally*,
    A. are written as if the reader is familiar with the vocabulary and technical background of the writer
    B. do not have a "subject line" which describes the major topic covered in the text
    C. include a listing of reference materials which support the memo writer's conclusions
    D. require that a letter of transmittal be attached

11. It is *preferable* to print information on a field report rather than write it out longhand MAINLY because
    A. printing takes less time to write than writing long hand
    B. printing is usually easier to read than longhand writing
    C. longhand writing on field reports is not acceptable in court cases
    D. printing occupies less space on a report than longhand writing

12. Of the following characteristics of a written report, the one that is MOST important is its
    A. length   B. accuracy   C. organization   D. grammar

13. A written report to your superior contains many spelling errors.
    Of the following statements relating to spelling errors, the one that is MOST NEARLY correct is that
    A. this is unimportant as long as the meaning of the report is clear
    B. readers of the report will ignore the many spelling errors
    C. readers of the report will get a poor opinion of the writer of the report
    D. spelling errors are unimportant as long as the grammar is correct

14. Written reports to your superior should have the same general arrangement and layout.
    The BEST reason for this requirement is that the
    A. report will be more accurate
    B. report will be more complete
    C. person who reads the report will know what the subject of the report is
    D. person who reads the report will know where to look for information in the report

15. The first paragraph of a report usually contains detailed information on the subject of the report.
    Of the following, the BEST reason for this requirement is to enable the
    A. reader to quickly find the subject of the report
    B. typist to immediately determine the subject of the report so that she will understand what she is typing
    C. clerk to determine to whom copies of the report will be needed
    D. typist to quickly determine how many copies of the report will be needed

16. Of the following statements concerning reports, the one which is LEAST valid is:
    A. A case report should contain factual material to support conclusions made
    B. An extremely detailed report may be of less value than a brief report giving the essential facts
    C. Highly technical language should be avoided as far as possible in preparing a report to be used at a court trial
    D. The position of the important facts in a report does not influence the emphasis placed on them by the reader

17. Suppose that you realize that you have made an error in a report that has been forwarded to another unit. You know that this error is not likely to be discovered for some time.
    Of the following, the MOST advisable course of action for you to take is to
    A. approach the supervisor of the other unit on an informal basis, and ask him to correct the error
    B. say nothing about it since most likely one error will not invalidate the entire report
    C. tell your supervisor immediately that you have made an error so that it may be corrected, if necessary
    D. wait until the error is discovered and then admit that you had made it

17.____

18. In a report, words in a sentence must be arranged properly to make sure that the intended meaning of the sentence is clear.
    The sentence below that does NOT make sense because a clause has been separated from the word on which its meaning depends is:
    A. To be a good writer, clarity is necessary.
    B. To be a good writer, you must write clearly.
    C. You must write clearly to be a good writer.
    D. Clarity is necessary to good writing.

18.____

19. The use of a graph to show statistical data in a report is *superior* to a table because it
    A. emphasizes approximations
    B. emphasizes facts and relationships more dramatically
    C. presents data more accurately
    D. is easily understood by the average reader

19.____

20. Of the following, the degree of formality required of a written report is, MOST likely to depend on the
    A. subject matter of the report
    B. frequency of its occurrence
    C. amount of time available for its preparation
    D. audience for whom the report is intended

20.____

Questions 21-25.

DIRECTIONS: Questions 21 through 25 consist of sets of four sentences lettered A, B, C, and D. For each question, choose the sentence which is grammatically and stylistically MOST appropriate for use in a formal written report.

21. A. It is recommended, therefore, that the impasse panel hearings are to be convened on September 30.
    B. It is therefore recommended that the impasse panel hearings be convened on September 30.
    C. Therefore, it is recommended to convene the impasse panel hearings on September 30.
    D. It is recommended that the impasse panel hearings therefore should be convened on September 30.

21.____

22. A. Penalties have been assessed for violating the Taylor Law by several unions.
    B. When they violated provisions of the Taylor Law, several unions were later penalized.
    C. Several unions have been penalized for violating provisions of the Taylor Law.
    D. Several unions' violating provisions of the Taylor Law resulted in them being penalized.

22.____

23. A. The number of disputes settled through mediation has increased significantly over the past two years.
    B. The number of disputes settled through mediation are increasing significantly over two-year periods.
    C. Over the past two years, through mediation, the number of disputes settled increased significantly.
    D. There is a significant increase over the past two years of the number of disputes settled through mediation.

23.____

24. A. The union members will vote to determine if the contract is to be approved.
    B. It is not yet known whether the union members will ratify the proposed contract.
    C. When the union members vote, that will determine the new contract.
    D. Whether the union members will ratify the proposed contract, it is not yet known.

24.____

25. A. The parties agreed to an increase in fringe benefits in return for greater work productivity.
    B. Greater productivity was agreed to be provided in return for increased fringe benefits.
    C. Productivity and fringe benefits are interrelated; the higher the former, the more the latter grows.
    D. The contract now provides that the amount of fringe benefits will depend upon the level of output by the workers.

25.____

KEY (CORRECT ANSWERS)

1.	A	11.	B
2.	B	12.	B
3.	D	13.	C
4.	C	14.	D
5.	C	15.	A
6.	A	16.	D
7.	A	17.	C
8.	A	18.	A
9.	A	19.	B
10.	A	20.	D

21. B
22. C
23. A
24. B
25. A

TEST 2

DIRECTIONS: Each question or incomplete statement is followed by several suggested answers or completions. Select the one that BEST answers the question or completes the statement. *PRINT THE LETTER OF THE CORRECT ANSWER IN THE SPACE AT THE RIGHT.*

Questions 1-4.

DIRECTIONS: Questions 1 through 4 are to be answered on the basis of the following report which was prepared by a supervisor for inclusion in his agency's annual report.

Line #

1   On Oct. 13, I was assigned to study the salaries paid
2   to clerical employees in various titles by the city and by
3   private industry in the area.
4   In order to get the data I needed, I called Mr. Johnson at
5   the Bureau of the Budget and the payroll officers at X Corp.-
6   a brokerage house, Y Co. –an insurance company, and Z Inc. –
7   a publishing firm. None of them was available and I had to call
8   all of them again the next day.
9   When I finally got the information I needed, I drew up a
10 chart, which is attached. Note that not all of the companies I
11 contacted employed people at all the different levels used in the
12 city service.
13 The conclusions I draw from analyzing this information is
14 as follows: The city's entry-level salary is about average for
15 the region; middle-level salaries are generally higher in the
16 city government than in private industry; but salaries at the
17 highest levels in private industry are better than city em-
18 ployees' pay.

1. Which of the following criticisms about the style in which this report is written is MOST valid?
    A. It is too informal.
    B. It is too concise.
    C. It is too choppy.
    D. The syntax is too complex.

2. Judging from the statements made in the report, the method followed by this employee in performing his research was
    A. *good*; he contacted a representative sample of businesses in the area
    B. *poor*; he should have drawn more definite conclusions
    C. *good*; he was persistent in collecting information
    D. *poor*; he did not make a thorough study

3. One sentence in this report contains a grammatical error. This sentence *begins* on line number
    A. 4   B. 7   C. 10   D. 13

4. The type of information given in this report which should be presented in footnotes or in an appendix, is the
   A. purpose of the study
   B. specifics about the businesses contacted
   C. reference to the chart
   D. conclusions drawn by the author

4._____

5. Of the following, a DISTINGUISHING characteristic of a written report intended for the head of your agency as compared to a report prepared for a lower-echilon staff member is that the report for the agency head should, *usually*, include
   A. considerably more detail, especially statistical data
   B. the essential details in an abbreviated form
   C. all available source material
   D. an annotated bibliography

5._____

6. Assume that you are asked to write a lengthy report for use by the administrator of your agency, the subject of which is "The Impact of Proposed New Data Processing Operations on Line Personnel" in your agency. You decide that the *most* appropriate type of report for you to prepare is an analytical report, including recommendations.
   The MAIN reason for your decision is that
   A. the subject of the report is extremely complex
   B. large sums of money are involved
   C. the report is being prepared for the administrator
   D. you intend to include charts and graphs

6._____

7. Assume that you are preparing a report based on a survey dealing with the attitudes of employees in Division X regarding proposed new changes in compensating employees for working overtime. Three percent of the respondents to the survey voluntarily offer an unfavorable opinion on the method of assigning overtime work, a question not specifically asked of the employees. On the basis of this information, the MOST appropriate and significant of the following comments for you to make in the report with regard to employees' attitudes on assigning overtime work is that
   A. an insignificant percentage of employees dislike the method of assigning overtime work
   B. three percent of the employees in Division X dislike the method of assigning overtime work
   C. three percent of the sample selected for the survey voiced an unfavorable opinion on the method of assigning overtime work
   D. some employees voluntarily voiced negative feelings about the method of assigning overtime work, making it impossible to determine the extent of this attitude

7._____

8. Assume that you have been asked to prepare a narrative summary of the monthly reports submitted by employees in your division.
   In preparing your summary of this month's reports, the FIRST step to take is to
   A. read through the reports, noting their general content and any unusual features
   B. decide how many typewritten pages your summary should contain
   C. make a written summary of each separate report, so that you will not have to go back to the original reports again
   D. ask each employee which points he would prefer to see emphasized in your summary

8.____

9. Assume that an administrative officer is writing a brief report to his superior outlining the advantages of matrix organization.
   Of the following, it would be INCORRECT to state that
   A. in matrix organization, a project is emphasized by designating one individual as the focal point for all matters pertaining to it
   B. utilization of manpower can be flexible in matrix organization because reservoir of specialists is maintained in the line operations
   C. the usual line-staff management is generally reversed in matrix organization
   D. in matrix organization, responsiveness to project needs is generally faster due to establishing needed communication lines and decision points

9.____

10. Written reports dealing with inspections of work and installations SHOULD be
    A. as long and detailed as practicable
    B. phrased with personal interpretations
    C. limited to the important facts of the inspection
    D. technically phrased to create an impression on superiors

10.____

11. It is important to use definite, exact words in preparing a descriptive report and to avoid, as much as possible, nouns that have vague meanings and, possibly, a different meaning for the reader than for the author.
    Which of the following sentences contains only nouns that are *definite* and *exact*?
    A. The free enterprise system should be vigorously encouraged in the United States.
    B. Arley Swopes climbed Mount Everest three times last year.
    C. Beauty is a characteristic of all the women at the party.
    D. Gil Noble asserts that he is a real democrat.

11.____

12. One way of shortening n unnecessarily long report is to reduce sentence length by eliminating the use of several words where a single one that does not alter the meaning will do.
    Which of the following sentences CANNOT be shortened without losing some of its information content?
    A. After being polished, the steel ball bearings ran at maximum speed.
    B. After the close of the war, John Taylor was made the recipient of a pension.
    C. In this day and age, you can call anyone up on the telephone.
    D. She is attractive in appearance, but she is a rather selfish person.

12.____

13. Employees are required to submit written reports of all unusual occurrences promptly.
    The BEST reason for such promptness is that the
    A. report may be too long if made at one's convenience
    C. report will tend to be more accurate as to facts
    D. employee is likely to make a better report under pressure

14. In making a report, it is poor practice to erase information on the report in order to make a change because
    A. there may be a question of what was changed and why it was changed
    B. you are likely to erase through the paper and tear the report
    C. the report will no longer look neat and presentable
    D. the duplicate copies will be smudged

15. The one of the following which BEST describes a periodic report is that it
    A. provides a record of accomplishments for a given time span and a comparison with similar time spans in the past
    B. covers the progress made in a project that has been postponed
    C. integrates, summarizes, and, perhaps, interprets published data on technical or scientific material
    D. describes a decision, advocates a policy or action, and presents facts in support of the writer's position

16. The PRIMARY purpose of including pictorial illustrations in a formal report is *usually* to
    A. amplify information which has been adequately treated verbally
    B. present details that are difficult to describe verbally
    C. provide the reader with a pleasant, momentary distraction
    D. present supplementary information incidental to the main ideas developed in the report

KEY (CORRECT ANSWERS)

1.	A	6.	A
2.	D	7.	D
3.	D	8.	A
4.	B	9.	C
5.	B	10.	C

11.	B.
12.	A.
13.	C
14.	A.
15.	A.
16	B.

EXAMINATION SECTION

TEST 1

DIRECTIONS: Each question or incomplete statement is followed by several suggested answers or completions. Select the one that BEST answers the question or completes the statement. *PRINT THE LETTER OF THE CORRECT ANSWER IN THE SPACE AT THE RIGHT.*

1. A specialist is meeting with a panel of local community leaders to determine their perceptions about the effectiveness of a recent outreach program. The leaders seem unresponsive to the specialist's questions, looking at the floor or each other without directly answering the specialist's questions.
   One strategy that might work to elicit the desired information would be to
   A. try to discern the hidden meaning of their silence
   B. adopt a mildly confrontational tone and remind them of what's at stake in the community
   C. keep asking open-ended questions and wait patiently for responses
   D. tell them to come back when they're ready to tell you their opinions

2. Each of the following statements about maintaining a community's attention is true, EXCEPT:
   A. The more challenging it is to pay attention to a message, the more likely it is that it will be attended to
   B. Listeners will be more motivated to pay attention if a speech is personally meaningful
   C. People will be more likely to attend if a speaker pauses to suggest natural transitions in a speech
   D. Listeners will attend to messages that stand out

3. Each of the following is a key strategy to integrative bargaining among community members in conflict, EXCEPT
   A. focusing on positions, rather than interests
   B. separating the people from the problem
   C. aiming for an outcome based on an objectively identified standard
   D. using active listening skills, such as rephrasing and questioning

4. Which of the following is NOT one of the major variables to take into account when considering a community needs assessment?
   A. State of program development   B. Resources available
   C. Demographics   D. Community attitudes

5. Which of the following groups would probably be formed specifically for, or be involved in, the purpose of addressing a specific unmet community need?
   A. An existing consumer group
   B. A council of community representatives
   C. A committee
   D. An existing community organization

6. If a public outreach campaign designed to mobilize a community fails, the MOST likely reason for this failure is that the campaign
   A. was not specific about what it wanted people to do
   B. was overly serious and did not appeal to people's sense of humor
   C. offered no incentive for the audience to make a change
   D. did not use language that appealed to the audience's emotions

7. Nationwide, the rate of involvement of elderly people in community-based programs demonstrates that they are
   A. under-served when compared to other age groups
   B. served at about the same rate as other age groups
   C. over-served when compared to other age groups
   D. hardly served at all

8. In projecting the likelihood of an education program's success, a domestic violence specialist identifies every single event that must occur to complete the project. The specialist then arranges these events in sequential order and allocates time requirements for each. Finally, the total time is calculated and a model showing all their events and timelines is charted.
   The specialist has used
   A. a PERT chart
   B. a simulation
   C. a Markov model
   D. the critical path method

9. When working with members of a predominantly African-American community, specialists from other cultural backgrounds should be aware that African-Americans tend to express thoughts and feelings through descriptions of
   A. physically tangible sensations
   B. problems to be analyzed
   C. corresponding analogies
   D. spiritual issues

10. Local nonprofessionals should be considered useful to a specialist who is looking to undertake a community outreach or educational initiative.
    Which of the following is LEAST likely to be a characteristic or role demonstrated by these community members?
    A. Undertaking support functions at the agency
    B. Serving as a communication channel between the agency and clients
    C. Encouraging greater agency acceptance and credibility within the community
    D. Helping the agency to accomplish meaningful change

11. In working with Native American groups or clients, it is important to recognize that the GREATEST health problem facing their communities today is
    A. domestic violence
    B. depression and suicide
    C. alcoholism
    D. tuberculosis

12. A specialist is facilitating a cooperative conflict resolution session between community members who have different opinions about what kinds of intervention services should be offered by the local adult protective services agency.
    Which of the following is NOT a guideline that should be followed in this process?
    A. Early in the negotiations, ask each party to name the issues on which they will positively not yield.
    B. Try to get the parties to view the issue from other points of view, beside the two or three conflicting ones.
    C. Have each side volunteer what it would be willing to do to resolve the conflict.
    D. At the end of the session, draw up a formal agreement with agreed-upon actions for both parties.

13. A specialist wants to evaluate the effectiveness of a local women's shelter. The shelter has suffered from lax participation, given the number of women who have been abused in the surrounding area. The specialist wants to speak with the women in the community who did not follow up on referrals to the shelter, and begins by visiting some of these women. After gaining the trust of these women, the specialist asks for the names of women they know who might be in need of help with a domestic violence situation.
    The specialist's approach in this case is _____ sampling.
    A. maximum variation   B. snowball
    C. convenience   D. typical case

14. When it comes to perceiving messages, people typically DON'T
    A. tend to simplify causal connections and sometimes even seek a single cause to explain what may be a highly complex effect
    B. tend to perceive messages independently of a categorical framework, especially if the message may be distorted by such an interpretation
    C. have a predisposition toward accepting any pattern that a speaker offers to explain seemingly unconnected facts
    D. tend to interpret things in the way they are viewed by their reference group

15. The elder members of Native American communities, regardless of kinship, are MOST commonly referred to as
    A. the ancients   B. father or mother
    C. grandfather or grandmother D. chiefs

16. Each of the following is typically an objective of community mobilization, EXCEPT:
    A. To convince existing community resources to alter their services or work together to address an unmet need
    B. To gather and distribute information to consumers and agencies about unmet needs

C. To publicize existing community resources and make them more accessible
D. To bring an unmet community need to public attention in order to achieve acceptance of and support for fulfilling the need

17. Research in community outreach shows that women often build friendships through shared positive feelings, whereas men often build friendships through
    A. metacommunication
    B. catharsis
    C. impression management
    D. shared activities

18. Typically, the FIRST step in a community-needs assessment is to
    A. identify community's strengths
    B. explore the nature of the neighborhood
    C. get to know the area and its residents
    D. talk to people in the community

19. Most public relations experts agree that _____ exposure(s) to a message is the minimum just to get the message noticed. If the aim of a public outreach campaign is action or a change in behavior, the agency budget must plan for more exposures.
    A. one
    B. two
    C. three
    D. four

20. In the program development/community liaison model of community work and public outreach, the PRIMARY constituency is considered to be
    A. community representatives and the service agency board or administrators
    B. elected officials, social agencies, and interagency organizations
    C. marginalized or oppressed population groups in a city or region
    D. residents of a neighborhood, parish or rural county

21. Social or interpersonal problems in many African-American communities have their roots in
    A. personality deficits
    B. unresolved family conflicts
    C. poor communication
    D. external stressors

22. A public outreach campaign should
    I. focus on short-term, measurable goals, rather than ultimate outcomes
    II. try to alter entrenched attitudes within a short time, with powerfully worded messages
    III. proceed in steps or phases, each of which lays out a mechanism that leads to the desired effect
    IV. ignore causes that led to a problem, and instead focus on solutions

    The CORRECT answer is:
    A. I and II
    B. II and III
    C. III only
    D. I, II, III and IV

23. Research findings indicate that in listing preferences for helping professional attributes, individuals from culturally diverse groups are MOST likely to consider _____ as more important than _____.
    A. personality similarity; either race/ethnic similarity or attitude similarity
    B. therapist experience; any kind of similarity
    C. race/ethnic similarity; attitude similarity
    D. attitude similarity; race/ethnic similarity

24. Each of the following is considered to be an objective of community organization EXCEPT
    A. effecting changes in the distribution of decision-making power
    B. helping people develop and strengthen the traits of self-direction and cooperation
    C. effecting and maintaining the balance between needs and resources in a community
    D. helping people deal with their problems by developing alternative behaviors

25. A specialist is helping the adult protective services agency to design a public outreach campaign. The topic to be addressed is complex, public understanding is low, and most professionals at the agency feel that having more complete information might change the opinions of community members. Which method of pre-campaign research is probably MOST appropriate?
    A. Deliberative polling
    B. Attitude scales
    C. Surveys or questionnaires
    D. Focus groups

KEY (CORRECT ANSWERS)

1.	C		11.	C
2.	A		12.	A
3.	A		13.	B
4.	C		14.	B
5.	C		15.	C
6.	A		16.	B
7.	A		17.	D
8.	D		18.	B
9.	C		19.	C
10.	A		20.	A

21.	D
22.	C
23.	D
24.	D
25.	A

TEST 2

DIRECTIONS: Each question or incomplete statement is followed by several suggested answers or completions. Select the one that BEST answers the question or completes the statement. *PRINT THE LETTER OF THE CORRECT ANSWER IN THE SPACE AT THE RIGHT.*

1. A specialist has been called in to resolve a dispute between two community leaders who have been arguing about the level of service needed within the community. The discussion has been going on for several hours when the specialist arrives, and both people seem to be upset.
After calming the two down and getting each of them to agree on a statement of the problem, the specialist should ask each person to
    A. summarize his or her argument in three main points
    B. explain why he or she became so upset
    C. clearly state, in objective terms, the position of the other in a form that meets with the other's approval
    D. identify the best alternative outcome, other than their presumed ideal

2. In evaluating the impact of a public outreach campaign, the _____ model can be used early in the campaign to address first impressions.
    A. exposure or advertising
    B. expert interview
    C. impact monitoring or process
    D. experimental or quasi-experimental

3. When trying to motivate an older population to take action on a community problem, it is helpful to remember that older people
    A. are more self-reliant in their decision-making than other members of the same family
    B. often need more time to decide than younger people
    C. are more likely than younger people to view community problems self-referentially
    D. tend to take a pragmatic, rather than philosophical, view of life

4. The method of group or community decision-making that is normally MOST time-consuming is
    A. majority opinion   B. consensus
    C. expert opinion   D. authority rule

5. A local adult protective services agency has identified one of the goals of its recent public outreach campaign to be the mobilization of activists.
The campaign should probably
    A. target neutral audiences
    B. home in on supporters
    C. stick to purely factual information
    D. try to persuade community fence-sitters

6. Research of Native American youths' perceptions of family concerns for their well-being has generally found that these youths
   A. have a high degree of uncertainty about their families' feelings toward them
   B. believe their families don't care about them
   C. believe that their mothers care a great deal about them, but their fathers don't
   D. believe their families care a great deal about them

6.____

7. A domestic violence specialist is developing a new outreach program for the local community. The specialist has defined the target problem, set program goals, and planned the actions that will take place as a result of the program. Most likely, the next step will be to
   A. evaluate the resources available to achieve program goals
   B. define and sequence the steps that will be taken to achieve program goals
   C. determine how the program will be evaluated
   D. decide how the program will operate

7.____

8. Elder: *I'm so glad to have someone to talk to, someone who really understands my problem.*
   Specialist: *It is nice to be able to talk to someone who will listen.*
   Elder: *That's for sure.*
   In the above exchange, what listening skill is evident in the underlined statement?
   A. Verbatim response
   B. Paraphrasing
   C. Advising
   D. Evaluation

8.____

9. Which of the following activities is involved in the specialist's task of mobilizing?
   A. Meeting individuals in the community with problems and assisting them in finding help
   B. Identifying unmet community needs
   C. Speaking out against an unjust policy or procedure
   D. Developing new services or linking presently available services to meet community needs

9.____

10. The preliminary research associated with a public outreach campaign should FIRST be aimed at determining
    A. the budget
    B. the message's ultimate audience
    C. what media to use
    D. the short-term behavioral goals of the campaign

10.____

11. A specialist in a low-income community wants to plan programs that will deal with the influence of unemployment on domestic disturbances. The specialist needs to know not only how many unemployed people are in the community now, but also how many people will be unemployed at any particular tie in the future, and how those numbers will vary given certain conditions.

11.____

Probably the BEST way to trace employment rates over time and within differing conditions is through the use of
   A. the critical path
   B. linear programming
   C. difference equations
   D. the Markov model

12. Generally, public outreach programs—whatever their stated goal—should
    I. create a sense of urgency about a problem
    II. decline to identify opponents of the issue or idea
    III. propose concrete, easily understandable solutions
    IV. urge a specific action

    The CORRECT answer is:
    A. I only   B. I, III and IV   C. II and III   D. I, II, III and IV

12.____

13. Which of the following methods of community needs assessment relies to the GREATEST degree on existing public records?
    A. Social indicators
    B. Field study
    C. Rates under treatment
    D. Key informant

13.____

14. During an interview with a Native American client, a specialist is careful to maintain close and nearly constant eye contact.
    The client is MOST likely to interpret this as a(n)
    A. show of high concern
    B. sign of disrespect
    C. uncomfortable assumption of intimacy
    D. attempt to intimidate

14.____

15. The BEST strategy for addressing an audience that is known to be captive, or even hostile, is to
    A. refer to experiences in common
    B. flatter the audience
    C. joke about things in or near the audience
    D. plead for fairness

15.____

16. Integrative conflict resolution is characterized by
    A. an overriding concern to maximize joint outcomes
    B. one side's interests opposing the other's
    C. a fixed and limited amount of resources to be divided, so that the more one group gets, the less another gets
    D. manipulation and withholding information as negotiation strategies

16.____

17. A specialist wants to learn how to interact with the members of a largely Latino community in a more culturally sensitive way.
    Which of the following is NOT a guideline for interacting with members of a Latino community?
    A. Efforts to foster independence and self-reliance may be interpreted by many Latinos as a lack of concern for others.
    B. Efforts to deal one-on-one with an adolescent client may serve to alienate the parents, especially the mother.

17.____

C. A nonverbal gesture, such as lowering the eyes, is interpreted by many Latinos as a sign of respect and deference to authority.
D. In much of Latino culture, the focus of control for problems tends to be much more external than internal.

18. Each of the following is a supporting assumption of community organization, EXCEPT:
    A. Democracy requires cooperative participation.
    B. In order for communities to change, it is necessary for each individual in the community to be willing to change.
    C. Communities often need help with organization and planning.
    D. Holistic approaches work better than fragmented or ad-hoc programs.

19. Helping professionals often have difficulty to bring community resources together to fulfill unmet community needs.
    Which of the following is NOT usually a reason for this?
    A. Some community groups resist assistance when it is offered.
    B. Few community groups make their needs known.
    C. Community resources frequently change the type of services they offer.
    D. Often, community resources prefer to work alone.

20. When dealing with groups or populations of elderly clients, specialists should be mindful that about _____ of the nation's elderly suffer from mental health problems.
    A. a tenth   B. a quarter   C. a third   D. half

21. In an African-American community, a specialist from another culture should recognize that church participation, for most African-Americans, is viewed as a
    A. method for maintaining control and communicating competency
    B. way of depersonalizing problems or troubles
    C. way to divert attention away from problems
    D. means of cathartic emotional release

22. Adult protective service programs supported by state statutes protect elderly people from abuse and neglect under the doctrine of
    A. parens patriae   B. habeas corpus
    C. in loco parentis   D. volenti non fit injuria

23. In terms of public outreach, which of the following statements about an audience is NOT generally true?
    A. The more heterogeneous the audience, the more necessary it will be to use specific examples and appeals to certain types of people.
    B. The smaller the audience, the more likely that its members will share assumptions and values.
    C. When the speaker does not know the status of an audience, it is best to assume that they are captive rather than voluntary.
    D. The larger an audience, the more formal a presentation is likely to be.

24. A specialist often spends time in the places frequented by community residents. She listens carefully to what residents seem most concerned about, and engages many in conversations, asking them how they see the problems in the community. During these conversations, she makes mental notes about whether the statements of the problems are the same things that are mentioned in their conversations. From these conversations, the worker determines what she thinks the unmet needs of the community are.
Which of the key issues in identifying unmet needs has the worker neglected to address?
    A. The different points of view regarding the issues, and whether there is any common ground
    B. Whether the stated problems and conversations with community residents reflect the same concerns
    C. How community residents define the issues
    D. What the residents talk about with one another in a community

25. Which of the following political styles should be used to promote an issue that could become controversial if it is perceived to involve major reforms?
    A. High-conflict, polarized
    B. High-conflict, consensual
    C. Moderate conflict, compromise-oriented
    D. Low-conflict, technical

KEY (CORRECT ANSWERS)

1. C
2. A
3. B
4. B
5. B

6. D
7. A
8. B
9. D
10. B

11. D
12. B
13. A
14. B
15. A

16. A
17. D
18. B
19. C
20. B

21. D
22. A
23. A
24. A
25. D

COMMUNICATION
EXAMINATION SECTION
TEST 1

DIRECTIONS: Each question or incomplete statement is followed by several suggested answers or completions. Select the one that BEST answers the question or completes the statement. *PRINT THE LETTER OF THE CORRECT ANSWER IN THE SPACE AT THE RIGHT.*

1. In some agencies the counsel to the agency head is given the right to bypass the chain of command and issue orders directly to the staff concerning matters that involve certain specific processes and practices.
   This situation MOST nearly illustrates the principle of _____ authority.
   A. the acceptance theory of
   B. multiple-linear
   C. splintered
   D. functional

   1.____

2. It is commonly understood that communication is an important part of the administrative process.
   Which of the following is NOT a valid principle of the communication process in administration?
   A. The channels of communication should be spontaneous.
   B. The lines of communication should be as direct and as short as possible.
   C. Communications should be authenticated.
   D. The persons serving in communications centers should be competent.

   2.____

3. Of the following, the one factor which is generally considered LEAST essential to successful committee operations is
   A. stating a clear definition of the authority and scope of the committee
   B. selecting the committee chairman carefully
   C. limiting the size of the committee to four persons
   D. limiting the subject matter to that which can be handled in group discussion

   3.____

4. Of the following, the failure by line managers to accept and appreciate the benefits and limitations of a new program or system VERY FREQUENTLY can be traced to the
   A. budgetary problems involved
   B. resultant need to reduce staff
   C. lack of controls it engenders
   D. failure of top management to support its implementation

   4.____

5. If a manager were thinking about using a committee of subordinates to solve an operating problem, which of the following would generally NOT be an advantage of such use of the committee approach?
   A. Improved coordination
   B. Low cost
   C. Increased motivation
   D. Integrated judgment

   5.____

6. Every supervisor has many occasions to lead a conference or participate in a conference of some sort.
   Of the following statements that pertain to conferences and conference leadership, which is generally considered to be MOST valid?
   A. Since World War II, the trend has been toward fewer shared decisions and more conferences.
   B. The most important part of a conference leader's job is to direct discussion.
   C. In providing opportunities for group interaction, management should avoid consideration of its past management philosophy.
   D. A good administrator cannot lead a good conference if he is a poor public speaker.

7. Of the following, it is usually LEAST desirable for a conference leader to
   A. call the name of a person after asking a question
   B. summarize proceedings periodically
   C. make a practice of repeating questions
   D. ask a question without indicating who is to reply

8. Assume that, in a certain organization, a situation has developed in which there is little difference in status or authority between individuals.
   Which of the following would be the MOST likely result with regard to communication in this organization?
   A. Both the accuracy and flow of communication will be improved.
   B. Both the accuracy and flow of communication will substantially decrease.
   C. Employees will seek more formal lines of communication.
   D. Neither the flow nor the accuracy of communication will be improved over the former hierarchical structure.

9. The main function of many agency administrative officers is "information management." Information that is received by an administrative officer may be classified as active or passive, depending upon whether or not it requires the recipient to take some action.
   Of the following, the item received which is clearly the MOST active information is
   A. an appointment of a new staff member
   B. a payment voucher for a new desk
   C. a press release concerning a past event
   D. the minutes of a staff meeting

10. Of the following, the one LEAST considered to be a communication barrier is
    A. group feedback   B. charged words
    C. selective perception D. symbolic meanings

11. Management studies support the hypothesis that, in spite of the tendency of employees to censor the information communicated to their supervisor, subordinates are more likely to communicate problem-oriented information UPWARD when they have a
    A. long period of service in the organization
    B. high degree of trust in the supervisor
    C. high educational level
    D. low status on the organizational ladder

    11.____

12. Electronic data processing equipment can produce more information faster than can be generated by any other means.
    In view of this, the MOST important problem faced by management at present is to
    A. keep computers fully occupied
    B. find enough computer personnel
    C. assimilate and properly evaluate the information
    D. obtain funds to establish appropriate information systems

    12.____

13. A well-designed management information system essentially provides each executive and manager the information he needs for
    A. determining computer time requirements
    B. planning and measuring results
    C. drawing a new organization chart
    D. developing a new office layout

    13.____

14. It is generally agreed that management policies should be periodically reappraised and restated in accordance with current conditions.
    Of the following, the approach which would be MOST effective in determining whether a policy should be revised is to
    A. conduct interviews with staff members at all levels in order to ascertain the relationship between the policy and actual practice
    B. make proposed revisions in the policy and apply it to current problems
    C. make up hypothetical situations using both the old policy and a revised version in order to make comparisons
    D. call a meeting of top level staff in order to discuss ways of revising the policy

    14.____

15. Your superior has asked you to notify division employees of an important change in one of the operating procedures described in the division manual. Every employee presently has a copy of this manual.
    Which of the following is normally the MOST practical way to get the employees to understand such a change?
    A. Notify each employee individually of the change and answer any questions he might have
    B. Send a written notice to key personnel, directing them to inform the people under them

    15.____

C. Call a general meeting, distribute a corrected page for the manual, and discuss the change
D. Send a memo to employees describing the change in general terms and asking them to make the necessary corrections in their copies of the manual

16. Assume that the work in your department involves the use of any technical terms.
In such a situation, when you are answering inquiries from the general public, it would usually be BEST to
    A. use simple language and avoid the technical terms
    B. employ the technical terms whenever possible
    C. bandy technical terms freely, but explain each term in parentheses
    D. apologize if you are forced to use a technical term

17. Suppose that you receive a telephone call from someone identifying himself as an employee in another city department who asks to be given information which your own department regards as confidential.
Which of the following is the BEST way of handling such a request?
    A. Give the information requested, since your caller as official standing
    B. Grant the request, provided the caller gives you a signed receipt
    C. Refuse the request, because you have no way of knowing whether the caller is really who he claims to be
    D. Explain that the information is confidential and inform the caller of the channels he must go through to have the information released to him

18. Studies show that office employees place high importance on the social and human aspects of the organization. What office employees like best about their jobs is the kind of people with whom they work. So strive hard to group people who are most likely to get along well together.
Based on this information, it is MOST reasonable to assume that office workers are most pleased to work in a group which
    A. is congenial   B. has high productivity
    C. allows individual creativity D. is unlike other groups

19. A certain supervisor does not compliment members of his staff when they come up with good ideas. He feels that coming up with good ideas is part of the job and does not merit special attention.
This supervisor's practice is
    A. *poor*, because recognition for good ideas is a good motivator
    B. *poor*, because the staff will suspect that the supervisor has no good ideas of his own
    C. *good*, because it is reasonable to assume that employees will tell their supervisor of ways to improve office practice
    D. *good*, because the other members of the staff are not made to seem inferior by comparison

20. Some employees of a department have sent an anonymous letter containing many complaints to the department head.
Of the following, what is this MOST likely to show about the department?
    A. It is probably a good place to work.
    B. Communications are probably poor.
    C. The complaints are probably unjustified.
    D. These employees are probably untrustworthy.

    20.____

21. Which of the following actions would usually be MOST appropriate for a supervisor to take after receiving an instruction sheet from his superior explaining a new procedure which is to be followed?
    A. Put the instruction sheet aside temporarily until he determines what is wrong with the old procedure.
    B. Call his superior and ask whether the procedure is one he must implement immediately.
    C. Write a memorandum to the superior asking for more details.
    D. Try the new procedure and advise the superior of any problems or possible improvements.

    21.____

22. Of the following, which one is considered the PRIMARY advantage of using a committee to resolved a problem in an organization?
    A. No one person will be held accountable for the decision since a group of people was involved.
    B. People with different backgrounds give attention to the problem.
    C. The decision will take considerable time so there is unlikely to be a decision that will later be regretted.
    D. One person cannot dominate the decision-making process.

    22.____

23. Employees in a certain office come to their supervisor with all their complaints about the office and the work. Almost every employee has had at least one minor complaint at some time.
The situation with respect to complaints in this office may BEST be described as probably
    A. *good*; employees who complain care about their jobs and work hard
    B. *good*; grievances brought out into the open can be corrected
    C. *bad*; only serious complaints should be discussed
    D. *bad*; it indicates the staff does not have confidence in the administration

    23.____

24. The administrator who allows his staff to suggest ways to do their work will usually find that
    A. this practice contributes to high productivity
    B. the administrator's ideas produce greater output
    C. clerical employees suggest inefficient work methods
    D. subordinate employees resent performing a management function

    24.____

25. The MAIN purpose for a supervisor's questioning the employees at a conference he is holding is to
 A. stress those areas of information covered but not understood by the participants
 B. encourage participants to think through the problem under discussion
 C. catch those subordinates who are not paying attention
 D. permit the more knowledgeable participants to display their grasp of the problems being discussed

KEY (CORRECT ANSWERS)

1.	D		11.	B
2.	A		12.	C
3.	C		13.	B
4.	D		14.	A
5.	B		15.	C
6.	B		16.	A
7.	C		17.	D
8.	D		18.	A
9.	A		19.	A
10.	A		20.	B

21. D
22. B
23. B
24. A
25. B

TEST 2

DIRECTIONS: Each question or incomplete statement is followed by several suggested answers or completions. Select the one that BEST answers the question or completes the statement. *PRINT THE LETTER OF THE CORRECT ANSWER IN THE SPACE AT THE RIGHT.*

1. For a superior to use *consultative supervision* with his subordinates effectively, it is ESSENTIAL that he
   A. accept the fact that his formal authority will be weakened by the procedure
   B. admit that he does not know more than all his men together and that his ideas are not always best
   C. utilize a committee system so that the procedure is orderly
   D. make sure that all subordinates are consulted so that no one feels left out

   1.____

2. The *grapevine* is an informal means of communication in an organization. The attitude of a supervisor with respect to the grapevine should be to
   A. ignore it since it deals mainly with rumors and sensational information
   B. regard it as a serious danger which should be eliminated
   C. accept it as a real line of communication which should be listened to
   D. utilize it for most purposes instead of the official line of communication

   2.____

3. The supervisor of an office that must deal with the public should realize that planning in this type of work situation
   A. is useless because he does not know how many people will request service or what service they will request
   B. must be done at a higher level but that he should be ready to implement the results of such planning
   C. is useful primarily for those activities that are not concerned with public contact
   D. is useful for all the activities of the office, including those that relate to public contact

   3.____

4. Assume that it is your job to receive incoming telephone calls. Those calls which you cannot handle yourself have to be transferred to the appropriate office.
   If you receive an outside call for an extension line which is busy, the one of the following which you should do FIRST is to
   A. interrupt the person speaking on the extension and tell him a call is waiting
   B. tell the caller the line is busy and let him know every thirty seconds whether or not it is free
   C. leave the caller on "hold" until the extension is free
   D. tell the caller the line is busy and ask him if he wishes to wait

   4.____

5. Your superior has subscribed to several publications directly related to your division's work, and he has asked you to see to it that the publications are circulated among the supervisory personnel in the division. There are eight supervisors involved.
The BEST method of insuring that all eight see these publications is to
   A. place the publication in the division's general reference library as soon as it arrives
   B. inform each supervisor whenever a publication arrives and remind all of them that they are responsible for reading it
   C. prepare a standard slip that can be stapled to each publication, listing the eight supervisors and saying, "Please read, initial your name, and pass along"
   D. send a memo to the eight supervisors saying that they may wish to purchase individual subscriptions in their own names if they are interested in seeing each issue

6. Your superior has telephoned a number of key officials in your agency to ask whether they can meet at a certain time next month. He has found that they can all make it, and he has asked you to confirm the meeting.
Which of the following is the BEST way to confirm such a meeting?
   A. Note the meeting on your superior's calendar.
   B. Post a notice of the meeting on the agency bulletin board.
   C. Call the officials on the day of the meeting to remind them of the meeting.
   D. Write a memo to each official involved, repeating the time and place of the meeting.

7. Assume that a new city regulation requires that certain kinds of private organizations file information forms with your department. You have been asked to write the short explanatory message that will be printed on the front cover of the pamphlet containing the forms and instructions.
Which of the following would be the MOST appropriate way of beginning this message?
   A. Get the readers' attention by emphasizing immediately that there are legal penalties for organizations that fail to file before a certain date.
   B. Briefly state the nature of the enclosed forms and the types of organizations that must file.
   C. Say that your department is very sorry to have to put organizations to such an inconvenience.
   D. Quote the entire regulation adopted by the city, even if it is quite long and is expressed din complicated legal language.

8. Suppose that you have been told to make up the vacation schedule for the 18 employees in a particular unit. In order for the unit to operate effectively, only a few employees can be on vacation at the same time.
Which of the following is the MOST advisable approach in making up the schedule?
   A. Draw up a schedule assigning vacations in alphabetical order
   B. Find out when the supervisors want to take their vacations, and randomly assign whatever periods are left to the non-supervisory personnel

C. Assign the most desirable times to employees of longest standing and the least desirable times to the newest employees
D. Have all employees state their own preference, and then work out any conflicts in consultation with the people involved

9. Assume that you have been asked to prepare job descriptions for various positions in your department.
Which of the following are the basic points that should be covered in a *job description*?
    A. General duties and responsibilities of the position, with examples of day-to-day tasks
    B. Comments on the performances of present employees
    C. Estimates of the number of openings that may be available in each category during the coming year
    D. Instructions for carrying out the specific tasks assigned to your department

9.____

10. Of the following, the biggest DISADVANTAGE in allowing a free flow of communications in an agency is that such a free flow
    A. decreases creativity
    B. increases the use of the *grapevine*
    C. lengthens the chain of command
    D. reduces the executive's power to direct the flow of information

10.____

11. A downward flow of authority in an organization is one example of _____ communication.
    A. horizontal   B. informal   C. circular   D. vertical

11.____

12. Of the following, the one that would MOST likely block effective communication is
    A. concentration only on the issues at hand
    B. lack of interest or commitment
    C. use of written reports
    D. use of charts and graphs

12.____

13. An ADVANTAGE of the *lecture* as a teaching tool is that it
    A. enables a person to present his ideas to a large number of people
    B. allows the audience to retain a maximum of the information given
    C. holds the attention of the audience for the longest time
    D. enables the audience member to easily recall the main points

13.____

14. An ADVANTAGE of the *small-group* discussion as a teaching tool is that
    A. it always focuses attention on one person as the leader
    B. it places collective responsibility on the group as a whole
    C. its members gain experience by summarizing the ideas of others
    D. each member of the group acts as a member of a team

14.____

15. The one of the following that is an ADVANTAGE of a *large-group* discussion, when compared to a small-group discussion, is that the large-group discussion
    A. moves along more quickly than a small-group discussion
    B. allows its participants to feel more at ease, and speak out more freely
    C. gives the whole group a chance to exchange ideas on a certain subject at the same occasion
    D. allows its members to feel a greater sense of personal responsibility

15.____

KEY (CORRECT ANSWERS)

1.	D	6.	D	11.	D
2.	C	7.	B	12.	B
3.	D	8.	D	13.	A
4.	D	9.	A	14.	D
5.	C	10.	D	15.	C

PREPARING WRITTEN MATERIAL

PARAGRAPH REARRANGEMENT
COMMENTARY

The sentences that follow are in scrambled order. You are to rearrange them in proper order and indicate the letter choice containing the correct answer at the space at the right.

Each group of sentences in this section is actually a paragraph presented in scrambled order. Each sentence in the group has a place in that paragraph; no sentence is to be left out. You are to read each group of sentences and decide upon the best order in which to put the sentences so as to form a well-organized paragraph.

The questions in this section measure the ability to solve a problem when all the facts relevant to its solution are not given.

More specifically, certain positions of responsibility and authority require the employee to discover connection between events sometimes, apparently, unrelated. In order to do this, the employee will find it necessary to correctly infer that unspecified events have probably occurred or are likely to occur. This ability becomes especially important when action must be taken on incomplete information.

Accordingly, these questions require competitors to choose among several suggested alternatives, each of which presents a different sequential arrangement of the events. Competitors must choose the MOST logical of the suggested sequences.

In order to do so, they may be required to draw on general knowledge to infer missing concepts or events that are essential to sequencing the given events. Competitors should be careful to infer only what is essential to the sequence. The plausibility of the wrong alternatives will always require the inclusion of unlikely events or of additional chains of events which are NOT essential to sequencing the given events.

It's very important to remember that you are looking for the best of the four possible choices, and that the best choice of all may not even be one of the answers you're given to choose from.

There is no one right way to solve these problems. Many people have found it helpful to first write out the order of the sentences, as they would have arranged them, on their scrap paper before looking at the possible answers. If their optimum answer is there, this can save them some time. If it isn't, this method can still give insight into solving the problem. Others find it most helpful to just go through each of the possible choices, contrasting each as they go along. You should use whatever method feels comfortable and works for you.

While most of these types of questions are not that difficult, we've added a higher percentage of the difficult type, just to give you more practice. Usually there are only one or two questions on this section that contain such subtle distinctions that you're unable to answer confidently. And you then may find yourself stuck deciding between two possible choices, neither of which you're sure about.

EXAMINATION SECTION
TEST 1

DIRECTIONS: The sentences that follow are in scrambled order. You are to rearrange them in proper order and indicate the letter choice containing the correct answer. *PRINT THE LETTER OF THE CORRECT ANSWER IN THE SPACE AT THE RIGHT.*

1. Below are four statements labeled W, X, Y and Z.
   W. He was a strict and fanatic drillmaster.
   X. The word is always used in a derogatory sense and generally shows resentment and anger on the part of the user.
   Y. It is from the name of this Frenchman that we derive our English word, martinet.
   Z. Jean Martinet was the Inspector-General of Infantry during the reign of King Louis XIV.
   The PROPER order in which these sentences should be placed in a paragraph is:
   A. X, Z, W, Y   B. X, Z, Y, W   C. Z, W, Y, X   D. Z, Y, W, X

1.____

2. In the following paragraph, the sentences, which are numbered, have been jumbled.
   I. Since then it has undergone changes.
   II. It was incorporated in 1955 under the laws of the State of New York.
   III. Its primary purposes, a cleaner city, has, however, remained the same.
   IV. The Citizens Committee works in cooperation with the Mayor's Inter-departmental Committee for a Clean City.
   The order in which these sentences should be arranged to form a well-organized paragraph is:
   A. II, IV, I, III   B. III, IV, I, II   C. IV, II, I, III   D. IV, III, II, I

2.____

3.____

Questions 3-5.

DIRECTIONS: The sentences listed below are part of a meaningful paragraph but they are not given in their proper order. You are to decide what would be the BEST order in which to put the sentences so as to form a well-organized paragraph. Each sentence has a place in the paragraph; there are no extra sentences. You are then to answer Questions 3 through 5 inclusive on the basis of your rearrangements of these scrambled sentences into a properly organized paragraph.

In 1887 some insurance companies organized an Inspection Department to advise their clients on all phases of fire prevention and protection. Probably this has been due to the smaller annual fire losses in Great Britain than in the United States. It tests various fire prevention devices and appliances and determines manufacturing hazards and their safeguards. Fire research began earlier in the United States and is more advanced than in Great Britain. Later they established a laboratory specializing in electrical, mechanical, hydraulic, and chemical fields.

155

2 (#1)

3. When the five sentences are arranged in proper order, the paragraph starts with the sentence which begins
    A. "In 1887..."   B. "Probably this..."   C. "It tests..."
    D. "Fire research..."   E. "Later they..."

3.____

4. In the last sentence listed above, "they" refers to
    A. the insurance companies   B. the United States and Great Britain
    C. the Inspection Department   D. clients
    E. technicians

4.____

5. When the above paragraph is properly arranged, it ends with the words
    A. "...and protection."   B. "...the United States."
    C. "...their safeguards."   D. "...in Great Britain."
    E. "...chemical fields."

5.____

KEY (CORRECT ANSWERS)

1. C
2. C
3. D
4. A
5. C

TEST 2

DIRECTIONS: In each of the questions numbered I through V, several sentences are given. For each question, choose as your answer the group of number that represents the MOST logical order of these sentences if they were arranged in paragraph form. *PRINT THE LETTER OF THE CORRECT ANSWER IN THE SPACE AT THE RIGHT.*

1. I. It is established when one shows that the landlord has prevented the tenant's enjoyment of his interest in the property leased.
    II. Constructive eviction is the result of a breach of the covenant of quiet enjoyment implied in all leases.
    III. In some parts of the United States, it is not complete until the tenant vacates within a reasonable time.
    IV. Generally, the acts must be of such serious and permanent character as to deny the tenant the enjoyment of his possessing rights.
    V. In this event, upon abandonment of the premises, the tenant's liability for that ceases.
    The CORRECT answer is:
    A. II, I, IV, III, V
    B. V, II, III, I, IV
    C. IV, III, I, II, V
    D. I, III, V, IV, II

    1.____

2. I. The powerlessness before private and public authorities that is the typical experience of the slum tenant is reminiscent of the situation of blue-collar workers all through the nineteenth century.
    II. Similarly, in recent years, this chapter of history has been reopened by anti-poverty groups which have attempted to organize slum tenants to enable them to bargain collectively with their landlords about the conditions of their tenancies.
    III. It is familiar history that many of the worker remedied their condition by joining together and presenting their demands collectively.
    IV. Like the workers, tenants are forced by the conditions of modern life into substantial dependence on these who possess great political aid and economic power.
    V. What's more, the very fact of dependence coupled with an absence of education and self-confidence makes them hesitant and unable to stand up for what they need from those in power.
    The CORRECT answer is:
    A. V, IV, I, II, III
    B. II, III, I, V, IV
    C. III, I, V, IV, II
    D. I, IV, V, III, II

    2.____

3. I. A railroad, for example, when not acting as a common carrier may contract away responsibility for its own negligence.
    II. As to a landlord, however, no decision has been found relating to the legal effect of a clause shifting the statutory duty of repair to the tenant.
    III. The courts have not passed on the validity of clauses relieving the landlord of this duty and liability.
    IV. They have, however, upheld the validity of exculpatory clauses in other types of contracts.

    3.____

V. Housing regulations impose a duty upon the landlord to maintain leased premises in safe condition.
VI. As another example, a bailee may limit his liability except for gross negligence, willful acts, or fraud.

The CORRECT answer is:
A. II, I, VI, IV, III, V
B. I, III, IV, V, VI, II
C. III, V, I, IV, II, VI
D. V, III, IV, I, VI, II

4. I. Since there are only samples in the building, retail or consumer sales are generally eschewed by mart occupants, and in some instances, rigid controls are maintained to limit entrance to the mart only to those persons engaged in retailing.
    II. Since World War I, in many larger cities, there has developed a new type of property, called the mart building.
    III. It can, therefore, be used by wholesalers and jobbers for the display of sample merchandise.
    IV. This type of building is most frequently a multi-storied, finished interior property which is a cross between a retail arcade and a loft building.
    V. This limitation enables the mart occupants to ship the orders from another location after the retailer or dealer makes his selection from the samples.

    The CORRECT answer is:
    A. II, IV, III, I, V
    B. IV, III, V, I, II
    C. I, III, II, IV, V
    D. I, IV, II, III, V

5. I. In general, staff-line friction reduces the distinctive contribution of staff personnel.
    II. The conflicts, however, introduce an uncontrolled element into the managerial system.
    III. On the other hand, the natural resistance of the line to staff innovations probably usefully restrains over-eager efforts to apply untested procedures on a large scale.
    IV. Under such conditions, it is difficult to know when valuable ideas are being sacrificed.
    V. The relatively weak position of staff, requiring accommodation to the line, tends to restrict their ability to engage in free, experimental innovation.

    The CORRECT answer is:
    A. IV, II, III, I, V
    B. I, V, III, II, IV
    C. V, III, I, II, IV
    D. II, I, IV, V, III

KEY (CORRECT ANSWERS)

1. A
2. D
3. D
4. A
5. B

TEST 3

DIRECTIONS: Questions 1 through 4 consist of six sentences which can be arranged in a logical sequence. For each question, select the choice which places the numbered sentences in the MOST logical sequent. *PRINT THE LETTER OF THE CORRECT ANSWER IN THE SPACE AT THE RIGHT.*

1. I. The burden of proof as to each issue is determined before trial and remains upon the same party throughout the trial.
    II. The jury is at liberty to believe one witness' testimony as against a number of contradictory witnesses.
    III. In a civil case, the party bearing the burden of proof is required to prove his contention by a fair preponderance of the evidence.
    IV. However, it must be noted that a fair preponderance of evidence does not necessarily mean a greater number of witnesses.
    V. The burden of proof is the burden which rests upon one of the parties to an action to persuade the trier of the facts, generally the jury, that a proposition he asserts is true.
    VI. If the evidence is equally balanced, or if it leaves the jury in such doubt as to be unable to decide the controversy either way, judgment must be given against the party upon whom the burden of proof rests.
    The CORRECT answer is:
    A. III, II, V, IV, I, VI
    B. I, II, VI, V, III, IV
    C. III, IV, V, I, II, VI
    D. V, I, III, VI, IV, II

    1.____

2. I. If a parent is without assets and is unemployed, he cannot be convicted of the crime of non-support of a child.
    II. The term "sufficient ability" has been held to mean sufficient financial ability.
    III. It does not matter if his unemployment is by choice or unavoidable circumstances.
    IV. If he fails to take any steps at all, he may be liable to prosecution for endangering the welfare of a child.
    V. Under the penal law, a parent is responsible for the support of his minor child only if the parent is "of sufficient ability."
    VI. An indigent parent may meet his obligation by borrowing money or by seeking aid under the provisions of the Social Welfare Law.
    The CORRECT answer is:
    A. VI, I, V, III, II, IV
    B. I, III, V, II, IV, VI
    C. V, II, I, III, VI, IV
    D. I, VI, IV, V, II, III

    2.____

3. I. Consider, for example, the case of a rabble rouser who urges a group of twenty people to go out and break the windows of a nearby factory.
    II. Therefore, the law fills the indicated gap with the crime of inciting to riot.
    III. A person is considered guilty of inciting to riot when he urges ten or more persons to engage in tumultuous and violent conduct of a kind likely to create public alarm.
    IV. However, if he has not obtained the cooperation of at least four people, he cannot be charged with unlawful assembly.

    3.____

159

V. The charge of inciting to riot was added to the law to cover types of conduct which cannot be classified as either the crime of "riot" or the crime of "unlawful assembly."
VI. If he acquires the acquiescence of at least four of them, he is guilty of unlawful assembly even if the project does not materialize.

The CORRECT answer is:
- A. III, V, I, VI, IV, II
- B. V, I, IV, VI, II, III
- C. III, IV, I, V, II, VI
- D. V, I, IV, VI, III, II

4.
I. If, however, the rebuttal evidence presents an issue of credibility, it is for the jury to determine whether the presumption has, in fact, been destroyed.
II. Once sufficient evidence to the contrary is introduced, the presumption disappears from the trial.
III. The effect of a presumption is to place the burden upon the adversary to come forward with evidence to rebut the presumption.
IV. When a presumption is overcome and ceases to exist in the case, the fact or facts which gave rise to the presumption still remain.
V. Whether a presumption has been overcome is ordinarily a question for the court.
VI. Such information may furnish a basis for a logical inference.

The CORRECT answer is:
- A. IV, VI, II, V, I, III
- B. III, II, V, I, IV, VI
- C. V, III, VI, IV, II, I
- D. V, IV, I, II, VI, III

KEY (CORRECT ANSWERS)

1. D
2. C
3. A
4. B

PREPARING WRITTEN MATERIAL
EXAMINATION SECTION
TEST 1

DIRECTIONS: Each of the sentences in this test may be classified under one of the following four categories:
    A. Faulty because of incorrect grammar or word usage
    B. Faulty because of incorrect punctuation
    C. Faulty because of incorrect capitalization or incorrect spelling
    D. Correct

Examine each sentence carefully to determine under which of the above four options it is best classified. Then, in the space to the right, print the capital letter preceding the option which is the BEST of the four suggested above. (Note that each faulty sentence contains but one type of error. Consider a sentence to be correct if it contains none of the types of errors mentioned, even though there may be other correct ways of expressing the same thought.)

1. He sent the notice to the clerk who you hired yesterday.

2. It must be admitted, however that you were not informed of this change.

3. Only the employee who have served in this grade for at least two years are eligible for promotion.

4. The work was divided equally between she and Mary.

5. He thought that you were not available at that time.

6. When the messenger returns; please give him this package.

7. The new secretary prepared, typed, addressed, and delivered, the notices.

8. Walking into the room, his desk can be seen at the rear.

9. Although John has worked here longer than She, he produces a smaller amount of work.

10. She said she could of typed this report yesterday.

11. Neither one of these procedures are adequate for the efficient performance of this task.

12. The typewriter is the tool of the typist; the cash register, the tool of the cashier.

13. "The assignment must be completed as soon as possible" said the supervisor.   13.____

14. As you know, office handbooks are issued to all new Employees.   14.____

15. Writing a speech is sometimes easier than to deliver it before an audience.   15.____

16. Mr. Brown our accountant, will audit the accounts next week.   16.____

17. Give the assignment to whomever is able to do it most efficiently.   17.____

18. The supervisor expected either your or I to file these reports.   18.____

KEY (CORRECT ANSWERS)

1. A   11. A
2. B   12. C
3. D   13. B
4. A   14. C
5. D   15. A

6. B   16. B
7. B   17. A
8. A   18. A
9. C
10. A

TEST 2

DIRECTIONS: Each of the sentences in this test may be classified under one of the following four categories:
- A. Faulty because of incorrect grammar or word usage
- B. Faulty because of incorrect punctuation
- C. Faulty because of incorrect capitalization or incorrect spelling
- D. Correct

Examine each sentence carefully to determine under which of the above four options it is best classified. Then, in the space to the right, print the capital letter preceding the option which is the BEST of the four suggested above. (Note that each faulty sentence contains but one type of error. Consider a sentence to be correct if it contains none of the types of errors mentioned, even though there may be other correct ways of expressing the same thought.)

1. The fire apparently started in the storeroom, which is usually locked. 1._____
2. On approaching the victim, two bruises were noticed by this officer. 2._____
3. The officer, who was there examined the report with great care. 3._____
4. Each employee in the office had a seperate desk. 4._____
5. All employees including members of the clerical staff, were invited to the lecture. 5._____
6. The suggested Procedure is similar to the one now in use. 6._____
7. No one was more pleased with the new procedure than the chauffeur. 7._____
8. He tried to persaude her to change the procedure. 8._____
9. The total of the expenses charged to petty cash were high. 9._____
10. An understanding between him and I was finally reached. 10._____

KEY (CORRECT ANSWERS)

1. D 6. C
2. A 7. D
3. B 8. C
4. C 9. A
5. B 10. A

TEST 3

DIRECTIONS: Each of the sentences in this test may be classified under one of the following four categories:
- A. Faulty because of incorrect grammar or word usage
- B. Faulty because of incorrect punctuation
- C. Faulty because of incorrect capitalization or incorrect spelling
- D. Correct

Examine each sentence carefully to determine under which of the above four options it is best classified. Then, in the space to the right, print the capital letter preceding the option which is the BEST of the four suggested above. (Note that each faulty sentence contains but one type of error. Consider a sentence to be correct if it contains none of the types of errors mentioned, even though there may be other correct ways of expressing the same thought.)

1. They told both he and I that the prisoner had escaped.   1.____

2. Any superior officer, who, disregards the just complaint of his subordinates, is remiss in the performance of his duty.   2.____

3. Only those members of the national organization who resided in the Middle West attended the conference in Chicago.   3.____

4. We told him to give the national organization assignment to whoever was available.   4.____

5. Please do not disappoint and embarass us by not appearing in court.   5.____

6. Although the office's speech proved to be entertaining, the topic was not relevent to the main theme of the conference.   6.____

7. In February all new officers attended a training course in which they were learned in their principal duties and the fundamental operating procedure of the department.   7.____

8. I personally seen inmate Jones threaten inmates Smith and Green with bodily harm if they refused to participate in the plot.   8.____

9. To the layman, who on a chance visit to the prison observes everything functioning smoothly, the maintenance of prison discipline may seem to be a relatively easily realizable objective.   9.____

10. The prisoners in cell block fourty were forbidden to sit on the cell cots during the recreation hour.   10.____

KEY (CORRECT ANSWERS)

1. A 6. C
2. B 7. A
3. C 8. A
4. D 9. D
5. C 10. C

TEST 4

DIRECTIONS: Each of the sentences in this test may be classified under one of the following four categories:
- A. Faulty because of incorrect grammar or word usage
- B. Faulty because of incorrect punctuation
- C. Faulty because of incorrect capitalization or incorrect spelling
- D. Correct

Examine each sentence carefully to determine under which of the above four options it is best classified. Then, in the space to the right, print the capital letter preceding the option which is the BEST of the four suggested above. (Note that each faulty sentence contains but one type of error. Consider a sentence to be correct if it contains none of the types of errors mentioned, even though there may be other correct ways of expressing the same thought.)

1. I cannot encourage you any.   1.____
2. You always look well in those sort of clothes.   2.____
3. Shall we go to the park?   3.____
4. The man whome he introduced was Mr. Carey.   4.____
5. She saw the letter laying here this morning.   5.____
6. It should rain before the Afternoon is over.   6.____
7. They have already went home.   7.____
8. That Jackson will be elected is evident.   8.____
9. He does not hardly approve of us.   9.____
10. It was he, who won the prize.   10.____

KEY (CORRECT ANSWERS)

1.	A	6.	C
2.	A	7.	A
3.	D	8.	D
4.	C	9.	A
5.	A	10.	B

TEST 5

DIRECTIONS: Each of the sentences in this test may be classified under one of the following four categories:
- A. Faulty because of incorrect grammar or word usage
- B. Faulty because of incorrect punctuation
- C. Faulty because of incorrect capitalization or incorrect spelling
- D. Correct

Examine each sentence carefully to determine under which of the above four options it is best classified. Then, in the space to the right, print the capital letter preceding the option which is the BEST of the four suggested above. (Note that each faulty sentence contains but one type of error. Consider a sentence to be correct if it contains none of the types of errors mentioned, even though there may be other correct ways of expressing the same thought.)

1. Shall we go to the park. 1.____
2. They are, alike, in this particular way. 2.____
3. They gave the poor man sume food when he knocked on the door. 3.____
4. I regret the loss caused by the error. 4.____
5. The students' will have a new teacher. 5.____
6. They sweared to bring out all the facts. 6.____
7. He decided to open a branch store on 33rd street. 7.____
8. His speed is equal and more than that of a racehorse. 8.____
9. He felt very warm on that Summer day. 9.____
10. He was assisted by his friend, who lives in the next house. 10.____

KEY (CORRECT ANSWERS)

1.	B	6.	A
2.	B	7.	C
3.	C	8.	A
4.	D	9.	C
5.	B	10.	D

TEST 6

DIRECTIONS: Each of the sentences in this test may be classified under one of the following four categories:
- A. Faulty because of incorrect grammar or word usage
- B. Faulty because of incorrect punctuation
- C. Faulty because of incorrect capitalization or incorrect spelling
- D. Correct

Examine each sentence carefully to determine under which of the above four options it is best classified. Then, in the space to the right, print the capital letter preceding the option which is the BEST of the four suggested above. (Note that each faulty sentence contains but one type of error. Consider a sentence to be correct if it contains none of the types of errors mentioned, even though there may be other correct ways of expressing the same thought.)

1. The climate of New York is colder than California. 1._____
2. I shall wait for you on the corner. 2._____
3. Did we see the boy who, we think, is the leader. 3._____
4. Being a modest person, John seldom talks about his invention. 4._____
5. The gang is called the smith street bos. 5._____
6. He seen the man break into the store. 6._____
7. We expected to lay still there for quite a while. 7._____
8. He is considered to be the Leader of his organization. 8._____
9. Although I recieved an invitation, I won't go. 9._____
10. The letter must be here some place. 10._____

KEY (CORRECT ANSWERS)

1.	A	6.	A
2.	D	7.	A
3.	B	8.	C
4.	D	9.	C
5.	C	10.	A

TEST 7

DIRECTIONS: Each of the sentences in this test may be classified under one of the following four categories:
- A. Faulty because of incorrect grammar or word usage
- B. Faulty because of incorrect punctuation
- C. Faulty because of incorrect capitalization or incorrect spelling
- D. Correct

Examine each sentence carefully to determine under which of the above four options it is best classified. Then, in the space to the right, print the capital letter preceding the option which is the BEST of the four suggested above. (Note that each faulty sentence contains but one type of error. Consider a sentence to be correct if it contains none of the types of errors mentioned, even though there may be other correct ways of expressing the same thought.)

1. I though it to be he. 1.____
2. We expect to remain here for a long time. 2.____
3. The committee was agreed. 3.____
4. Two-thirds of the building are finished. 4.____
5. The water was froze. 5.____
6. Everyone of the salesmen must supply their own car. 6.____
7. Who is the author of Gone With the Wind? 7.____
8. He marched on and declaring that he would never surrender. 8.____
9. Who shall I say called? 9.____
10. Everyone has left but they. 10.____

KEY (CORRECT ANSWERS)

1.	A	6.	A
2.	D	7.	B
3.	D	8.	A
4.	A	9.	D
5.	A	10.	D

TEST 8

DIRECTIONS: Each of the sentences in this test may be classified under one of the following four categories:
   A. Faulty because of incorrect grammar or word usage
   B. Faulty because of incorrect punctuation
   C. Faulty because of incorrect capitalization or incorrect spelling
   D. Correct

Examine each sentence carefully to determine under which of the above four options it is best classified. Then, in the space to the right, print the capital letter preceding the option which is the BEST of the four suggested above. (Note that each faulty sentence contains but one type of error. Consider a sentence to be correct if it contains none of the types of errors mentioned, even though there may be other correct ways of expressing the same thought.)

1. Who did we give the order to? 1.____
2. Send your order in immediately. 2.____
3. I believe I paid the Bill. 3.____
4. I have not met but one person. 4.____
5. Why aren't Tom, and Fred, going to the dance? 5.____
6. What reason is there for him not going? 6.____
7. The seige of Malta was a tremendous event. 7.____
8. I was there yesterday I assure you 8.____
9. Your ukulele is better than mine. 9.____
10. No one was there only Mary. 10.____

KEY (CORRECT ANSWERS)

1. A 6. A
2. D 7. C
3. C 8. B
4. A 9. C
5. B 10. A

TEST 9

DIRECTIONS: In each of the following groups of sentences, one of the four sentences is faulty in grammar, punctuation, or capitalization. Select the INCORRECT sentence in each case.

1. A. If you had stood at home and done your homework, you would not have failed in arithmetic.
   B. Her affected manner annoyed every member of the audience.
   C. How will the new law affect our income taxes?
   D. The plants were not affected by the long, cold winter, but they succumbed to the drought of summer.

   1.____

2. A. He is one of the most able men who have been in the Senate.
   B. It is he who is to blame for the lamentable mistake.
   C. Haven't you a helpful suggestion to make at this time?
   D. The money was robbed from the blind man's cup.

   2.____

3. A. The amount of children in this school is steadily increasing.
   B. After taking an apple from the table, she went out to play.
   C. He borrowed a dollar from me.
   D. I had hoped my brother would arrive before me.

   3.____

4. A. Whom do you think I hear from every week?
   B. Who do you think is the right man for the job?
   C. Who do you think I found in the room?
   D. He is the man whom we considered a good candidate for the presidency.

   4.____

5. A. Quietly the puppy laid down before the fireplace.
   B. You have made your bed; now lie in it.
   C. I was badly sunburned because I had lain too long in the sun.
   D. I laid the doll on the bed and left the room.

   5.____

KEY (CORRECT ANSWERS)

1. A
2. D
3. A
4. C
5. A

PHILOSOPHY, PRINCIPLES, PRACTICES, AND TECHNICS OF SUPERVISION, ADMINISTRATION, MANAGEMENT, AND ORGANIZATION

TABLE OF CONTENTS

	Page
MEANING OF SUPERVISION	1
THE OLD AND THE NEW SUPERVISION	1
THE EIGHT (8) BASIC PRINCIPLES OF THE NEW SUPERVISION	1
I. Principle of Responsibility	1
II. Principle of Authority	2
III. Principle of Self-Growth	2
IV. Principle of Individual Worth	2
V. Principle of Creative Leadership	2
VI. Principle of Success and Failure	2
VII. Principle of Science	3
VIII. Principle of Cooperation	3
WHAT IS ADMINISTRATION?	3
I. Practices Commonly Classed as "Supervisory"	3
II. Practices Commonly Classed as "Administrative"	3
III. Practices Commonly Classed as Both "Supervisory" and "Administrative"	4
RESPONSIBILITIES OF THE SUPERVISOR	4
COMPETENCIES OF THE SUPERVISOR	4
THE PROFESSIONAL SUPERVISOR-EMPLOYEE RELATIONSHIP	4
MINI-TEXT IN SUPERVISION, ADMINISTRATION, MANAGEMENT, AND ORGANIZATION	5
I. Brief Highlights	5
A. Levels of Management	6
B. What the Supervisor Must Learn	6
C. A Definition of Supervision	6
D. Elements of the Team Concept	6
E. Principles of Organization	6
F. The Four Important Parts of Every Job	7
G. Principles of Delegation	7
H. Principles of Effective Communications	7
I. Principles of Work Improvement	7
J. Areas of Job Improvement	7
K. Seven Key Points in Making Improvements	8

	L.	Corrective Techniques for Job Improvement	8
	M.	A Planning Checklist	8
	N.	Five Characteristics of Good Directions	9
	O.	Types of Directions	9
	P.	Controls	9
	Q.	Orienting the New Employee	9
	R.	Checklist for Orienting New Employees	9
	S.	Principles of Learning	10
	T.	Causes of Poor Performance	10
	U.	Four Major Steps in On-the-Job Instructions	10
	V.	Employees Want Five Things	10
	W.	Some Don'ts in Regard to Praise	11
	X.	How to Gain Your Workers' Confidence	11
	Y.	Sources of Employee Problems	11
	Z.	The Supervisor's Key to Discipline	11
	AA.	Five Important Processes of Management	12
	BB.	When the Supervisor Fails to Plan	12
	CC.	Fourteen General Principles of Management	12
	DD.	Change	12
II.	Brief Topical Summaries		13
	A.	Who/What is the Supervisor?	13
	B.	The Sociology of Work	13
	C.	Principles and Practices of Supervision	14
	D.	Dynamic Leadership	14
	E.	Processes for Solving Problems	15
	F.	Training for Results	15
	G.	Health, Safety, and Accident Prevention	16
	H.	Equal Employment Opportunity	16
	I.	Improving Communications	16
	J.	Self-Development	17
	K.	Teaching and Training	17
		1. The Teaching Process	17
		a. Preparation	17
		b. Presentation	18
		c. Summary	18
		d. Application	18
		e. Evaluation	18
		2. Teaching Methods	18
		a. Lecture	18
		b. Discussion	18
		c. Demonstration	19
		d. Performance	19
		e. Which Method to Use	19

PHILOSOPHY, PRINCIPLES, PRACTICES, AND TECHNICS
OF
SUPERVISION, ADMINISTRATION, MANAGEMENT, AND ORGANIZATION

MEANING OF SUPERVISION

The extension of the democratic philosophy has been accompanied by an extension in the scope of supervision. Modern leaders and supervisors no longer think of supervision in the narrow sense of being confined chiefly to visiting employees, supplying materials, or rating the staff. They regard supervision as being intimately related to all the concerned agencies of society, they speak of the supervisor's function in terms of "growth," rather than the "improvement" of employees.

This modern concept of supervision may be defined as follows: Supervision is leadership and the development of leadership within groups which are cooperatively engaged in inspection, research, training, guidance, and evaluation.

THE OLD AND THE NEW SUPERVISION

TRADITIONAL
1. Inspection
2. Focused on the employee
3. Visitation
4. Random and haphazard
5. Imposed and authoritarian
6. One person usually

MODERN
1. Study and analysis
2. Focused on aims, materials, methods, supervisors, employees, environment
3. Demonstrations, intervisitation, workshops, directed reading, bulletins, etc.
4. Definitely organized and planned (scientific)
5. Cooperative and democratic
6. Many persons involved (creative)

THE EIGHT (8) BASIC PRINCIPLES OF THE NEW SUPERVISION

I. Principle of Responsibility
   Authority to act and responsibility for acting must be joined.
   A. If you give responsibility, give authority.
   B. Define employee duties clearly.
   C. Protect employees from criticism by others.
   D. Recognize the rights as well as obligations of employees.
   E. Achieve the aims of a democratic society insofar as it is possible within the area of your work.
   F. Establish a situation favorable to training and learning.
   G. Accept ultimate responsibility for everything done in your section, unit, office, division, department.
   H. Good administration and good supervision are inseparable.

II. Principle of Authority
The success of the supervisor is measured by the extent to which the power of authority is not used.
   A. Exercise simplicity and informality in supervision
   B. Use the simplest machinery of supervision
   C. If it is good for the organization as a whole, it is probably justified.
   D. Seldom be arbitrary or authoritative.
   E. Do not base your work on the power of position or of personality.
   F. Permit and encourage the free expression of opinions.

III. Principle of Self-Growth
The success of the supervisor is measured by the extent to which, and the speed with which, he is no longer needed.
   A. Base criticism on principles, not on specifics.
   B. Point out higher activities to employees.
   C. Train for self-thinking by employees to meet new situations.
   D. Stimulate initiative, self-reliance, and individual responsibility
   E. Concentrate on stimulating the growth of employees rather than on removing defects.

IV. Principle of Individual Worth
Respect for the individual is a paramount consideration in supervision.
   A. Be human and sympathetic in dealing with employees.
   B. Don't nag about things to be done.
   C. Recognize the individual differences among employees and seek opportunities to permit best expression of each personality.

V. Principle of Creative Leadership
The best supervision is that which is not apparent to the employee.
   A. Stimulate, don't drive employees to creative action.
   B. Emphasize doing good things.
   C. Encourage employees to do what they do best.
   D. Do not be too greatly concerned with details of subject or method.
   E. Do not be concerned exclusively with immediate problems and activities.
   F. Reveal higher activities and make them both desired and maximally possible.
   G. Determine procedures in the light of each situation but see that these are derived from a sound basic philosophy.
   H. Aid, inspire, and lead so as to liberate the creative spirit latent in all good employees.

VI. Principle of Success and Failure
There are no unsuccessful employees, only unsuccessful supervisors who have failed to give proper leadership.
   A. Adapt suggestions to the capacities, attitudes, and prejudices of employees.
   B. Be gradual, be progressive, be persistent.
   C. Help the employee find the general principle; have the employee apply his own problem to the general principle.
   D. Give adequate appreciation for good work and honest effort.
   E. Anticipate employee difficulties and help to prevent them.
   F. Encourage employees to do the desirable things they will do anyway.
   G. Judge your supervision by the results it secures.

VII. Principle of Science
Successful supervision is scientific, objective, and experimental. It is based on facts, not on prejudices.
   A. Be cumulative in results.
   B. Never divorce your suggestions from the goals of training.
   C. Don't be impatient of results.
   D. Keep all matters on a professional, not a personal, level.
   E. Do not be concerned exclusively with immediate problems and activities.
   F. Use objective means of determining achievement and rating where possible.

VIII. Principle of Cooperation
Supervision is a cooperative enterprise between supervisor and employee.
   A. Begin with conditions as they are.
   B. Ask opinions of all involved when formulating policies.
   C. Organization is as good as its weakest link.
   D. Let employees help to determine policies and department programs.
   E. Be approachable and accessible—physically and mentally.
   F. Develop pleasant social relationships.

WHAT IS ADMINISTRATION

Administration is concerned with providing the environment, the material facilities, and the operational procedures that will promote the maximum growth and development of supervisors and employees. (Organization is an aspect and a concomitant of administration.)

There is no sharp line of demarcation between supervision and administration; these functions are intimately interrelated and, often, overlapping. They are complementary activities.

I. Practices Commonly Classed as "Supervisory"
   A. Conducting employees' conferences
   B. Visiting sections, units, offices, divisions, departments
   C. Arranging for demonstrations
   D. Examining plans
   E. Suggesting professional reading
   F. Interpreting bulletins
   G. Recommending in-service training courses
   H. Encouraging experimentation
   I. Appraising employee morale
   J. Providing for intervisitation

II. Practices Commonly Classified as "Administrative"
   A. Management of the office
   B. Arrangement of schedules for extra duties
   C. Assignment of rooms or areas
   D. Distribution of supplies
   E. Keeping records and reports
   F. Care of audio-visual materials
   G. Keeping inventory records
   H. Checking record cards and books

I. Programming special activities
J. Checking on the attendance and punctuality of employees

III. Practices Commonly Classified as Both "Supervisory" and "Administrative"
  A. Program construction
  B. Testing or evaluating outcomes
  C. Personnel accounting
  D. Ordering instructional materials

RESPONSIBILITIES OF THE SUPERVISOR

A person employed in a supervisory capacity must constantly be able to improve his own efficiency and ability. He represent the employer to the employees and only continuous self-examination can make him a capable supervisor.

Leadership and training are the supervisor's responsibility. An efficient working unit is one in which the employees work with the supervisor. It is his job to bring out the best in his employees. He must always be relaxed, courteous, and calm in his association with his employees. Their feelings are important, and a harsh attitude does not develop the most efficient employees.

COMPETENCES OF THE SUPERVISOR

I. Complete knowledge of the duties and responsibilities of his position.
II. To be able to organize a job, plan ahead, and carry through.
III. To have self-confidence and initiative.
IV. To be able to handle the unexpected situation and make quick decisions.
V. To be able to properly train subordinates in the positions they are best suited for.
VI. To be able to keep good human relations among his subordinates.
VII. To be able to keep good human relations between his subordinates and himself and to earn their respect and trust.

THE PROFESSIONAL SUPERVISOR-EMPLOYEE RELATIONSHIP

There are two kinds of efficiency: one kind is only apparent and is produced in organizations through the exercise of mere discipline; this is but a simulation of the second, or true, efficiency which springs from spontaneous cooperation. If you are a manager, no matter how great or small your responsibility, it is your job, in the final analysis, to create and develop this involuntary cooperation among the people whom you supervise. For, no matter how powerful a combination of money, machines, and materials a company may have, this is a dead and sterile thing without a team of willing, thinking, and articulate people to guide it.

The following 21 points are presented as indicative of the exemplary basic relationship that should exist between supervisor and employee:

1. Each person wants to be liked and respected by his fellow employee and wants to be treated with consideration and respect by his superior.
2. The most competent employee will make an error. However, in a unit where good relations exist between the supervisor and his employees, tenseness and fear do not exist. Thus, errors are not hidden or covered up, and the efficiency of a unit is not impaired.

3. Subordinates resent rules, regulations, or orders that are unreasonable or unexplained.
4. Subordinates are quick to resent unfairness, harshness, injustices, and favoritism.
5. An employee will accept responsibility if he knows that he will be complimented for a job well done, and not too harshly chastised for failure; that his supervisor will check the cause of the failure, and, if it was the supervisor's fault, he will assume the blame therefore. If it was the employee's fault, his supervisor will explain the correct method or means of handling the responsibility.
6. An employee wants to receive credit for a suggestion he has made, that is used. If a suggestion cannot be used, the employee is entitled to an explanation. The supervisor should not say "no" and close the subject.
7. Fear and worry slow up a worker's ability. Poor working environment can impair his physical and mental health. A good supervisor avoids forceful methods, threats, and arguments to get a job done.
8. A forceful supervisor is able to train his employees individually and as a team, and is able to motivate them in the proper channels.
9. A mature supervisor is able to properly evaluate his subordinates and to keep them happy and satisfied.
10. A sensitive supervisor will never patronize his subordinates.
11. A worthy supervisor will respect his employees' confidences.
12. Definite and clear-cut responsibilities should be assigned to each executive.
13. Responsibility should always be coupled with corresponding authority.
14. No change should be made in the scope or responsibilities of a position without a definite understanding to that effect on the part of all persons concerned.
15. No executive or employee, occupying a single position in the organization, should be subject to definite orders from more than one source.
16. Orders should never be given to subordinates over the head of a responsible executive. Rather than do this, the officer in question should be supplanted.
17. Criticisms of subordinates should, whoever possible, be made privately, and in no case should a subordinate be criticized in the presence of executives or employees of equal or lower rank.
18. No dispute or difference between executives or employees as to authority or responsibilities should be considered too trivial for prompt and careful adjudication.
19. Promotions, wage changes, and disciplinary action should always be approved by the executive immediately superior to the one directly responsible.
20. No executive or employee should ever be required, or expected, to be at the same time an assistant to, and critic of, another.
21. Any executive whose work is subject to regular inspection should, wherever practicable, be given the assistance and facilities necessary to enable him to maintain an independent check of the quality of his work.

MINI-TEXT IN SUPERVISION, ADMINISTRATION, MANAGEMENT, AND ORGANIZATION

I. Brief Highlights

Listed concisely and sequentially are major headings and important data in the field for quick recall and review.

A. Levels of Management
Any organization of some size has several levels of management. In terms of a ladder, the levels are:

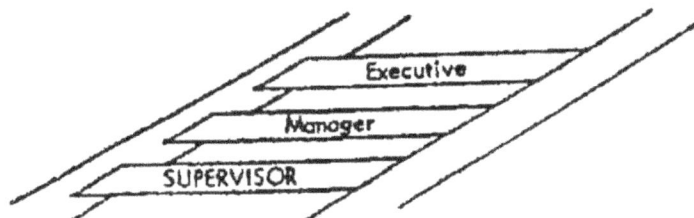

The first level is very important because it is the beginning point of management leadership.

B. What the Supervisor Must Learn
A supervisor must learn to:
1. Deal with people and their differences
2. Get the job done through people
3. Recognize the problems when they exist
4. Overcome obstacles to good performance
5. Evaluate the performance of people
6. Check his own performance in terms of accomplishment

C. A Definition of Supervisor
The term supervisor means any individual having authority, in the interests of the employer, to hire, transfer, suspend, lay-off, recall, promote, discharge, assign, reward, or discipline other employees or responsibility to direct them, or to adjust their grievances, or effectively to recommend such action, if, in connection with the foregoing, exercise of such authority is not of a merely routine or clerical nature but requires the use of independent judgment.

D. Elements of the Team Concept
What is involved in teamwork? The component parts are:
1. Members
2. A leader
3. Goals
4. Plans
5. Cooperation
6. Spirit

E. Principles of Organization
1. A team member must know what his job is.
2. Be sure that the nature and scope of a job are understood.
3. Authority and responsibility should be carefully spelled out.
4. A supervisor should be permitted to make the maximum number of decisions affecting his employees.
5. Employees should report to only one supervisor.
6. A supervisor should direct only as many employees as he can handle effectively.
7. An organization plan should be flexible.

8. Inspection and performance of work should be separate.
9. Organizational problems should receive immediate attention.
10. Assign work in line with ability and experience.

F. The Four Important Parts of Every Job
1. Inherent in every job is the *accountability* for results.
2. A second set of factors in every job is *responsibilities*.
3. Along with duties and responsibilities one must have the *authority* to act within certain limits without obtaining permission to proceed.
4. No job exists in a vacuum. The supervisor is surrounded by key *relationships*.

G. Principles of Delegation
Where work is delegated for the first time, the supervisor should think in terms of these questions:
1. Who is best qualified to do this?
2. Can an employee improve his abilities by doing this?
3. How long should an employee spend on this?
4. Are there any special problems for which he will need guidance?
5. How broad a delegation can I make?

H. Principles of Effective Communications
1. Determine the media.
2. To whom directed?
3. Identification and source authority.
4. Is communication understood?

I. Principles of Work Improvement
1. Most people usually do only the work which is assigned to them.
2. Workers are likely to fit assigned work into the time available to perform it.
3. A good workload usually stimulates output.
4. People usually do their best work when they know that results will be reviewed or inspected.
5. Employees usually feel that someone else is responsible for conditions of work, workplace layout, job methods, type of tools/equipment, and other such factors.
6. Employees are usually defensive about their job security.
7. Employees have natural resistance to change.
8. Employees can support or destroy a supervisor.
9. A supervisor usually earns the respect of his people through his personal example of diligence and efficiency.

J. Areas of Job Improvement
The areas of job improvement are quite numerous, but the most common ones which a supervisor can identify and utilize are:
1. Departmental layout
2. Flow of work
3. Workplace layout
4. Utilization of manpower
5. Work methods
6. Materials handling

7. Utilization
8. Motion economy

K. Seven Key Points in Making Improvements
1. Select the job to be improved
2. Study how it is being done now
3. Question the present method
4. Determine actions to be taken
5. Chart proposed method
6. Get approval and apply
7. Solicit worker participation

l. Corrective Techniques of Job Improvement
Specific Problems
1. Size of workload
2. Inability to meet schedules
3. Strain and fatigue
4. Improper use of men and skills
5. Waste, poor quality, unsafe conditions
6. Bottleneck conditions that hinder output
7. Poor utilization of equipment and machine
8. Efficiency and productivity of labor

General Improvement
1. Departmental layout
2. Flow of work
3. Work plan layout
4. Utilization of manpower
5. Work methods
6. Materials handling
7. Utilization of equipment
8. Motion economy

Corrective Techniques
1. Study with scale model
2. Flow chart study
3. Motion analysis
4. Comparison of units produced to standard allowance
5. Methods analysis
6. Flow chart and equipment study
7. Down time vs. running time
8. Motion analysis

M. A Planning Checklist
1. Objectives
2. Controls
3. Delegations
4. Communications
5. Resources
6. Manpower

7. Equipment
8. Supplies and materials
9. Utilization of time
10. Safety
11. Money
12. Work
13. Timing of improvements

N. Five Characteristics of Good Directions
In order to get results, directions must be:
1. Possible of accomplishment
2. Agreeable with worker interests
3. Related to mission
4. Planned and complete
5. Unmistakably clear

O. Types of Directions
1. Demands or direct orders
2. Requests
3. Suggestion or implication
4. volunteering

P. Controls
A typical listing of the overall areas in which the supervisor should establish controls might be:
1. Manpower
2. Materials
3. Quality of work
4. Quantity of work
5. Time
6. Space
7. Money
8. Methods

Q. Orienting the New Employee
1. Prepare for him
2. Welcome the new employee
3. Orientation for the job
4. Follow-up

R. Checklist for Orienting New Employees   Yes   No
1. Do you appreciate the feelings of new employees when they first report for work? ___ ___
2. Are you aware of the fact that the new employee must make a big adjustment to his job? ___ ___
3. Have you given him good reasons for liking the job and the organization? ___ ___
4. Have you prepared for his first day on the job? ___ ___
5. Did you welcome him cordially and make him feel needed? ___ ___

		Yes	No
6.	Did you establish rapport with him so that he feels free to talk and discuss matters with you?	___	___
7.	Did you explain his job to him and his relationship to you?	___	___
8.	Does he know that his work will be evaluated periodically on a basis that is fair and objective?	___	___
9.	Did you introduce him to his fellow workers in such a way that they are likely to accept him?	___	___
10.	Does he know what employee benefits he will receive?	___	___
11.	Does he understand the importance of being on the job and what to do if he must leave his duty station?	___	___
12.	Has he been impressed with the importance of accident prevention and safe practice?	___	___
13.	Does he generally know his way around the department?	___	___
14.	Is he under the guidance of a sponsor who will teach the right way of doing things?	___	___
15.	Do you plan to follow-up so that he will continue to adjust successfully to his job?	___	___

S. Principles of Learning
1. Motivation
2. Demonstration or explanation
3. Practice

T. Causes of Poor Performance
1. Improper training for job
2. Wrong tools
3. Inadequate directions
4. Lack of supervisory follow-up
5. Poor communications
6. Lack of standards of performance
7. Wrong work habits
8. Low morale
9. Other

U. Four Major Steps in On-The-Job Instruction
1. Prepare the worker
2. Present the operation
3. Tryout performance
4. Follow-up

V. Employees Want Five Things
1. Security
2. Opportunity
3. Recognition
4. Inclusion
5. Expression

W. Some Don'ts in Regard to Praise
1. Don't praise a person for something he hasn't done.
2. Don't praise a person unless you can be sincere.
3. Don't be sparing in praise just because your superior withholds it from you.
4. Don't let too much time elapse between good performance and recognition of it

X. How to Gain Your Workers' Confidence
Methods of developing confidence include such things as:
1. Knowing the interests, habits, hobbies of employees
2. Admitting your own inadequacies
3. Sharing and telling of confidence in others
4. Supporting people when they are in trouble
5. Delegating matters that can be well handled
6. Being frank and straightforward about problems and working conditions
7. Encouraging others to bring their problems to you
8. Taking action on problems which impede worker progress

Y. Sources of Employee Problems
On-the-job causes might be such things as:
1. A feeling that favoritism is exercised in assignments
2. Assignment of overtime
3. An undue amount of supervision
4. Changing methods or systems
5. Stealing of ideas or trade secrets
6. Lack of interest in job
7. Threat of reduction in force
8. Ignorance or lack of communications
9. Poor equipment
10. Lack of knowing how supervisor feels toward employee
11. Shift assignments

Off-the-job problems might have to do with:
1. Health
2. Finances
3. Housing
4. Family

Z. The Supervisor's Key to Discipline
There are several key points about discipline which the supervisor should keep in mind:
1. Job discipline is one of the disciplines of life and is directed by the supervisor.
2. It is more important to correct an employee fault than to fix blame for it.
3. Employee performance is affected by problems both on the job and off.
4. Sudden or abrupt changes in behavior can be indications of important employee problems.
5. Problems should be dealt with as soon as possible after they are identified.
6. The attitude of the supervisor may have more to do with solving problems than the techniques of problem solving.
7. Correction of employee behavior should be resorted to only after the supervisor is sure that training or counseling will not be helpful.

8. Be sure to document your disciplinary actions.
9. Make sure that you are disciplining on the basis of facts rather than personal feelings.
10. Take each disciplinary step in order, being careful not to make snap judgments, or decisions based on impatience.

AA. Five Important Processes of Management
1. Planning
2. Organizing
3. Scheduling
4. Controlling
5. Motivating

BB. When the Supervisor Fails to Plan
1. Supervisor creates impression of not knowing his job
2. May lead to excessive overtime
3. Job runs itself—supervisor lacks control
4. Deadlines and appointments missed
5. Parts of the work go undone
6. Work interrupted by emergencies
7. Sets a bad example
8. Uneven workload creates peaks and valleys
9. Too much time on minor details at expense of more important tasks

CC. Fourteen General Principles of Management
1. Division of work
2. Authority and responsibility
3. Discipline
4. Unity of command
5. Unity of direction
6. Subordination of individual interest to general interest
7. Remuneration of personnel
8. Centralization
9. Scalar chain
10. Order
11. Equity
12. Stability of tenure of personnel
13. Initiative
14. Esprit de corps

DD. Change

Bringing about change is perhaps attempted more often, and yet less well understood, than anything else the supervisor does. How do people generally react to change? (People tend to resist change that is imposed upon them by other individuals or circumstances.

Change is characteristic of every situation. It is a part of every real endeavor where the efforts of people are concerned.

1. Why do people resist change?
   People may resist change because of:
   a. Fear of the unknown
   b. Implied criticism
   c. Unpleasant experiences in the past
   d. Fear of loss of status
   e. Threat to the ego
   f. Fear of loss of economic stability

2. How can we best overcome the resistance to change?
   In initiating change, take these steps:
   a. Get ready to sell
   b. Identify sources of help
   c. Anticipate objections
   d. Sell benefits
   e. Listen in depth
   f. Follow up

II. Brief Topical Summaries

   A. Who/What is the Supervisor?
      1. The supervisor is often called the "highest level employee and the lowest level manager."
      2. A supervisor is a member of both management and the work group. He acts as a bridge between the two.
      3. Most problems in supervision are in the area of human relations, or people problems.
      4. Employees expect: Respect, opportunity to learn and to advance, and a sense of belonging, and so forth.
      5. Supervisors are responsible for directing people and organizing work. Planning is of paramount importance.
      6. A position description is a set of duties and responsibilities inherent to a given position.
      7. It is important to keep the position description up-to-date and to provide each employee with his own copy.

   B. The Sociology of Work
      1. People are alike in many ways; however, each individual is unique.
      2. The supervisor is challenged in getting to know employee differences. Acquiring skills in evaluating individuals is an asset.
      3. Maintaining meaningful working relationships in the organization is of great importance.
      4. The supervisor has an obligation to help individuals to develop to their fullest potential.
      5. Job rotation on a planned basis helps to build versatility and to maintain interest and enthusiasm in work groups.
      6. Cross training (job rotation) provides backup skills.

14

7. The supervisor can help reduce tension by maintaining a sense of humor, providing guidance to employees, and by making reasonable and timely decisions. Employees respond favorably to working under reasonably predictable circumstances.
8. Change is characteristic of all managerial behavior. The supervisor must adjust to changes in procedures, new methods, technological changes, and to a number of new and sometimes challenging situations.
9. To overcome the natural tendency for people to resist change, the supervisor should become more skillful in initiating change.

C. Principles and Practices of Supervision
1. Employees should be required to answer to only one superior.
2. A supervisor can effectively direct only a limited number of employees, depending upon the complexity, variety, and proximity of the jobs involved.
3. The organizational chart presents the organization in graphic form. It reflects lines of authority and responsibility as well as interrelationships of units within the organization.
4. Distribution of work can be improved through an analysis using the "Work Distribution Chart."
5. The "Work Distribution Chart" reflects the division of work within a unit in understandable form.
6. When related tasks are given to an employee, he has a better chance of increasing his skills through training.
7. The individual who is given the responsibility for tasks must also be given the appropriate authority to insure adequate results.
8. The supervisor should delegate repetitive, routine work. Preparation of recurring reports, maintaining leave and attendance records are some examples.
9. Good discipline is essential to good task performance. Discipline is reflected in the actions of employees on the job in the absence of supervision.
10. Disciplinary action may have to be taken when the positive aspects of discipline have failed. Reprimand, warning, and suspension are examples of disciplinary action.
11. If a situation calls for a reprimand, be sure it is deserved and remember it is to be done in private.

D. Dynamic Leadership
1. A style is a personal method or manner of exerting influence.
2. Authoritarian leaders often see themselves as the source of power and authority.
3. The democratic leader often perceives the group as the source of authority and power.
4. Supervisors tend to do better when using the pattern of leadership that is most natural for them.
5. Social scientists suggest that the effective supervisor use the leadership style that best fits the problem or circumstances involved.
6. All four styles—telling, selling, consulting, joining—have their place. Using one does not preclude using the other at another time.

7. The theory X point of view assumes that the average person dislikes work, will avoid it whenever possible, and must be coerced to achieve organizational objectives.
8. The theory Y point of view assumes that the average person considers work to be a natural as play, and, when the individual is committed, he requires little supervision or direction to accomplish desired objectives.
9. The leader's basic assumptions concerning human behavior and human nature affect his actions, decisions, and other managerial practices.
10. Dissatisfaction among employees is often present, but difficult to isolate. The supervisor should seek to weaken dissatisfaction by keeping promises, being sincere and considerate, keeping employees informed, and so forth.
11. Constructive suggestions should be encouraged during the natural progress of the work.

E. Processes for Solving Problems
1. People find their daily tasks more meaningful and satisfying when they can improve them.
2. The causes of problems, or the key factors, are often hidden in the background. Ability to solve problems often involves the ability to isolate them from their backgrounds. There is some substance to the cliché that some persons "can't see the forest for the trees."
3. New procedures are often developed from old ones. Problems should be broken down into manageable parts. New ideas can be adapted from old one.
4. People think differently in problem-solving situations. Using a logical, patterned approach is often useful. One approach found to be useful includes these steps:
   a. Define the problem
   b. Establish objectives
   c. Get the facts
   d. Weigh and decide
   e. Take action
   f. Evaluate action

F. Training for Results
1. Participants respond best when they feel training is important to them.
2. The supervisor has responsibility for the training and development of those who report to him.
3. When training is delegated to others, great care must be exercised to insure the trainer has knowledge, aptitude, and interest for his work as a trainer.
4. Training (learning) of some type goes on continually. The most successful supervisor makes certain the learning contributes in a productive manner to operational goals.
5. New employees are particularly susceptible to training. Older employees facing new job situations require specific training, as well as having need for development and growth opportunities.
6. Training needs require continuous monitoring.
7. The training officer of an agency is a professional with a responsibility to assist supervisors in solving training problems.

8. Many of the self-development steps important to the supervisor's own growth are equally important to the development of peers and subordinates. Knowledge of these is important when the supervisor consults with others on development and growth opportunities.

G. Health, Safety, and Accident Prevention
1. Management-minded supervisors take appropriate measures to assist employees in maintaining health and in assuring safe practices in the work environment.
2. Effective safety training and practices help to avoid injury and accidents.
3. Safety should be a management goal. All infractions of safety which are observed should be corrected without exception.
4. Employees' safety attitude, training and instruction, provision of safe tools and equipment, supervision, and leadership are considered highly important factors which contribute to safety and which can be influenced directly by supervisors.
5. When accidents do occur, they should be investigated promptly for very important reasons, including the fact that information which is gained can be used to prevent accidents in the future.

H. Equal Employment Opportunity
1. The supervisor should endeavor to treat all employees fairly, without regard to religion, race, sex, or national origin.
2. Groups tend to reflect the attitude of the leader. Prejudice can be detected even in very subtle form. Supervisors must strive to create a feeling of mutual respect and confidence in every employee.
3. Complete utilization of all human resources is a national goal. Equitable consideration should be accorded women in the work force, minority-group members, the physically and mentally handicapped, and the older employee. The important question is: "Who can do the job?"
4. Training opportunities, recognition for performance, overtime assignments, promotional opportunities, and all other personnel actions are to be handled on an equitable basis.

I. Improving Communications
1. Communications is achieving understanding between the sender and the receiver of a message. It also means sharing information—the creation of understanding.
2. Communication is basic to all human activity. Words are means of conveying meanings; however, real meanings are in people.
3. There are very practical differences in the effectiveness of one-way, impersonal, and two-way communications. Words spoken face-to-face are better understood. Telephone conversations are effective, but lack the rapport of person-to-person exchanges. The whole person communicates.
4. Cooperation and communication in an organization go hand in hand. When there is a mutual respect between people, spelling out rules and procedures for communicating is unnecessary.
5. There are several barriers to effective communications. These include failure to listen with respect and understanding, lack of skill in feedback, and misinterpreting the meanings of words used by the speaker. It is also common

practice to listen to what we want to hear, and tune out things we do not want to hear.
6. Communication is management's chief problem. The supervisor should accept the challenge to communicate more effectively and to improve interagency and intra-agency communications.
7. The supervisor may often plan for and conduct meetings. The planning phase is critical and may determine the success or the failure of a meeting.
8. Speaking before groups usually requires extra effort. Stage fright may never disappear completely, but it can be controlled.

J. Self-Development
1. Every employee is responsible for his own self-development.
2. Toastmaster and toastmistress clubs offer opportunities to improve skills in oral communications.
3. Planning for one's own self-development is of vital importance. Supervisors know their own strengths and limitations better than anyone else.
4. Many opportunities are open to aid the supervisor in his developmental efforts, including job assignments; training opportunities, both governmental and non-governmental—to include universities and professional conferences and seminars.
5. Programmed instruction offers a means of studying at one's own rate.
6. Where difficulties may arise from a supervisor's being away from his work for training, he may participate in televised home study or correspondence courses to meet his self-development needs.

K. Teaching and Training
1. The Teaching Process
Teaching is encouraging and guiding the learning activities of students toward established goals. In most cases this process consists of five steps: preparation, presentation, summarization, evaluation, and application.

   a. Preparation
   Preparation is two-fold in nature; that of the supervisor and the employee. Preparation by the supervisor is absolutely essential to success. He must know what, when, where, how, and whom he will teach. Some of the factors that should be considered are:
   1) The objectives
   2) The materials needed
   3) The methods to be used
   4) Employee participation
   5) Employee interest
   6) Training aids
   7) Evaluation
   8) Summarization

   Employee preparation consists in preparing the employee to receive the material. Probably the most important single factor in the preparation of the employee is arousing and maintaining his interest. He must know the objectives of the training, why he is there, how the material can be used, and its importance to him.

b. Presentation
In presentation, have a carefully designed plan and follow it. The plan should be accurate and complete, yet flexible enough to meet situations as they arise. The method of presentation will be determined by the particular situation and objectives.

c. Summary
A summary should be made at the end of every training unit and program. In addition, there may be internal summaries depending on the nature of the material being taught. The important thing is that the trainee must always be able to understand how each part of the new material relates to the whole.

d. Application
The supervisor must arrange work so the employee will be given a chance to apply new knowledge or skills while the material is still clear in his mind and interest is high. The trainee does not really know whether he has learned the material until he has been given a chance to apply it. If the material is not applied, it loses most of its value.

e. Evaluation
The purpose of all training is to promote learning. To determine whether the training has been a success or failure, the supervisor must evaluate this learning.
In the broadest sense, evaluation includes all the devices, methods, skills, and techniques used by the supervisor to keep himself and the employees informed as to their progress toward the objectives they are pursuing. The extent to which the employee has mastered the knowledge, skills, and abilities, or changed his attitudes, as determined by the program objectives, is the extent to which instruction has succeeded or failed.
Evaluation should not be confined to the end of the lesson, day, or program but should be used continuously. We shall note later the way this relates to the rest of the teaching process.

2. Teaching Methods
A teaching method is a pattern of identifiable student and instructor activity used in presenting training material.
All supervisors are faced with the problem of deciding which method should be used at a given time.

a. Lecture
The lecture is direct oral presentation of material by the supervisor. The present trend is to place less emphasis on the trainer's activity and more on that of the trainee.

b. Discussion
Teaching by discussion or conference involves using questions and other techniques to arouse interest and focus attention upon certain areas, and by doing so creating a learning situation. This can be one of the most

valuable methods because it gives the employees an opportunity to express their ideas and pool their knowledge.

    c. Demonstration
The demonstration is used to teach how something works or how to do something. It can be used to show a principle or what the results of a series of actions will be. A well-staged demonstration is particularly effective because it shows proper methods of performance in a realistic manner.

    d. Performance
Performance is one of the most fundamental of all learning techniques or teaching methods. The trainee may be able to tell how a specific operation should be performed but he cannot be sure he knows how to perform the operation until he has done so.
As with all methods, there are certain advantages and disadvantages to each method.

    e. Which Method to Use
Moreover, there are other methods and techniques of teaching. It is difficult to use any method without other methods entering into it. In any learning situation, a combination of methods is usually more effective than any one method alone.

Finally, evaluation must be integrated into the other aspects of the teaching-learning process.

It must be used in the motivation of the trainees; it must be used to assist in developing understanding during the training; and it must be related to employee application of the results of training.

This is distinctly the role of the supervisor.

CHILD DEVELOPMENT

I - MIDDLE YEARS: AGES 6-12

The ages six to twelve are commonly known as the middle years of childhood. This is the time when children are in full bloom: they are no longer babies but the demands of adult life are still far away. All through this period children continue to develop their special personalities. They are getting to know more about themselves and the world in which they live, and their slow, steady growth can be observed. They grow in independence and are more able to take care of themselves. They also are eager adventurers who learn from their explorations but who often find, to their dismay and to the dismay of the adults around them, that they still have a lot to learn.

Each child is different and there are no set rules for rearing or teaching children. How children grow depends on the characteristics they inherit from their parents and, to a great extent, it depends on the guidance provided by parents and other adults. It also depends on the experiences they have inside and outside of their homes.

Although each child's temperament makes her special, certain guidelines of child growth apply to most youngsters, and parents and other caregivers may find these guidelines helpful when working with the middle-years child.

Physical Development

Growth is of many different kinds and a child's development during the middle years includes increases in height, weight, and strength. The different rates of growth of various body parts account for the awkwardness of the youngster in the late childhood years. Height and weight increase much more slowly and evenly during the middle years than in early childhood. Children usually gain about two or three inches in height each year. Just as height increases at a slow steady pace, so, too, does weight. At the age of six, a child will be about seven times his birth weight. For example, a child who weighed seven pounds at birth will weigh almost fifty pounds at age six. Body proportions also change. The trunk becomes slimmer and more elongated in contrast to the chunky body of the preschooler. The chest becomes broader and flatter, causing the shoulders to droop. Arms and legs become long and thin with little evidence of muscles. It is this thinning-out of the trunk, combined with the elongation of the arms and legs, that gives the middle-years child the "all arms and legs" gawky appearance.

Sexual Differentiation

During the middle years, boys and girls gradually become aware of sexual differences in behavior, attitudes, and manners. These sex differences still can be seen in many play activities. Fortunately, however, both boys and girls now receive more encouragement to try activities traditionally reserved for the opposite sex. This helps to break down sex-role stereotypes. For example, girls learn that they can be good at tasks requiring physical skill, and boys learn that they can be caring young persons without losing their "masculinity." Opportunities for different kinds of play also mean that children develop a variety of skills to carry with them into adulthood.

Psychological Development

Middle-years children can find themselves in conflict with the need to grow up and the desire to remain a child forever, a conflict known as the Peter Pan fantasy. They want to grow up so that they can enjoy the prerogatives of adult life: staying up late, driving the car, wearing adult-styled clothes, and being privy to adult secrets. They want to be able to understand and laugh at adult jokes and be accepted into adult confidences and discussions.

On the other hand, they also want to hold on to all the privileges of childhood. Boys who quarrel, fight, and roughhouse and girls who dress up in their mothers' clothing and makeup are regarded as amusing by adults who would not tolerate such behavior in teenagers.

Social Development

There is a culture of childhood that is passed on solely by oral tradition. Many childrens' games, like hopscotch, marbles, kick-the-can, and blindman's buff, are passed down verbally from one generation to the next. Jokes, riddles, and sayings also are transmitted orally.

Georgie Porgie, pudding and pie Kissed the girls and made them cry.
or
Sticks and stones may break my bones, But names will never hurt me.
or
Ladybug, ladybug fly away home. Your house is on fire your children are gone Except for the little one under the stone Ladybug, ladybug fly away home.
or
Rain, rain go away Come again another day.

This culture of childhood that finds itself rooted in the past gives a clue to the child's relationship to her family. In contrast to the upheaval an adolescent experiences, the young child may appear to be a staid traditionalist who accepts the authority of the family just as she accepts the games and superstitions of previous generations of children. The middle-years child is more likely to defend than attack her family and what it stands for. The family is the main base of security and identity and is still more important than the child's peer group.

Ages and Stages

Information presented here about the ages and stages of children is only a *guide* for adults working with children. Physically, emotionally, and intellectually, each child grows and develops at his own rate. Some youngsters may be early bloomers. That is, they may have reached a stage of emotional or physical development beyond their chronological years. It is not unusual for a six-year-old to be as tall as a ten-year-old. But when interacting with this child, adults must remember that he *is* six and not ten and they should not expect him to behave as though he were a ten-year-old. Another example is an eight-year-old with an extensive vocabulary who can converse with adults as though she were twelve. In a relationship with this child, it is important for adults to remember that although she may be conversationally mature, she may be mentally, physically and emotionally still an eight-year-old.

Understanding the characteristics of an age can be helpful to adults who work with or care for children. But, if adults are to foster optimal growth and development in children, they also must remain sensitive and responsive to children as individuals.

Six-Year-Olds

General
The sixth year is the age of transition.
• At this age, children are active, outgoing, and self-centered. Their own activities take precedence over everything else.
• They are in constant motion: jiggling, shoving, and pushing. They like to roughhouse and their play may go too far because they don't know when to stop.
• They can play organized games with rules, but only at beginning levels because strategy and foresight are not highly developed at the age of six.
• Six-year-olds may be clumsy and tend to dawdle. For example, they may be slow at dressing to go to school or other places. On the other hand, they want their needs met at once and get upset when adults do not drop everything to do their bidding.

Self-Concept and Independence
• They want to be the center of everything to be first and to win. They are the center of their very own universe and their way of

doing things seems the best and only way. They do not lose gracefully or accept criticism.

• They are assertive, bossy, and extremely sensitive to real or imagined slights. They dominate every situation and are always ready with advice.

• Growing up may be a strain at times for six-year-olds and there may be a period of regression during which they engage in baby talk and display babyish behavior.

• Six-year-olds are extremely possessive of their belongings.

• When the outside world impinges adversely upon them, they are stubborn, obstinate, and unreasonable.

• They tend to project their own feelings onto others and then criticize other people because of this. "She thinks she's-everything" or "He's so fresh."

• They are ashamed of their mistakes and fears and of being seen crying and are careful not to expose themselves to criticism.

Relating to Other Children and Adults

• Six-year-olds often pair up and have best friends with whom they spend a good deal of time. Such pairs often take pleasure in "keeping out" a third child who wants to join them.

• Friendships are erratic and may change many times. Lots of tattling and putting-down of other children goes on, for example, "He's dumb."

• Boys and girls occasionally play together at this age, but the movement toward same-sexed friends has already begun.

• Six-year-olds can be highly sensitive to their parents' moods. For instance, they are quick to notice changes in facial expressions.

Although the six-year-old is most loving of his mother, he is also building his sense of self by trying to break away from her. Many temper tantrums are directed at her and the six-year-old may often refuse to obey his mother's directions. On the other hand, the six-year-old can be sympathetic toward his mother when she is not feeling well.

Parents can find the six-year-old trying. Adults working with six-year-olds need to keep a sense of perspective and their sense of humor. If parents and other caregivers remember the transitional nature of this age, six will become a more manageable and less trying age.

Games and Activities

• Their activities center on the physical. Riding a bicycle is an activity they enjoy. Roller skating and swimming also are favorites.

• They are poor at games requiring strategy and foresight like chess, checkers, and tic-tac-toe, but like running games such as tag and hide-and-seek.

• Six-year-olds like making things as well as cooking activities. They also like to paint, color, and draw.

Seven-Year-Olds

General

Seven is the age of quieting down.

• Toward the beginning of the seventh year the child begins to assimilate the wealth of new experiences and information she learned in first grade.

• They begin to sift and sort information into categories and link the bits of information that they have acquired. Seven-year-olds begin to reason and may at times appear serious and reflective.

• Seven-year-olds can be moody and brooding and pensive and sad because their assimilation of knowledge is not always smooth. Action has shifted and may now take place within their minds rather than within a physical space.

• Although they are self-absorbed they are not isolationists. They are becoming more aware not only of themselves, but of others as well.

Self-Concept and Independence

• The increased introspection of seven-year-olds also means that they have an increased sense of self and are acquiring sensitivity to the reactions of others. This sensitivity is to what others do and say, but not to what other people think. To the seven-year-old, thinking and doing are the same thing.

• They are sensitive about their bodies, which they do not like to have exposed or touched, and they may refuse to use the bathroom at school if it has no door on it.

• Because the physical self and the psychic self are so closely related at this stage, seven-year-olds are reluctant to expose themselves to failure and criticism. They often leave the scene rather than put themselves in a position where they might be subject to criticism or disapproval.

Relating to Other Children and Adults

• They want to be helpful and to become real members of the family group.

• They can take on tasks and responsibilities. When performing chores, they are careful and persistent, and they will demand guidance from adults as to "What do we do now?" or "How do we do this?"

• They can be polite and considerate toward adults. Seven-year-olds are less resistant and less stubborn than six-year-olds.

• They play easily with other children and seem to be in control. Although they are active and boisterous, they know when to stop before someone gets hurt.

Games and Activities

• Seven-year-olds have more capacity to play alone than they had at six, and they enjoy solitary activities such as reading and drawing.

• Group play is still not well organized and is carried out to individual ends.

• They like building things but need to know where things go and where they end. They can understand a simple model and a blueprint.

• Seven-year-olds continue to skate, swim, and are better at bike riding.

• They are avid collectors of anything and everything from stones to bottle tops.

• Seven-year-olds are fond of table games and jigsaw puzzles and can tackle a complicated game like Monopoly.

Eight-Year-Olds
General

Eight-year-olds are expansive, but on a higher level than when they were six.

• They are outgoing, curious, and extremely social and self-confident.

• They tend to be critical of themselves and judgmental of others.

• They now concern themselves with the why of events, and they are active and expansive as they seek out new experiences.

• Eight-year-olds talk constantly and love to gossip.

Self-Concept and Independence

• Eight-year-olds have a greater awareness of self; they are less sensitive, less introspective, and less apt to withdraw. They are becoming individuals who are aware of themselves in the social world.

• They are able to judge and appraise themselves and are conscious of the ways in which they differ from other people.

• Eight-year-olds are concerned about how other people feel about them, and they can be demanding in their efforts to get information about themselves.

• They can work independently, but need direction.

Relating to Other Children and Adults

• Eight-year-olds are mature in their social relationships with others. Relationships with friends are positive. Friendships are closer and very important.

• There is a noticeable separation between boys and girls and both play at games that tend to exclude the opposite sex.

• They are usually friendly and cooperative, preferring mature jobs that resemble adult-like activities.

• They are more polite with strangers than they are at home and are able to hold their own in conversations with adults.

Games and Activities

• Eight-year-olds dislike playing alone. They prefer to be with an adult or another child. Action becomes the focus of all their play.

• Both boys and girls like cooking and baking and show an interest in foreign places and children from different times.

• The collections they began at seven now become more organized and classified.

• They tend to make up their own rules for games and they may even invent new games.

• Eight-year-olds like dramatic play, especially where they take the role of characters they have read about, seen, or heard about.

• Table games such as cards, parchesi, checkers, and dominoes are very popular.

When working with eight-year-olds, adults must remember that they are very social and like to be with peers. They gossip and talk constantly, passing notes from one to the other. This often gets out-of-hand when they are in group situations. In addition to their tendency to judge others, eight-year-olds are increasingly self-critical. For example, many children who liked artwork at six or seven may give it up at eight because they see the difference between the quality of their drawings and those of a friend.

In Summary

Children are individuals with their own special temperaments and idiosyncracies. The ages and stages children go through can vary tremendously from one child to the next and, by respecting the variousness of children, parents and other caregivers can help them develop strong and healthy self-concepts.

II - MIDDLE YEARS: AGES 9-11

The ages six to twelve are commonly known as the middle years of childhood. This is the time when children are in full bloom; they are no longer babies but the demands of adult life are still far away. All through this period children continue to develop their special personalities. They are getting to know more about themselves and the world in which they live and their slow steady growth can be observed. They grow in independence and become more able to take care of themselves. They also are eager adventurers who learn from their explorations but who often find, to their dismay and to the dismay of the adults around them, that they still have a lot to learn.

Each child is different and there are no set rules for rearing or teaching children. How children grow depends on the characteristics they inherit from their parents and, to a good extent, it depends on the guidance provided by parents and other adults. It also depends on the experiences youngsters have inside and outside of their homes.

Although each child's temperament makes her special, certain guidelines of child growth apply to most youngsters, and parents and other caregivers may find these guidelines helpful when working with the middle-years child.

• **In physical development,** height and weight increase slowly and evenly. Children gain about two or three inches in height each year. Body proportions also change. In contrast to the chunky body of the preschooler, during the middle years the trunk becomes slimmer, the chest becomes broader, and the arms and legs thin out.

• **In psychological development,** middle-years children can find themselves in conflict between the need to grow up and the desire to remain a child forever. They want to grow up so that they can enjoy the prerogatives of adult life, but they also want to hold on to all the privileges of childhood.

During the middle years, boys and girls gradually become aware of sexual differences. Fortunately, children now are encouraged to try activities traditionally reserved for the opposite sex-a trend that is helping to break down sex-role stereotypes.

• **In social development,** the middle-years child may appear to be a staid traditionalist who accepts the authority of the family. The family is the main base of security and identity, although around the age of eleven the child begins to place more and more value on the peer group.

Ages and Stages

The information presented here about the ages and stages of children is only a *guide*. Physically, emotionally, and intellectually, each child grows and develops at his own rate. Some youngsters may be early bloomers. That is, they may have reached a stage of emotional or physical development beyond their chronological years. Understanding the characteristics of an age can be helpful to adults who work with or care for children. But, if adults are to foster optimal growth and development in children, they also must remain sensitive and responsive to children as individuals.

Nine-Year-Olds
General
Nine is a developmental middle zone.

• The nine-year-old shows a new maturity, self-confidence, and independence from adults.

• There is an increase in maturity and refinement of behavior. Judgmental tendencies are more discerning and objective. Nine-year-olds can evaluate themselves, find that they are lacking, but not feel guilty about it.

Self-Concept and Independence
• Nine-year-olds tend to be inner-directed and self-motivated.

• They have occasions of intense emotion and impatience, but their outbursts are less frequent and they show greater self-control. The inner-directed quality of their behavior allows nine-year-olds to become intently involved in activities.

• If forced to interrupt an activity, nine-year-olds will usually come back to it on their own.

• They can think and reason for themselves.

• They can be trusted.

• They may withdraw from surroundings to get a sense of self. They do not, however, retreat as much as they did when they were seven.

• Nine-year-olds do not feel impelled to boast and attack to protect themselves.

Relating to Other Children and Adults
• In their relationships with both adults and peers, they show consideration and fairness beyond that shown at *a* younger age.

• They can accept their own failures and mistakes, and they are willing to take responsibility for their own actions.

• Nine-year-olds have an increased awareness of sex and sex-differentiated behaviors.

• Girls can become concerned about their clothing and appearance. They take more interest in the "right" fashion.

• Friendships tend to be more solid, but occasionally nine-year-olds can have an intense dislike of the opposite sex, preferring to be with children of their own age and sex. Boys and girls both may begin to form clubs around various activities.

• Although their independence can be trying at times, they are often easier to work with than younger children who make great demands on adults.

• They are anxious to please and love to be chosen.

• Most of the mother-child conflict of the eight-year-old has disappeared, and the nine-year-old makes fewer demands on parents.

• Nine-year-olds usually have no problems with young children or older brothers and sisters. In fact, they can be very loyal to siblings.

Games and Activities

• Nine-year-olds spend much time in solitary activities of their own choosing.

• Bicycling, roller and ice skating, and swimming are physical activities they enjoy.

• They continue to enjoy the advanced table games they learned at eight.

• Materials and information attract the nine-year-old. Organized games or activities such as baseball, football, and basketball are popular. Many children at this age also have mastered basic reading and arithmetic and can use these skills to gain information, to solve problems, and to participate in games and recreation.

Ten-Year-Olds

General
Ten is the high point of childhood. Ten-year-olds have worked through the difficulties of home, school, and community. They now can take pride in their ability to fit in at home, at school, and at play with their peers. On occasion, there can be outbursts of anger, depression, or sadness, but these moods are short lived and soon forgotten.

• Girls are slightly more advanced sexually than boys and already there is some evidence of the rapid sprint to maturity that will make them taller and heavier than boys their own age in a couple of years. Their bodies are rounding out and the softening of contours may begin. Some girls may even experience the first stages of breast development. Girls become concerned about their bodies and menstruation and about sexual activity in general.

• For boys physical changes are less marked, thus concern for the body and physical maturity is much less noticeable.

Self-Concept and Independence

• Ten-year-olds accept themselves as they are without worrying too much about their strengths and weaknesses. They are much less interested in evaluating themselves. They like their bodies and like what they can do both athletically and academically. Their self-acceptance is heightened by the acceptance accorded them by peers, families, and school.

Relating to Other Children and Adults

• Ten-year-olds like and enjoy their friends. Boys may move into loosely organized groups. Within these groups, boys may have particular friends, but there is a lot of switching around. Girls usually move in smaller groups and are likely to form more intense friendships and have more serious "falling outs" with their friends being "mad" and "not playing" or "not speaking" to one another as a result. There are times when ten-year-olds may seem to value their peer group more than their families.

• Teachers and other adults who interact with this age group are popular if they are fair and not partial to particular children in the group. Adults working with ten-year-olds need to be firm but not strict. At this age children like adult leaders to schedule activities and like to keep to the schedule.

Games and Activities
• They like outings and trips.
• They like organized games and belonging to clubs and groups.
• When working on a project they may need to get up and move about.

Eleven-Year-Olds

General
At this age, there is an accelerated growth pace.
- The eleven-year-old's activity level increases; energy and appetite also increase.
- There is a tendency at this age to forget manners, to be loud, rude, and boorish, and to take unnecessary chances as a means of defying adult authority. Riding bicycles in heavy traffic is an example of this kind of behavior.
- Eleven-year-olds quarrel a good deal with adults and lack emotional control although they can be cooperative and friendly with strangers. They need firmness and understanding from adults.

Self-Concept and Independence
- They can be belligerent because of their high energy level, which pushes them toward activities, but which sometimes leads to carelessness.
- The eleven-year-old is looking for new self-definition.
- They will often confront others with criticism in an effort to get attention. They can, however, admit faults.
- They will sometimes differ with parents on careers and have dreams of being famous while their parents try to temper such fantasies.
- An eleven-year-old, on occasion, will challenge parents and other adults on child-rearing practices.

Relating to Other Children and Adults
- Boys and girls have best friends and a group of other friends who are selected because of common interests and temperaments.
- Both boys and girls admit to being interested in the opposite sex and show their interest by teasing, joking, and showing off.
- Eleven-year-olds like to quarrel with others, but don't like others to argue with them.
- They can be cooperative, friendly, and pleasant with adults, but they need to be treated with understanding and firmness.
- Eleven-year-olds can feel left out from their peer group.

Games and Activities
- They don't like to work with materials that are complex, but they do like things that show off their rote skills.
- Eleven-year-olds have trouble understanding relationships and the complex combinations of events.

In Summary

Children are individuals with their own special temperaments and idiosyncracies. The ages and stages children go through can vary tremendously from one child to the next and, by respecting the variousness of children, parents and other caregivers can help them develop strong and healthy self-concepts.

III - ADOLESCENTS

> *The young are prone to desire and in regard to sexual desire they exercise no self-restraint. They are changeful, too, and fickle in their desires. They are passionate, irascible, and apt to be carried away by their impulses. They are slaves, too, of their passion.*

A distinguished scientist and philosopher made this observation over 2000 years ago. To some, Aristotle's lament might suggest that adolescents haven't changed much since the days of ancient Athens, but recent research indicates that what hasn't changed is adults' *perceptions* of adolescents. Surveys of adolescents and their parents show that their values and attitudes are generally quite compatible. The famous "generation gap" appears to be an invention of the news media in response to a small but highly visible group of adolescents whose challenge to the older generation in the 1960s was mistakenly interpreted as representative.

What is it about the stage of life between childhood and adulthood that makes it so difficult for adults to understand? Although adolescence is not equally troublesome in all societies and for all families, adults' reports of its stressful nature are sufficiently widespread to warrant attention.

Change-physical, mental, and social change-is the most notable quality of adolescence and accounts for a good deal of the difficulty.

Physical Changes

The most obvious physical change during adolescence is rapid acceleration of growth. Within two years before or after age 12 for girls and age 14 for boys, a growth spurt occurs. The rate of gain in height and weight typically doubles for a year or more. Physical growth takes place in a fairly consistent sequence, beginning at the extremities and moving inward. Head, hands, and feet enlarge first, followed by arms and legs, then trunk. The broadening of male shoulders and female hips that characterizes adult body form occurs last. Overall growth is accompanied, though not always in the same order or at the same rate, by maturation of the reproductive organs and glands and by the appearance of pubic and underarm hair, and facial hair in males.

Together, these physical changes accomplish the biological aspect of adolescence, which is known as pubescence: they transform a child into an adult, one who is able to have children.

But this physical transformation is not as simple for the person going through it as it sounds when described in the abstract. For one thing, the ages at which pubescence begins and is completed vary as much as four years among different young people. Furthermore, the period from beginning to completion may be as little as 18 months for some and as much as six years for others. As a result of this variation, any group of early adolescents is likely to include young people who are at very different points in pubescence. Because girls enter pubescence, on the average, two years earlier than boys, the greatest variation among girls' physical maturation occurs during ages 11-13, while in boys it is during ages 13-15.

Rapid change combined with wide variation among individuals tend to make adolescents extremely sensitive to their appearance. At no other time in life are feelings about the self (self-esteem) so closely tied to feelings about the body (body image). Physical appearance also affects the ways in which other people treat an adolescent. Adults tend to expect adult behavior from a 15-year-old boy who is six feet tall and shaves regularly, but they will readily excuse childish behavior on the part of his classmate who, though the same age, has not yet begun his growth spurt. Perhaps even more importantly, peers judge one another on the basis of physical size and appearance. Early maturation can be an advantage for boys but often is not for girls because it puts them out-of-step with their peers.

The physical changes of pubescence, therefore, have direct effects on adolescents' social relations. They also affect emotions. The maturation of the gonads reproductive glandschanges the balance of hormones in the body, which can result in new sensitivities to the environment. For example, an adolescent may have a heightened sensitivity to loss of sleep, which results in moodiness or outbursts of temper. Cyclical changes in hormonal balance, especially among girls but also to some extent among boys, are associated with changes in emotions, behavior, and thinking. Since these cycles are new to adolescents, they may not be handled well.

Mental Changes

The most important mental change during adolescence is the growth in capacity for abstract thinking. Before age 11 or 12, children think in terms of concrete objects and groups of objects. Their reasoning is simple and direct. It does not allow for much complexity or subtlety. Given a problem to solve, the child tends to plunge into it with first one possible solution and then another until she either finds the correct solution or gives up. Confronted with a moral dilemma, she responds on the basis of a rule, which may or may not be appropriately applied.

By age 16, most adolescents have transcended this simple way of thinking, though not all of them adopt the most complex forms of reasoning. Nor do all use the same types of reasoning about all issues, any more than adults do. Adolescents begin to achieve the capacity to approach a problem systematically. Instead of moving immediately into the trying out of an assortment of solutions, they can analyze the problem and arrive at some tentative conclusions about what sorts of solutions probably will and will not work. Then they can proceed in a logical fashion to test and evaluate solutions, gaining a greater understanding of the problem along the way.

Moral issues become much more complex than they are for young children because adolescents are able to understand that two sound rules or principles might conflict in some cases. For example, they will understand that in certain situations, the values of friendship and honesty conflict, and they will struggle with a question about whether someone should report a friend for breaking a rule. Younger children are more likely to choose either one principle or the other without recognizing the dilemma. Furthermore, adolescents outgrow the childish belief that only evil people do bad things. They understand accident and circumstances involve even the best-intentioned people in undesirable actions. They are, therefore, likely to be more understanding and forgiving of human frailty than young children, though their interest in principles can also make adolescents morally rigid at times.

Along with the capacity to think abstractly comes the realization that what exists is only one of many possibilities. Thinking about those possibilities becomes a fascinating activity. The real is frequently compared to the ideal and found wanting. Because they can conceive of a more ideal worJd without having to bother themselves with all the details of how it might be achieved and what drawbacks it might have, adolescents are often impatient with the real world and with the failure of adults to have made it better already.

This capacity to think about many possible realities is important, given the momentous choices adolescents will make as they move into adulthood and choose career directions, educational paths, and mates. Without it they are likely to drift into the first opportunities that arise without considering what the other possibilities might be, which are most desirable, and which are feasible.

Similarly, the ability to reason about moral issues is necessary if a person is to establish a personal moral code. Rules and principles simply accepted from parents and other authorities are essential to children, but adolescents need to think through rules and principles and consider the alternatives in order to adopt or adapt them for themselves. An adolescent who does not go through the process of questioning principles and values may be without guidance when confronted with a new and complex moral dilemma or when one or another of his/her basic principles is seriously challenged.

Social Changes

Because of their physical and mental growth, adolescents are no longer treated like children. The expectations adults and peers have of them change and their behavior changes. Thus the social world in which they live changes in important ways.

One of the most obvious social changes is the initiation of serious interest in and interactions with young people of the opposite sex. The physical and emotional changes of pubescence described above lead to strong new feelings between girls and boys. Even before they begin to act upon these feelings by dating and engaging in other heterosexual activities, many adolescents begin to have "crushes" on opposite-sex peers, and sometimes on same-sex peers and on adults. These one-way emotional attachments simply indicate the presence of new emotional capacities, but they can be difficult for the adolescent to understand and deal with. Learning to handle the emotions and behavior that go along with attracting and forming emotional attachments to members of the opposite sex can be stressful, in addition to being terribly exciting.

The social world of the adolescent changes in other ways as well. A sixteen-year-old may notice that adults are treating her more like one of them, engaging in real conversation, for example, instead of saying "My, how you've grown," and asking about school. She may also notice that she enjoys this adult conversation when just a year or two before she would have preferred to go out and play.

By the age of sixteen, adolescents are being given many privileges formerly reserved for adults. In most places they can drive a car, quit school, and hold a job. Although it is usually against the law, they can fairly easily smoke and drink alcoholic beverages.

Relations with parents change too. As they grow more mature, adolescents are less dependent on their parents than they were earlier. They might be able to live on their own. They have ideas of their own and are reconsidering some of the beliefs and values their parents have taught them. They receive emotional support from peers. Sometimes their peers' values are inconsistent with their parents'. For all these reasons, they become less deferent to their parents' wishes and opinions, adopting a more independent and often a more aggressive stance.

Modern industrial societies demand highly educated workers and do not need the labor of children. Therefore, most young people experience a long gap between the attainment of physical adulthood and adult status. Marriage, parenthood, and full-time paid employment are the principal indicators of adult status in our society. At least two ambiguities arise from this social definition of adulthood. One is that young people are expected to postpone marriage and to remain economically dependent on their parents for several years after they are physically capable of reproduction and full-time employment. A second is that while many young people "prolong their adolescence" by enrolling in college and then in graduate or professional school, many of their peers are entering full-time employment, getting married, and starting families. Although adolescence can be an enjoyable stage of life because of the freedom from adult obligations, it can also be a frustrating time because adult privileges are withheld.

Difficulties for Parents

Adolescents are no longer children; they and their parents have to work out new ways of dealing with each other that recognize their growing but not yet complete maturity. Parents must realize that they can no longer control their offspring in many important areas. Adolescents simply have too many opportunities to do as they please. Young people, who are often adamant in demanding relief from parental control, need to understand that freedom demands responsibility. They cannot expect their parents to give them adult privileges regarding their social activities and then excuse them from household obligations because they are only children.

One of the reasons adolescents often seem to be a burden to their parents is that parents have to change the way they treat their adolescents. Parental behavior that has developed over several years and has been rather effective becomes obsolete. New behavior, a new parental style, is called for.

Being required to deal with new challenges and to behave in different ways is always difficult, but it can be especially difficult for parents of adolescents who are simultaneously experiencing stress in other parts of their lives. The term "midlife crisis" has become popular in recent years in recognition that many people go through a period of self-examination and often of serious readjustment in middle age as they realize they have relatively few years left to accomplish what they aspire to. Two life cycle changes in the family are associated with this midlife crisis: one is the death of one's own parents and the other is the maturation of one's children. People at this point frequently have to accept the fact that they will not achieve the prominence in their careers that they might have wanted. Common responses to this "crisis" include career and marital changes.

Parents who are experiencing crises of this magnitude are likely to feel overwhelmed by the challenges of dealing with their rapidly changing adolescents. But even parents who feel satisfied and secure in most aspects of their lives may have difficulty coping with their adolescent children.

What Adults Can Do for Adolescents

There are times when the adolescent says, "Why don't you just leave me alone!" and the adult wants to say, "Alright, I will." That is not a solution, however, because adolescents need adults to help them achieve adulthood themselves. The following suggestions may prove helpful to adults who work with adolescents, but they cannot be treated as a cookbook. Just as adolescents refuse to follow many adult "recipes" for proper behavior because they need to work out their own behavioral code, adults must be flexible and resourceful in responding to adolescents. There is no single way to do it.

1. Be honest. With their newly developed capacity for abstract thinking, adolescents become fascinated with principles and with consistency. They are severe critics of adults they think are hypocritical or two-faced. Most adolescents are sophisticated enough to see through dishonesty or pretention in adults who are close to them. They tend to be skeptical at what adults tell them and to welcome any confirmation of that skepticism.

2. Be open. Adolescents want and need to talk about things with their parents and other adults close to them. But they also need to maintain their privacy and their independence. Therefore, adult-adolescent conversations cannot be one-sided, with the adolescent baring his soul and the adult listening and offering advice. Adolescents need to know that some of the same concerns they struggle with are concerns of adults too.

Sexuality is one of the most insistent concerns of adolescents because it is a new one, brought out by their sexual maturation. Adults cannot be very helpful to adolescents about sexual issues unless they, as adults, are comfortable with their own sexuality. They must be willing to acknowledge the complexity of the issues and the strength of the social and emotional pressures. In our society the "official" morality is that sexual relations are limited to marriage, yet television, movies, magazines, songs on the radio, and even billboards bombard us constantly with the message that sexual attractiveness is the most important personal quality and that unrestrained sexual behavior is good. Like adolescents, adults can find this contradiction confusing, and they should be willing to discuss it.

3. Set clear and consistent limits. Most children will abide by rules their parents or other adults set down just because they are rules, at least as long as the adult is looking. Adolescents are much more likely to want to know why a particular rule or expectation has been stated. Adults should respect this need for explanation and should allow for some negotiation regarding rules for behavior. But, consistent with the recommendation to be honest, adults should not hesitate to say what they believe is absolutely essential and is not open to negotiation.

There may be some rules or limits set by parents that adolescents continue to violate because they are independent enough to do so. Parents may have to acknowledge that they cannot control what the adolescent does away from home but make clear that they will not allow it in the home and then follow through with that prohibition.

4. Remember that growing up means becoming independent. Effective parents, and other adults who succeed in helping adolescents become adults, are able to accept young people making choices that they would not have made and behaving in ways they do not approve of. That is what independence means. Young adults who still do as they are told all the time are immature and unprepared to face a world in which they are constantly required to decide for themselves. Most adolescents become adults who are a source of pride and happiness for their parents and for the other adults who worked with them. But for this to happen, they must first establish some independence, and that can require a painful break.

Adolescents undergo dramatic physical and mental changes in a short period of time, and they are given a confusing in-between place in our society. The period can be painful for the adolescents and for the adults who are close to them. But it is a necessary process both for the adolescents to come of age and for our society to renew itself through the questions, the new perspective, and the new talents that each group of young people brings into adulthood.

www.ingramcontent.com/pod-product-compliance
Lightning Source LLC
Chambersburg PA
CBHW081808300426
44116CB00014B/2285